IELTS
Practice Tests

Mark Harrison

Russell Whitehead

HARROW COLLEGE
HH Learning Centre
Lowlands Road, Harrow
Middx HA1 3AQ
020 8909 6520

HEINLE
CENGAGE Learning™

Australia • Brazil • Japan • Korea • Mexico • Singapore • Spain • United Kingdom • United States

HEINLE
CENGAGE Learning

Heinle Exam Essentials: IELTS Practice Tests
Mark Harrison and Russell Whitehead

Publisher: Christopher Wenger

Director of Product Development: Anita Raducanu

Director of Marketing: Amy Mabley

Acquisitions Editor: Sean Bermingham

Editorial Manager: David Baker

Development Editor: Derek Mackrell

Production Editor: Tan Jin Hock

International Marketing Manager: Eric Bredenberg

Sr. Print Buyer: Mary Beth Hennebury

Project Manager: Howard Middle/HM ELT Services

Production Management: Process ELT

(www.process-elt.com)

Copy Editor: Georgia Zographou/Process ELT

Compositor: Process ELT

Illustrator: Oxford Designers & Illustrators

Cover/Text Designer: Studio Image & Photographic Art

(www.studio-image.com)

ISBN-13: 978-1-4130-0975-0 (with key)
ISBN-10: 1-4130-0975-1 (with key)
ISBN-13: 978-1-4130-0976-7 (without key)
ISBN-10: 1-4130-097-X (without key)

For product information and technology assistance, contact **emea.info@cengage.com**.

For permission to use material from this text or product, and for permission queries, email **clsuk.permissions@cengage.com**.

Heinle, Cengage Learning EMEA
Cheriton House, North Way, Andover, Hampshire, SP10 5BE, United Kingdom

Cengage Learning is a leading provider of customised learning solutions with office locations around the globe, including Singapore, the United Kingdom, Australia, Mexico, Brazil and Japan. Locate our local office at: **international.cengage.com/region**

Cengage Learning products are represented in Canada by Nelson Education Ltd.

Visit Heinle online at **elt.heinle.com**
Visit our corporate website at **cengage.com**

Text Credits
Page 24: From THE LIFE AND LEGEND OF LEADBELLY, by Charles Wolfe and Kip Lornell. Copyright © 1999 Charles Wolfe and Kip Lornell. Page 33: From NOT IN FRONT OF THE GROWN-UPS, by Alison Lurie. Copyright © 1991 Bloomsbury. Copyright © 1990 by Alison Lurie. Reprinted by permission of Melanie Jackson Agency, L.L.C. Page 38: From "The Birth of Our Modern Minds," by Roger Highfield. Copyright © Telegraph Group Limited 2003. Page 44: From 'A Regional Language Revival," THE LINGUIST. Copyright © 1999 Anne Judge. Page 66: From THE LONGMAN HISTORY OF THE UNITED STATES OF AMERICA, by Hugh Brogan. Copyright © 1990 Pearson Education Limited. Page 72: From "How Bugs Hitch-hike across the Galaxy," by David Derbyshire. Copyright © Telegraph Group Limited 2003. Page 78: From "Finding Out About the World from Television News," TELEVISION AND COMMON KNOWLEDGE, Routledge. Copyright © 1999 David Morley. Page 84: From "The Sunday Times 50 Best Small Companies to Work For." Copyright © The Sunday Times 2004. Page 96: Used by permission of Institute of the Translation & Interpreting, Bulletin, May/June 2003. Page 100: From "Hands-on Healing, or a Con?" by Orla Kennedy. Copyright © Telegraph Group Limited 2003. Page 105: From THE INVENTION OF CLOUDS by Richard Hamblyn. Macmillan, London, UK. Copyright © 2001. Page 108: Used by permission of the Home Office, United Kingdom. Copyright © Crown. Copyright © 1999 Department for Transport. Page 116: "Introduction" from GROUCHO MARX AND OTHER SHORT STORIES AND TALL TALES by Robert S. Bader. Copyright © 1993 by Robert S. Bader. Reprinted by permission of Faber and Faber, Inc., an affiliate of Farrar, Straus and Giroux, LLC. Page 120: From "Molehills Made out of Mountains," by Anna Grayson. Copyright © Telegraph Group Limited 2003. Page 124: From "Think Happy," by John Elliott. Copyright © The Sunday Times 2003. Page 128: From LOCAL HEROES DO-IT-YOURSELF SCIENCE, by Adam Hart-Davis and Paul Bader. Copyright © BBC Worldwide Limited 2000. Page 136: From LONDON THE BIOGRAPHY by Peter Ackroyd (Vintage). Copyright © 2001 Peter Ackroyd. Page 141: From PERSONALITY ASSESSMENT: A CRITICAL SURVEY, by P.E. Vernon. © 1964 Routledge. Page 144: First published in CAM, the University of Cambridge Alumni Magazine. Page 148: From THE LONDONER, February 2004. Page 156: From: "How to Run a ..." by David Harvey, in THE AUTHOR, Summer 2003. © David Harvey 2003. Page 161: Extract from SIGHTLINES by Simon Inglis published by Yellow Jersey Press. Used by permission of The Random House Group Limited. Page 164: Reprinted "Introduction" from A THEORY OF SHOPPING, by Daniel Miller. Copyright © 1998 Cornell University. Used by permission of the publishers, Cornell University Press and Polity Press Page 173: Copyright © Transport for London. Page 168: From "Language Incentives," ITI Bulletin May-June 2003. Reprinted by permission of the Institute of Translation and Interpreting. Page 175: Copyright © London Borough of Barnet. Pages 177-179: From Barnet College Prospectus, 2004-2005. Copyright © Barnet College. Page 181: From "To My Horror, I Couldn't Even Write," by Christine Doyle. Copyright © Telegraph Group Limited 2003. Page 187: From Walkers News Copyright (c) 2003 Countryside Agency. Page 189: From "Have Your Say on Library Plans." Reprinted by permission of Library Services, London Borough of Barnet. Pages 191-193: From Southgate College Prospectus, 2004-2005. Copyright © Southgate College. Page 194: From "Natural Assets Worth Saving in the Outback," by John Craven. Copyright © 2000 The Mail On Sunday.

Printed by Seng Lee Press, Singapore
6 7 8 9 10 – 11 10 09

Contents

Heinle Exam Essentials is a new series of materials for students preparing for the major EFL/ESL examinations, such as First Certificate in English (FCE), Certificate in Advanced English (CAE), Certificate of Proficiency in English (CPE), International English Language Testing System (IELTS), Test of English as a Foreign Language (TOEFL®), Test of English for International Communication (TOEIC®) and others. Each book in the series pays close attention to developing a detailed knowledge of the skills and strategies needed for success in each part or paper of the exams.

IELTS Practice Tests helps learners become aware of IELTS exam requirements, offers details about the format of the exam and helps learners develop the exam skills necessary for success. The book also offers extensive practice in all parts of the exam, using the actual test format. As well as students who are planning to take the IELTS exam, the book is also suitable for use by teachers of IELTS courses and by students and teachers involved in checking and improving academic English.

1 Taking the IELTS Exam

The IELTS exam, which is jointly managed by the University of Cambridge ESOL Examinations (Cambridge ESOL), the British Council and IDP: IELTS Australia, assesses the language ability of candidates who need to study or work where English is the language of communication. IELTS is recognised by universities and employers in many countries, such as Australia, Canada, New Zealand, the UK and the USA, as well as by professional bodies, immigration authorities and other government agencies.

There are four parts to the IELTS exam: Listening, Reading, Writing and Speaking. All candidates take the same Listening and Speaking Modules, while the Reading and Writing Modules are available in two formats – Academic and General Training.

The Academic Reading and Writing Modules assess whether a candidate is ready to study or train in the medium of English. The General Training Modules focus on basic survival skills in a broad social and educational context, and are more suitable for candidates who are going to English-speaking countries for the purposes of work experience, non-degree level training or immigration.

A full breakdown of the format, task types and timing of each Module can be found on the inside flap of this *Practice Test* book.

IELTS candidates receive a Band Score from 1 to 9 for each Module of the test, and an Overall Band Score from 1 to 9, which is an average of the four Module scores. A breakdown of the nine Bands can be found on the cover flap of this book.

One mark is awarded for each correct answer in the Listening and Reading Modules. A confidential Band Score

conversion table is then used to translate these total marks into IELTS band scores. Scores are reported as a whole Band or a half Band.

Writing tasks are assessed independently by certified IELTS examiners, according to the 9-Band scale. Writing scripts are assessed on the following criteria:

Content
Task 1: Has the writer included all the relevant information?
Task 2: Has the writer fully answered the question by dealing with all parts of it?

Organisation
Task 1: Does the answer flow well and is it clear and easy to read?
Task 2: Does the answer flow well and is there a clear progression of opinions and ideas?

Use of language
Task 1: Has the writer used appropriate linking words and phrases, and a good level of grammar? Is the vocabulary accurately used?
Task 2: Are ideas and opinions linked by appropriate words and phrases? Is the grammar and vocabulary accurate and not too simple?

The Speaking Module is also measured according to the 9-Band scale, based on the following criteria:

Fluency and coherence: Does the speaker talk in a logical and organised way? Is the speech reasonably continuous, without too many pauses or repetitions?

Lexical resource: Does the speaker use a variety of words and expressions in an appropriate way?

Grammatical range and accuracy: Does the speaker use a variety of grammatical structures, without too many mistakes, in order to convey his/her meaning effectively?

Pronunciation: Is the candidate's speech easy to understand? Is the pronunciation of sounds, words and phrases accurate, and does the speaker use appropriate intonation patterns?

For more information on the criteria used for assessing the Speaking Module, see page 88.

Further information about the exam can also be obtained from the IELTS website: **www.ielts.org**

2 *IELTS Practice Tests*: contents

IELTS Practice Tests prepares candidates for the IELTS examination by providing **six full practice tests**, which follow the latest exam specifications.

There are **two guided tests**, which provide clear, authoritative and complete guidance on the task types featured in each section of the exam.

These guided tests are followed by **four tests (without guidance)**, which offer students thorough practice at a realistic exam level.

An additional **General Training section** contains the Reading and Writing Modules for two practice tests.

Together, these tests provide at least two opportunities to practise every task type, whilst covering as full a range as possible of typical IELTS topic areas and situations.

The CDs and cassettes accompanying the book include the **audio materials** for the Listening Modules, recorded so as to reflect accurately the audio element of the actual exam.

A **writing bank** has sample answers for the writing tasks, for both Academic and General Training tests.

IELTS Practice Tests with key edition contains a comprehensive **answer key**, which includes detailed explanations of each answer for the Listening and Reading Modules, and an **annotated audio script**.

3 How to use *IELTS Practice Tests*

Students:
You can use this book in different ways, according to your needs: your level, your aims, how much time you have, if you are studying completely by yourself or with a class and teacher.

IELTS uses many task types and you need to be well prepared for them all in order to do well in the exam. *IELTS Practice Tests* will help you to do this.

Use the chart on the inside flap to understand the overall content and format of the test. Look through Test 3 to see how the description in the chart matches the test.

Teachers:
Remember that IELTS is not like an exam that has a specific syllabus that it will test. Your skills will be needed to diagnose and address your students' needs in terms of lexis, structure, discourse, and so on. Because *IELTS Practice Tests* covers the full range of exam tasks and a comprehensive range of typical IELTS exam topics, it can help you to concentrate on the linguistic aspects of the course you teach.

Tests 1 and 2
Students:
Tests 1 and 2 contain valuable help in preparing for the exam. All the exam task types are represented and they are clearly headed for easy reference.

For each task, there is a **Task guide**, which gives you important facts and advice for that particular task type.

There is also a **Step-by-step guide** for each task type, which takes you through a series of carefully designed steps that will help you understand how to approach doing the task.

Model answers (on pages 199–206) are provided for all the writing tasks.

One way to use Tests 1 and 2 is to work your way through both tests. This will help you become well informed about what the IELTS exam involves. Alternatively, use Tests 1 and 2 as a sort of reference tool. Practise taking other tests in the book and use Tests 1 and 2 to get advice on particular task types.

Teachers:
This part of the **IELTS Exam Essentials** series could constitute the basis of a short intensive IELTS preparation course. It is also a useful place to check details of particular task types. The exercises and model answers can also be used as the starting points for skills classes.

Tests 3–6
Students:
These four complete tests can be used in a variety of ways. For example, you may:

• work through Tests 1 and 2 first, and use Tests 3–6 to practise what you have studied or

• begin with Tests 3–6, and when you come to each task type, check the task guides in Tests 1 and 2 to make sure you understand how to approach it.

You can use the Tests to create a self-study course:

• Work your way through Tests 1 and 2.

• Do Tests 3 and 4, returning to the task guides in Tests 1 and 2 to prepare yourself for each task type.

• Check your answers carefully – including the audio scripts for the listening sections – and keep notes about the areas where you have problems.

• Do Test 5, while checking your notes; when you reach a task type where you have had a problem before, review the task guides for Tests 1 and 2.

• Take Test 6 under test conditions (correct timing, silence, no dictionaries or reference books, etc.).

When you get an answer wrong, check to see which of the following happened:

• Did you mishear a word in the Listening?

• Did you read the question too quickly and not understand what to look for in the Reading?

• Did you make the wrong interpretation of what the graph represents in the Writing?

• Did you misunderstand what a word or phrase means?

Every question you get wrong is an opportunity to learn something that will help you later in the exam.

Teachers:
You can use the above steps with your students, either in-class or as a structured self-study programme. Encourage your students to build their understanding of the test with the explanatory key and to develop their ability to evaluate their own language and learning needs.

Mark Harrison and Russell Whitehead, January 2005

IELTS TEST 1

Exam Essentials

LISTENING MODULE | READING MODULE | WRITING MODULE | SPEAKING MODULE

SECTION 1
SECTION 2
SECTION 3
SECTION 4

▶ **Questions 1–10**

Questions 1–4

Complete the notes below.

Write **NO MORE THAN TWO WORDS AND/OR A NUMBER** *for each answer.*

Easylet Accommodation Agency

Cheapest properties: £ **1** .... per week

Minimum period of contract: **2** ....

Office open Saturdays until **3** ....

List of properties available on **4** ....

Notes completion

Task guide

▶ This task requires you to write answers that are pieces of information given in the recording you hear.

▶ Read the instructions carefully. These will tell you the maximum number of words you can use to answer the questions – this may be as many as three, but may be only two or one. They may also tell you that numbers are required.

▶ The words or numbers you need are on the recording. Do not rephrase or change the form of the words on the recording.

▶ The questions follow the order of the recording.

Step-by-step guide

▶ **Step 1 – Think first**

Look at the notes. What sort of information is required in each gap?

Decide if each gap 1–4 will require: A word(s), B a number or C word(s) and a number.

▶ **Step 2 – Now listen and do the task**

▶ **Step 3 – Check what you heard**

Three things are important: (a) you must be ready for the information, (b) you must write the correct information, and (c) you must be careful not to write the wrong information.

Look at the tapescript for *Question 1*. For (a), the words which lead you to the answer are underlined. For (b), the number you must write for the answer is circled. For (c), words which you might wrongly think could be the answer are in *italics*.

Tapescript

Man: Easylet. Good morning. How can I help you?
Woman: Hello. I saw your advertisement in the paper and I'm calling to ask about renting a flat.
Man: Certainly. What kind of flat had you in mind?
Woman: Well, er, I don't know exactly ... I mean, it depends on price, to some extent.
Man: OK, now we have properties across the whole range. *The average is probably £120 a week.*
Woman: Oh, I was hoping for something a little cheaper.
Man: They start at £90 that's the lowest we have usually. And *they go up to £200.*
Woman: I could manage the lowest figure.

Now look at the tapescript for *Question 2*. Underline the words that lead you to the answer and circle the correct answer.

Tapescript

Man: An important question is how long you're thinking of staying in the property. We don't do short lets.
Woman: I'd want a flat for nine months, perhaps longer.
Man: That would be fine. Our contracts are for a standard six months, and that can be extended.
Woman: Fine. I'd need to come in and see you?

Questions 5–7

Choose **THREE** *letters* **A–G**.

Which **THREE** *things are included for free with every property for rent from Easylet?*

5 ....

6 ....

7 ....

A heating bills
B kitchen equipment
C plates and glasses
D sheets and towels
E telephone
F television
G water bill

Multiple-choice with multiple answers (1)

Task guide

▸ This task requires you to choose correct answers from a list of possible answers.

▸ You get one mark for each correct answer.

▸ It's very important to read the instructions carefully. They will tell you what to listen for. You will probably hear something connected with all the options. The instructions will tell you the reason for choosing some of the options on the list.

▸ The options are usually listed in alphabetical order.

▸ The order of the options in the list will probably differ from the order of the recording.

▸ You may hear exactly the same words as appear in the options, or you may hear alternative phrases that have the same meaning.

▸ You can write the correct answers in any order.

▸ See also pages 10 and 16 for other types of multiple-choice tasks.

Step-by-step guide

▸ **Step 1 – Think first**

Look at the instructions. You are listening for things that are 'included for free' in 'every property for rent'.

Think about ways of giving this information.

▸ **Step 2 – Check what you hear**

Look at this part of the tapescript, which relates to options B and C.

Tapescript

Man: That depends on the flat, to a certain extent, although some things are standard in all flats. For example, **every flat has kitchen equipment provided for your use.**
Woman: Good. *Does that also mean tableware, cups, glasses, plates?*
Man: *In some flats, but not all.*

B is a correct answer. C is not a correct answer, although it is clearly mentioned. Plates and glasses are 'included for free', but not in 'every flat'.

▸ **Step 3 – Listen and do the task**

IELTS
TEST 1
Exam Essentials

| LISTENING MODULE | READING MODULE | WRITING MODULE | SPEAKING MODULE |

SECTION 1
SECTION 2
SECTION 3
SECTION 4

Questions 8–10

Label the map below.

*Write the correct letter **A–H** next to questions 8–10.*

Where are the following blocks of flats situated?

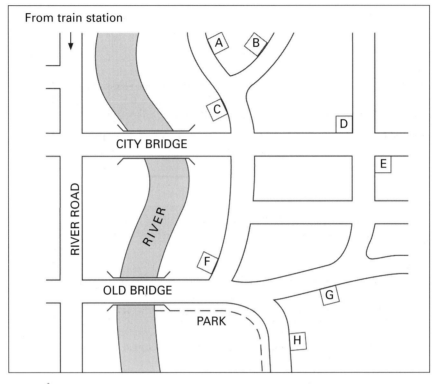

8   Eastern Towers   ....*A*..........

9   Granby Mansions   .....*H*........

10   Busby Garden `   ......*E*.........

Labelling a map/plan/diagram (1)

Task guide

▸ This task requires you to label a map with the correct places or points using the information you hear in the recording. Similar tasks may require you to label a plan or a diagram.

▸ The questions follow the order of the recording. If you realise you have missed one question, make sure you focus carefully for the next one.

▸ The map and the recording will give you a starting point. Listen carefully because finding the answers greatly depends on locating the starting point in the map.

▸ There are several more possible places than you need marked on the map. Follow the speaker's directions carefully before you decide which is the correct place.

▸ The information about the starting point is repeated for each question. Do not worry too much if you miss one question, or feel you have got one question wrong.

▸ See also pages 14 and 64 for other types of labelling tasks.

Step-by-step guide

▶ Step 1 – Think first

Look at the map and try to locate the starting point.

Remind yourself of the language of directions: turn left, go straight on, follow along, etc.

The possible places on the map will often be quite close together, so you need to listen carefully to decide which of two or three possibilities is correct in each case.

▶ Step 2 – Locate the starting point

Look at this section of the tapescript, which tells you where the starting point is, and locate it in the map.

Tapescript

Woman: Could you tell me where they are? I'm **at the train station** at the moment.
Man: Eastern Towers, if you're coming **from the station**, isn't very far.

In this case, you should start reading the map in the top left corner, which is clearly marked 'From train station'. This is your starting point for all three blocks of flats.

▶ Step 3 – Check what you will hear

Look at the next section of the script. Follow the speaker's directions carefully. Pay special attention to the different references to 'left' and 'right'.

Tapescript

Man: Eastern Towers, if you're coming **from the station**, isn't very far. **Cross over** City Bridge. Then **go left**, and where the road divides, you want the **right-hand fork**. You'll see Eastern Towers **on the left side** of the road. It's a lovely building, with trees around it.

The relevant information is in **bold**. Notice that the reference to trees will not help you find the answer.

▶ Step 4 – Listen and do the task

SECTION 1
SECTION 2
SECTION 3
SECTION 4

▸ *Questions 11–20*

Questions 11 and 12

For each question, choose **TWO** *letters* **A–E**.

11 Which **TWO** activities for school groups need to be booked one week in advance?
    A drama workshops
    B garden sculpture experience
    C painting demonstrations
    D tours for the blind
    E video making

12 Which **TWO** facilities are closed in winter?
    A adventure playground
    B artists' studio
    C café
    D mini zoo
    E shop

Multiple-choice with multiple answers (2)

Task guide

▸ This task requires you to answer each question by choosing two correct options.

▸ In order to receive one mark for these questions, you need to choose both correct options. There is no half mark for choosing only one correctly.

▸ The length of the recording that you hear in this type of task will be less than when there is one mark for each correct answer (see page 7).

▸ You will probably hear some reference to each of the options on the list. It is, therefore, important that you are clear what you are listening for. Only two of the options will be the correct answers to the question.

▸ The options are usually listed alphabetically. The options don't follow the order in which you will hear the information on the recording.

▸ Make sure you read the list of possible answers very carefully; they are often quite similar.

▸ See also pages 7 and 16 for other types of multiple-choice tasks.

Step-by-step guide

▶ Step 1 – Think first

The words on the recording may or may not be the same as the words in the options. Prepare yourself for hearing various ways of describing the options on the list.

For example, option A is 'drama workshops'. You may hear 'drama workshops', but you may also hear 'workshops involving drama', 'practical activities using drama', 'activities that involve acting', and so on.

If you prepare yourself like this, you will be more likely to understand whether option A is a correct answer to *Question 11*.

▶ Step 2 – Listen carefully

Look at options C and D. Can you think of different ways to describe them?

C painting demonstration: ....

D tours for the blind: ....

Now look at this part of the tapescript. <u>Underline</u> the words that relate to options C and D. Are the words used in the tapescript the same as in the options? Are they similar to words you predicted?

Tapescript

It's nice to see so many of you here. I'm going to tell you something about Hollylands – our facilities and activities, and the exhibitions we have coming up. I hope you'll find it interesting and bring your pupils along. For most of what we have to offer here, you can just turn up with your party. I'm pleased to say that recent work has meant that the whole centre is prepared for blind visitors. There are a couple of activities where we ask you to book a week in advance. We only have artists that you can watch painting at certain times, so we need notice of your coming for that.

▶ Step 3 – Think about what you hear

Option C: Blind visitors are mentioned, but there do not seem to be tours for the blind, and there is no requirement to book a certain number of days in advance. Although you hear something about blind people, you do not hear the answer to the question. You should not choose option C as an answer.

Option D: In this case, 'painting demonstrations' has become 'artists that you can watch painting'. You hear that because Hollylands only has 'artists ... at certain times' they 'need notice'. This 'notice' links to the previous sentence: 'activities where we ask you to book a week in advance'.

You hear something about options C and D, but only D is a correct answer to *Question 11*.

▶ Step 4 – Listen and do the task

IELTS TEST 1

Exam Essentials

LISTENING MODULE   READING MODULE   WRITING MODULE   SPEAKING MODULE

SECTION 1
SECTION 2
SECTION 3
SECTION 4

Questions 13–17

Complete the table below.

Write **NO MORE THAN THREE WORDS AND/OR A NUMBER** *for each answer.*

HOLLYLANDS MUSEUM & EDUCATION CENTRE

EXHIBITION	STARTING DATE	POINTS TO REMEMBER
History in Pictures	13	opportunity to go on an old bus
14	19ᵗʰ September	visitors can use 15 .... service
16	11ᵗʰ November	competition – prize: 17 .... for 2 people

Table completion

Task guide

▸ This task requires you to listen and fill in a table with the correct information.

▸ It is important to write in exactly what is required, so you should look carefully at the whole table to see how the information is organised.

▸ If there are words or numbers before and/or after the numbered gaps, these are likely not to be the actual words that you hear on the tape, but similar words that have the same meaning.

▸ You must fill in the numbered gaps with the exact words and numbers that you hear on the recording.

▸ Read the instructions carefully. Notice how many words you can use to fill in each gap. The number of words may vary; you may be asked to write a maximum of one, two or three words in each gap. The instructions will also tell you if you need to use a number for your answer.

▸ You need to listen carefully, as the recording may contain other information which may seem correct, but which will in fact be wrong for the purposes of completing the table.

▸ See also page 54 for another type of table completion task.

Step-by-step guide

> **Step 1 – Think first**

Prepare for this task by thinking about how the information might be presented on the recording.

For example, an 'exhibition' might be described as a 'show' or an 'event'. These exhibitions might 'have the name', 'have the title' or 'be called' something.

Think of different ways to talk about the 'starting date'.

Starting date: ....

> **Step 2 – Check what you hear**

Look at the tapescript for *Question 13*.

Tapescript

OK, now we run a programme of exhibitions through the year, so I'll tell you about the next few. Our current exhibition, *Local Lives*, ends on 26th August, and then one called *History in Pictures* starts on 28th August. This includes all sorts of objects and experiences from the past, such as farm machinery and some cars. We're sure children will love the chance to have a ride on an old bus.

1 What is the correct answer for *Question 13*?

....

2 What wrong answer might you write for *Question 13* if you didn't listen carefully?

....

3 How is the 'opportunity to go on an old bus' described in the tapescript?

....

4 Why should you not write 'on' as part of your answer to *Question 13*?

....

> **Step 3 – Listen and do the task**

SECTION 1
SECTION 2
SECTION 3
SECTION 4

Questions 18–20

Label the plan below.

*Choose three answers from the box and write the letters **A–F** next to questions 18–20.*

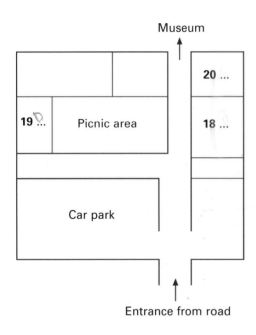

A	bicycle parking
B	drinks machine
C	first aid room
D	manager's office
E	telephones
F	ticket office
G	toilets

18 ....

19 ....

20 ....

Labelling a map/plan/diagram (2) (with choices)

Task guide

▶ This task requires you to label a plan (or map or diagram) correctly.

▶ You must use the information you hear on the recording to decide which of the possible answers are correct for the places marked on the plan.

▶ You may have to find two or more places from a list of several possible answers.

▶ It is important that you look carefully at the plan, so that you are ready to find your way around it while listening to the recording.

▶ The options will probably be listed alphabetically, but the order in which you hear them will probably be different.

▶ If you miss one answer, don't worry too much – move on to the next one. You should be able to find each answer independently of the other(s).

▶ See also pages 8 and 64 for other types of labelling tasks.

Step-by-step guide

> ▸ **Step 1 – Get in position**

In order to answer the questions correctly, you need to start reading the plan from the correct point. You need to locate the starting point on the plan.

On the plan here, there are two possible starting points: 'Entrance from road' and 'Museum'. Think about the position of the arrows as well. Where will the directions probably start?

> ▸ **Step 2 – Think first**

It is possible that the options will be expressed in a different way in the tapescript. Look at how option A is described in the tapescript.

Tapescript

So, whether you come by car or bicycle, you'll come in from the road. Cars then park to the left, through the gates into the car park, and bikes to the right, through the gates opposite.

1 Is option A a correct answer for *Question 18, 19* or *20*? ....

Now look at how option B is described in the tapescript.

Tapescript

Cyclists in particular might be feeling thirsty at this point, and you can get a drink from the machine at the end of the bike park, half way to the museum entrance.

2 Is option B a correct answer for *Question 18, 19* or *20*? ....

3 Options A and B have come first and second in the recording. Do we know if option C will come next? ....

> ▸ **Step 3 – Listen and do the task**

LISTENING MODULE	READING MODULE	WRITING MODULE	SPEAKING MODULE

SECTION 1
SECTION 2
SECTION 3
SECTION 4

▸ **Questions 21–30**

Questions 21–25

Choose the correct letter, **A, B** *or* **C.**

21 Before giving her presentation, Kate was worried about
   A being asked difficult questions.
   B using the projection equipment.
   C explaining statistical results.

22 During many presentations by students, Martin feels that
   A the discussion of research methods is not detailed enough.
   B lecturers do not show enough interest in their students' work.
   C the student does not make enough eye contact with the audience.

23 What is Kate's opinion of the tutorials she attends?
   A They involve too much preparation.
   B They should be held more frequently.
   C They do not have a clear focus.

24 What does Martin intend to do next semester?
   A make better use of the internet
   B improve his note-taking skills
   C prioritise reading lists effectively

25 What problem do Kate and Martin both have when using the library?
   A The opening hours are too short.
   B There are too few desks to work at.
   C The catalogue is difficult to use.

Multiple-choice with single answer

Task guide

- This task requires you to choose the correct answer to each question from three possible answers.

- There may be between one and ten questions.

- The questions follow the order of the recording.

- Within each question, you may hear reference to the three options in any order.

- If you realise you have missed a question, don't try to remember it, but move on, and make sure you do not miss the next question(s).

- Multiple-choice questions vary considerably in terms of complexity. In Section 1, they ask you to listen for relatively straightforward facts, but in Section 3 and Section 4, the questions will test your understanding of opinions, feelings, evidence, argument, and so on.

- Do not immediately choose an option simply because you hear the same word or words on the recording. It is your understanding of the meaning of the whole question that is tested here.

- See also pages 7 and 10 for other types of multiple-choice tasks.

Step-by-step guide

▸ **Step 1 – Think first**

It is very important that you read the question carefully.

The stems of some questions (here *Questions 21* and *22*) are partial sentences, to be completed by the possible answers, while the stems of others are complete questions (here *Questions 23, 24* and *25*.)

▸ **Step 2 – Watch out for possible dangers**

Look at *Question 21*. The question consists of two parts: 'Before giving her presentation' and 'Kate was worried about'. This is what you must listen for.

These are some dangers in choosing an answer:

You hear Kate say what worried her during or after the presentation, not **before** her presentation, and choose the wrong answer.

You hear Kate say what she was looking forward to, not what she was **worried about** before the presentation, and choose the wrong answer.

You hear another speaker, not **Kate**, say what he or she was worried about before his or her presentation, and choose the wrong answer.

▸ **Step 3 – Consider the possibilities**

Look at the tapescript for *Question 21* and answer the questions below about options A, B and C.

Tapescript

I was ever so nervous beforehand. It's silly, because I do know my stuff quite well. I must know those statistics inside out, but when you have to get each table of results to come up in the right order, it can make you nervous. It was my first time using the computerised projector, and I was sure I was going to get the controls wrong, or something. And of course, that's not a good situation, if you know you've got to listen to questions carefully and be ready to answer quickly.

Option A

1 Did Kate expect to be asked questions? ....

2 Does she talk about questions being difficult? ....

3 Is option A the correct answer? ....

Option B

1 Does she talk about using projection equipment? ....

2 Does she talk about problems in connection with projection equipment? ....

3 Is option B the correct answer? ....

Option C

1 Does she talk about statistical results? ....

2 Does she say that explaining statistical results was something she was worried about? ....

3 Is option C the correct answer? ....

▸ **Step 4 – Listen and do the task**

Questions 26–30

Who will do the following tasks?

A   Martin
B   Kate
C   both Martin and Kate

*Write the correct letter, **A, B** or **C** next to questions 26–30.*

26   compose questionnaire   ....

27   select people to interview   ....

28   conduct interviews   ....

29   analyse statistics   ....

30   prepare visuals for presentation   ....

Classification

Task guide

▸ This task requires you to answer a series of questions with the same choice of answers in each case.

▸ Although the possible answers are the same for each question, the questions do not depend on each other. You can get one question wrong, but the next one right.

▸ Do not try to 'break the code': it is not possible to predict how many answers will be the same, or to find a pattern of any kind.

▸ In some cases, option C may be the combination of options A and B. In other cases, the possible answers may consist of three distinct possibilities – three different people, places, periods of time, and so on.

▸ The questions follow the order of the recording.

▸ If you miss one question, leave it and go on to the next one.

Step-by-step guide

▶ **Step 1 – Think first**

What you hear on the recording may be different words from the questions, but with the same meaning.

For 'compose a questionnaire' in *Question 26*, you might hear 'write a questionnaire', 'create a questionnaire', 'produce questions for a questionnaire', 'put a questionnaire together', and so on.

Look at *Questions 27–30*. Think of what you might hear on the tape and write your ideas:

27 ....

28 ....

29 ....

30 ....

▶ **Step 2 – Check what you will hear**

Look at the tapescript for *Question 26*.

Tapescript

Kate: Yes. Well, we're going to need the questionnaire before we can do much else, aren't we? Do you want to handle that?
Martin: I'd assumed we'd do it together?
Kate: You have more experience than me. Maybe you could think up the main questions, you know, a first version of the whole thing, and then I could read it through.
Martin: And make suggestions? Well, OK.

Kate first suggests that Martin 'handles' the questionnaire. If you choose option A (Martin) at this point, you are answering the question too soon. At this point, it has not been confirmed who will do the task of composing the questionnaire.

Next, Martin suggests that they do the task together. This indicates that both Martin and Kate (option C) is the answer. However, you cannot be sure, because Kate has not agreed to this yet.

Then Kate accepts Martin's suggestion and clarifies how they will both do the task. But you still cannot be sure, because Martin has not agreed to this.

Finally, Martin confirms his agreement ('Well, OK.'), and you can now safely choose option C as the correct answer.

▶ **Step 3 – Listen and do the task**

IELTS TEST 1

Exam Essentials

| LISTENING MODULE | READING MODULE | WRITING MODULE | SPEAKING MODULE |

SECTION 1
SECTION 2
SECTION 3
SECTION 4

▶ **Questions 31–40**

Questions 31–34

Answer the questions below.

Write **NO MORE THAN ONE WORD AND/OR A NUMBER** *for each answer.*

31   Where was a Stone Age rubbish dump found?

   ....

32   In Medieval times, what type of waste was most common?

   ....

33   What did science link with waste?

   ....

34   Which invention is the biggest problem for the environment?

   ....

Short-answer questions (1)

Task guide

▶ This task requires you to write answers to separate questions by using information you hear on the recording.

▶ The questions follow the order of the recording.

▶ Read the instructions carefully. Notice how many words you can use to answer each question. If you use more words than you are told, your answer will be wrong.

▶ You must write the exact words that you hear on the recording. Do not try to use other words or to change the form of words.

▶ Remember that the wording used in the questions is not likely to be exactly the same as the wording you hear on the recording. It is likely to be paraphrased or to use synonyms.

▶ Sometimes you may think you know the answer to a question from your general knowledge. But remember that these questions are about what the speaker says. You must answer the question according to what information the speaker gives on the recording.

▶ See also page 22 for another type of short-answer task.

Step-by-step guide

▶ Step 1 – Think first

Look at *Questions 31–34*, and think about the kinds of answers you are required to write.

Questions 31–34 are about facts. *Questions 31, 33* and *34* will need to be answered with nouns. *Question 32* will need to be answered with an adjective.

While multiple-choice questions often test your understanding of opinion rather than plain fact, in short-answer questions you need to listen for and extract facts.

▶ Step 2 – Identify the correct answer

This task is likely, particularly when used in Section 4, to involve dealing with more than one apparently possible answer. It's important to distinguish between what is apparently possible and what is correct.

Look at the tapescript for *Questions 31* and *32* and answer the questions below.

Tapescript

We have evidence that in ancient Greece and Rome governments operated municipal waste collection, and a huge Stone Age mound was identified some years ago in Norway as waste disposal, so we can see that people have been generating waste for a very long time indeed. However, during the Dark Ages, sophisticated municipal waste processing disappeared. The medieval answer to waste was to throw it out of the window. But this waste, apart from broken pottery and a few metal objects, was largely organic.

Question 31

1 This question asks 'where': which three places are mentioned in the script?

....

2 Which words in the tapescript mean the same as 'rubbish dump'?

....

3 Which words in the tapescript mean the same as 'was ... found'?

....

4 What is the correct answer to *Question 31*?

....

Question 32

1 Can the words 'throw it out of the window' be an answer to *Question 32*?

....

2 Which three types of waste in medieval times are mentioned in the tapescript?

....

3 What word is the tapescript means the same as 'most common'?

....

4 What is the correct answer to *Question 32*?

....

▶ Step 3 – Listen and do the task

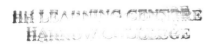

LISTENING MODULE	READING MODULE	WRITING MODULE	SPEAKING MODULE

SECTION 1
SECTION 2
SECTION 3
SECTION 4

Questions 35–37

List **THREE** factors which led to the increase in waste.

Write **NO MORE THAN TWO WORDS** for each answer.

35 ....

36 ....

37 ....

Short-answer questions (2)

Task guide

▸ This task requires you to answer the same question with a list of two or more things.

▸ The instructions tell you the maximum number of words you can use. Do not use more words than this.

▸ You can write your answers in any order.

▸ It is important that what you write in the list answers the question.

▸ See also page 20 for another type of short-answer task.

Step-by-step guide

▸ **Step 1 – Think first**

The question asks you to list 'factors which led to the increase in waste'.

Think of words which mean the same as 'factor'.
Think of words which mean the same as 'lead to'.
Think of words which mean the same as 'increase'.
Think of words which mean the same as 'waste'.

▸ **Step 2 – Select what to write**

Look at the tapescript for *Question 35*. The correct answer is 'mass manufacturing'.

Tapescript

As many countries became industrialised, we saw the advent of **mass manufacturing**. This has been enormously damaging as it has greatly increased the amount of things on the planet's surface which don't go away by themselves.

Why are these answers not correct?

1 industrialised

....

2 the advent of manufacturing

....

3 damaging

....

4 amount of things

....

▸ **Step 3 – Listen and do the task**

Questions 38–40

Which country uses the highest proportion of each method of waste disposal?

Choose your answers from the box and write the letters **A–F** *next to questions 38–40.*

> A Denmark
> B Germany
> C Japan
> D Switzerland
> E UK
> F USA

38 incineration: ....

39 landfill: ....

40 recycling: ....

Matching

Task guide

▸ This task requires you choose an answer for each question from the same list of possible answers.

▸ The options are usually listed alphabetically or similarly. For example, if the options are dates, they will be listed with the earliest first.

▸ The questions follow the order of the recording.

▸ You must read the question very carefully, as the possible answers will be mentioned several times in different ways.

Step-by-step guide

▸ **Step 1 – Read the question**

The question asks you to listen for the country 'which uses the highest proportion of each method of waste disposal'.

It is very likely that all the six countries listed will use all three waste disposal methods.

It is possible that a large country such as the US could incinerate 'a low proportion' of its waste, but this waste could be 'a higher quantity' of waste than that incinerated by another smaller country that incinerates 'a high proportion' of its waste.

Such questions will not depend on mathematics.

You need to read the question very carefully.

▸ **Step 2 – Check what you will hear**

Look at the tapescript for *Question 38*.

Tapescript

One of the main ways of dealing with MSW is incineration – burning it. This is adopted variously around the world. The UK burns relatively little waste, as does the US, while Denmark burns about half of all waste, and Japan uses this method for as much as three quarters.

You hear four countries, the UK, the US, Denmark and Japan, mentioned very closely together. The possible answers, A, C, E and F, are all heard, and you must be able to distinguish C as the only correct one.

▸ **Step 3 – Listen and do the task**

IELTS
TEST **1**

Exam Essentials

LISTENING MODULE   READING MODULE   WRITING MODULE   SPEAKING MODULE

PASSAGE 1
PASSAGE 2
PASSAGE 3

You should spend about 20 minutes on **Questions 1–13** *which are based on Reading Passage 1 on pages 24 and 25.*

The Dollar-a-Year Man

How John Lomax set out to record American folk music

A In the early 1930s, folklorist, platform lecturer, college professor and former banker John Avery Lomax was trying to recapture a sense of direction for his life. For two decades he had enjoyed a national reputation for his pioneering work in collecting and studying American folk songs; no less a figure than President Theodore Roosevelt had admired his work, and had written a letter of support for him as he sought grants for his research. He had always dreamed of finding a way of making a living by doing the thing he loved best, collecting folk songs, but he was now beginning to wonder if he would ever realise that dream.

B Lomax wanted to embark on a nationwide collecting project, resulting in as many as four volumes, and 'complete the rehabilitation of the American folk-song'. Eventually this was modified to where he envisioned a single book tentatively called *American Ballads and Folk Songs*, designed to survey the whole field. It called for first-hand field collecting, and would especially focus on the neglected area of black folk music.

C In 1932, Lomax travelled to New York, and stopped in to see a man named H.S. Latham

of the Macmillan Company. He informally outlined his plan to Latham, and read him the text of an earthy African American blues ballad called 'Ida Red'. Latham was impressed, and two days later Lomax had a contract, a small check to bind it, and an agreement to deliver the manuscript about one year later. The spring of 1932 began to look more green, lush and full of promise.

D Lomax immediately set to work. He travelled to libraries at Harvard, the Library of Congress, Brown University and elsewhere in order to explore unpublished song collections and to canvas the folk song books published over the past ten years. During his stay in Washington, D.C., Lomax became friendly with Carl Engel, Music Division chief of the Library of Congress. Engel felt that Lomax had the necessary background and energy to someday direct the Archive of Folk Song. Through funds provided by the Council of Learned Societies and the Library of Congress, Lomax ordered a state-of-the-art portable recording machine. More importantly, the Library of Congress agreed to furnish blank records and to lend their name to his collecting; Lomax simply had to agree to deposit the completed records at the Library of Congress. He did so without hesitation. On

July 15, 1933, Lomax was appointed an 'honorary consultant' for a dollar a year.

E Together with his eighteen-year-old son Alan, he began a great adventure to collect songs for *American Ballads and Folk Songs*, a task that was to last for many months. Lomax's library research had reinforced his belief that a dearth of black folk song material existed in printed collections. This fact, along with his early appreciation of African American folk culture, led Lomax to decide that black folk music from rural areas should be the primary focus. This bold determination resulted in the first major trip in the United States to capture black folk music in the field. In order to fulfill their quest, the two men concentrated on sections of the South with a high percentage of blacks. They also pinpointed laboring camps, particularly lumber camps, which employed blacks almost exclusively. But as they went along, prisons and penitentiaries also emerged as a focal point for research.

F The recordings made by the Lomaxes had historical significance. The whole idea of using a phonograph to preserve authentic folk music was still fairly new. Most of John Lomax's peers were involved in collecting songs the classic way: taking both words and melody down by hand, asking the singer to perform the song over and over until the collector had 'caught' it on paper. John Lomax sensed at once the limitations of this kind of method, especially when getting songs from African-American singers, whose quarter tones, blue notes and complex timing often frustrated white musicians trying to transcribe them with European notation systems.

G The whole concept of field recordings was, in 1933 and still is today, radically different from the popular notion of recording. Field recordings are not intended as commercial products, but as attempts at cultural preservation. There is no profit motive, nor any desire to make the singer a 'star'. As have hundreds of folk song collectors after him, John Lomax had to persuade his singers to perform, to explain to them why their songs were important, and to convince the various authorities – the wardens, the trusties, the bureaucrats – that this was serious, worthwhile work. He faced the moral problem of how to safeguard the records and the rights of the singers – a problem he solved in this instance by donating the discs to the Library of Congress. He had to overcome the technical problems involved in recording outside a studio; one always hoped for quiet, with no doors slamming or alarms going off, but it was always a risk. His new state-of-the-art recording machine sported a new microphone designed by NBC, but there were no wind baffles to help reduce the noise when recording outside. Lomax learned how to balance sound, where to place microphones, how to work echoes and walls, and soon was a skilled recordist.

IELTS TEST 1

Exam Essentials

| LISTENING MODULE | **READING MODULE** | WRITING MODULE | SPEAKING MODULE |

PASSAGE 1
PASSAGE 2
PASSAGE 3

Questions 1–5

Complete the summary below.

Choose **NO MORE THAN THREE WORDS** *from the passage for each answer.*

Write your answers in boxes 1–5 on your answer sheet.

JOHN LOMAX'S
P R O J E C T

Lomax began the research for this project by looking at 1 .... that were not available in book form, as well as at certain books. While he was doing this research, he met someone who ran a department at the 2 .... in Washington. As a result of this contact, he was provided with the very latest kind of 3 .... for his project.

Lomax believed that the places he should concentrate on were 4 .... in the South of the US. While he and his son were on their trip, they added 5 .... as places where they could find what they were looking for.

Summary (notes/table/flow chart) completion

Task guide

▸ This task requires you to find pieces of information in the reading passage in order to fill in the gaps in a summary (or notes or table or flow chart).

▸ This task often, but not always, focusses on one part or section of the reading passage, rather than on pieces of information spread throughout the text.

▸ This task requires you to use **exact words and phrases** from the text; the answers therefore all appear in the relevant part of the text. Do not try to use different words that have the same meaning – your answer will be marked wrong even if the meaning is correct.

▸ In completion tasks, the questions follow the same order as the relevant information in the reading passage.

▸ Read the instructions carefully. Notice how many words you can use to answer each question. The number of words may vary; you may be asked to write one, two or three words in each question. The instructions will also tell you if you need to use a number for your answer.

▸ In this case, you are asked to complete a summary. There is a flow-chart completion task on page 98, a table completion task on page 118 and a notes completion task on page 138. In all these tasks, the requirements are the same.

▸ See also page 80 for another type of summary completion task.

Step-by-step guide

▸ **Step 1 – Locate the task in the text**

First of all, you need to locate the task in the reading passage. Look for clues.

If the task has a title, it may refer to something that only appears in a particular section of the text.

In this case, the title ('JOHN LOMAX'S PROJECT') doesn't really help, because most of the text is about Lomax's project. You will need to look for clues in the summary.

1 The summary begins: 'Lomax began his research for this project ...'. In which section of the text (A–G) does he begin his research?

....

Which sentence in that section refers to him beginning his work?

....

2 The second sentence of the summary refers to Washington. Is Washington mentioned in the same section of the text?

....

3 The second paragraph of the summary mentions 'the South of the US'. Which section (A–G) of the text mentions 'the South'?

....

4 The second paragraph of the summary also mentions Lomax's son. Is his son mentioned in the same section of the text?

....

▸ **Step 2 – Find the answers**

Now look for the answers in the parts of the text you identified in step 1.

Remember that you must fill in the gaps with the exact words and phrases that appear in the text. However, the rest of the summary does not consist of words and phrases that are all repeated exactly from the text. Instead, the summary uses words and phrases that have the same meaning as those used in the text or that express the same ideas in a different way.

Question 1

Look at the words before and after the gap.

1 The verb after the gap is 'were'. What kind of word or phrase is required in the gap?

    A singular noun   **B** adjective   **C** plural noun

2 Which word in the text means 'look at' or 'study'?

....

3 Which word in the text means 'not available in book form?

....

Now use your answers for step 2 to find the answer to *Question 1*.

Question 2

Look at the sentence containing *Question 2*.

1 What is the word or phrase in the gap likely to refer to?
    A the name of a department
    B the name of an institution
    C the name of a person

2 Which word in the text means 'department'?

....

3 If someone 'runs' a place, they are the manager of it or in charge of it. Which word in the text means 'manager' or 'head'?

....

Now use your answers for step 2 to find the answer to *Question 2*.

Questions 3–5

Now answer Q*uestions 3–5* using the same process:

• Try to predict what kind of word is required in each gap by looking at the surrounding context.

• Look for words and phrases in the text that mean the same or express the same ideas as those used in the text surrounding the gaps in the summary.

PASSAGE 1
PASSAGE 2
PASSAGE 3

Questions 6–10

Reading Passage 1 has seven sections labelled **A–G**.

Which section contains the following information?

Write the correct letter **A–G** *in boxes 6–10 on your answer sheet.*

NB *You may use any letter more than once.*

6   a reference to the speed with which Lomax responded to a demand

7   a reason why Lomax doubted the effectiveness of a certain approach

8   reasons why Lomax was considered suitable for a particular official post

9   a reference to a change of plan on Lomax's part

10   a reference to one of Lomax's theories being confirmed

Matching information to sections of text

Task guide

▸ This task requires you to find the sections in which specific pieces of information appear in the reading passage.

▸ It is possible that the same section will be the answer to more than one question. If this is the case, the instructions will tell you that you can use any letter more than once. However, it is also possible that a section or sections of the text will not be the answer to any of the questions. The instructions will not tell you if this is the case, but do not worry if you have not chosen a particular section as the answer to any of the questions, because this may be correct.

▸ Be careful not to choose a section as your answer simply because it contains something on the same general subject as the question. It is likely that more than one section will contain information connected with the question, but only one section will contain the precise piece of information asked for in the question.

▸ Beware of 'word spotting'. Do not choose a section as your answer simply because it contains a word that also appears in the question. Other sections may also contain that word. It is very unlikely that the correct answer will involve simply finding the same word in both the question and a certain section of the reading passage.

▸ See also pages 34 and 74 for other types of matching tasks.

Step-by-step guide

The best approach to this task is to:

- read the first question and then look through the text to find the answer to it.
- move to the next question and repeat the process.

Question 6

▶ **Step 1 – Decide what you are looking for**

1 The question refers to a 'demand' that Lomax responded to. Therefore, you are looking for:
   A something he was required to do
   B something he asked for
   C something he was given

2 *Question 6* refers to 'speed'. Therefore, you are looking for a reference to him doing something:
   A well or badly
   B quickly or slowly
   C easily or with difficulty

▶ **Step 2 – Find the answer**

Now use your answers for step 1 to find the answer to *Question 6*.

When you are looking through the text, look for something that matches the ideas or information contained in the question.

In many questions, you will not find words and phrases in the reading passage that mean exactly the same as those used in the question. Instead, you will need to find places in the passage which refer to the idea expressed in the question.

When you have located the section which contains the relevant piece of information, you will be able to answer these questions:

1 What was Lomax required to do?

....

2 Which phrase in the text means 'very quickly' or 'immediately'?

....

Now write your answer for *Question 6*.

Question 7

▶ **Step 1 – Decide what you are looking for**

1 The question refers to why Lomax 'doubted the effectiveness' of an approach. Therefore, you are looking for a reference to him:
   A finding out how something worked
   B explaining how something worked
   C thinking that something didn't work very well

2 The question refers to an 'approach'. In this context, you are likely to be looking for:
   A a route taken on a journey
   B a research method
   C a type of music

▶ **Step 2 – Find the answer**

Now use your answers for step 1 to find the answer to *Question 7*.

Look for references in the reading passage that match the ideas and information contained in the question.

When you have located the section which contains the relevant piece of information, you will be able to answer these questions:

1 Which approach did Lomax consider ineffective?

....

2 Which word in the text means 'disadvantages' and refers to this approach, in his opinion?

....

Now write your answer for *Question 7*.

Questions 8–10

Now answer *Questions 8–10* using the same process:

- Read each question carefully and make sure that you understand exactly what you are looking for in the text.
- Find the section of the reading passage which matches exactly the ideas and information contained in the question.

IELTS TEST 1

Exam Essentials

LISTENING MODULE   **READING MODULE**   WRITING MODULE   SPEAKING MODULE

PASSAGE 1
PASSAGE 2
PASSAGE 3

Questions 11–13

Choose **THREE** *letters* **A–F**.

Write your answers in boxes 11–13 on your answer sheet.

Which **THREE** *of the following difficulties for Lomax are mentioned by the writer of the text?*

A   finding a publisher for his research

B   deciding exactly what kind of music to collect

C   the scepticism of others concerning his methods

D   the reluctance of people to participate in his project

E   making sure that participants in his project were not exploited

F   factors resulting from his choice of locations for recording

Multiple-choice with multiple answers

Task guide

▸ This task requires you to select a specified number of options which correctly answer the question.

▸ This task requires you to ask yourself two things for each option: (a) Is it true according to the text? and (b) Does it correctly answer the question?

▸ Be careful! An option may be true, but it may not answer the question. For example, if you are asked to select 'problems', an option may refer to something that did happen in the text but was not actually a problem.

▸ In these tasks, the options follow the same order as the relevant information in the text.

▸ Sometimes there is one mark for each correct option you choose; sometimes there is only one mark for the whole task, and you have to choose all the correct options in order to get a mark. If only one question number is given, you will know that only one mark will be given. In this task, there are three question numbers (*Question 11, 12* and *13*), which means that three marks will be given.

▸ See also page 68 for another type of multiple-choice task.

Step-by-step guide

▶ **Step-by-step guide**

The best approach to this task is to:

• take each option one by one

• find the relevant place in the text and

• decide whether the option is one of the answers to the question or not.

Option A

▶ **Step 1 – Locate the option in the text**

Look at option A and then read through the text.

Which section mentions a publisher?

....

▶ **Step 2 – Decide whether the option answers the question**

Look through the section you identified in step 1. Answer the questions below and decide whether option A is one of the answers or not.

1 What was the name of the publishing company Lomax visited?

....

2 What was the name of the man he went to see about publishing the book?

....

3 How long after they met did this man contact Lomax?

....

4 Did this man agree to publish Lomax's book?

....

Using your answers to these questions, decide whether option A refers to something that Lomax found difficult.

Option B

▶ **Step 1 – Locate the option in the text**

Look at option B and then read through the text.

Which section contains three specific references to the kind of music Lomax decided to collect?

....

▶ **Step 2 – Decide whether the option answers the question**

Look through the section you identified in step 1. Answer the questions below and decide whether option B is one of the answers or not.

1 What kind of music did Lomax decide to collect?

....

2 What two reasons are given for Lomax deciding to collect this kind of music?

....

3 Is there a reference to any other kind of music he considered collecting?

....

4 Is there a reference to Lomax taking a long time to decide what kind of music to collect?

....

Using your answers to these questions, decide whether option B refers to something that Lomax found difficult.

Options C–F

Now look at options C–F and use the same process to decide whether each one is an answer or not:

• Find the relevant part of the text.

• Read that part of the text carefully to find out whether each of the options was something that caused Lomax a problem or not.

▶ **Questions 14–26**

You should spend about 20 minutes on **Questions 14–26** *which are based on Reading Passage 2 on the following pages.*

Questions 14–20

Reading Passage 2 has seven paragraphs **A–G**.

Choose the correct heading for each paragraph from the list of headings below.

Write the correct numbers **i–x** *in boxes 14–20 on your answer sheet.*

List of Headings

i	Optimistic beliefs held by the writers of children's literature
ii	The attitudes of certain adults towards children's literature
iii	The attraction of children's literature
iv	A contrast that categorises a book as children's literature
v	A false assumption made about children's literature
vi	The conventional view of children's literature
vii	Some good and bad features of children's literature
viii	Classifying a book as children's literature
ix	The treatment of various themes in children's literature
x	Another way of looking at children's literature

---

14   Paragraph **A**

15   Paragraph **B**

16   Paragraph **C**

17   Paragraph **D**

18   Paragraph **E**

19   Paragraph **F**

20   Paragraph **G**

Children's literature

A I am sometimes asked why anyone who is not a teacher or a librarian or the parent of little kids should concern herself with children's books and folklore. I know the standard answers: that many famous writers have written for children, and that the great children's books are also great literature; that these books and tales are an important source of archetype and symbol, and that they can help us to understand the structure and functions of the novel.

B All this is true. But I think we should also take children's literature seriously because it is sometimes subversive: because its values are not always those of the conventional adult world. Of course, in a sense much great literature is subversive, since its very existence implies that what matters is art, imagination and truth. In what we call the real world, what usually counts is money, power and public success.

C The great subversive works of children's literature suggest that there are other views of human life besides those of the shopping mall and the corporation. They mock current assumptions and express the imaginative, unconventional, noncommercial view of the world in its simplest and purest form. They appeal to the imaginative, questioning, rebellious child within all of us, renew our instinctive energy, and act as a force for change. This is why such literature is worthy of our attention and will endure long after more conventional tales have been forgotten.

D An interesting question is what – besides intention – makes a particular story a 'children's book'? With the exception of picture books for toddlers, these works are not necessarily shorter or simpler than so-called adult fiction, and they are surely not less well written. The heroes and heroines of these tales, it is true, are often children: but then so are the protagonists of Henry James's *What Maisie Knew* and Toni Morrison's *The Bluest Eye*. Yet the barrier between children's books and adult fiction remains; editors, critics and readers seem to have little trouble in assigning a given work to one category or the other.

E In classic children's fiction a pastoral convention is maintained. It is assumed that the world of childhood is simpler and more natural than that of adults, and that children, though they may have faults, are essentially good or at least capable of becoming so. The transformation of selfish, whiny, disagreeable Mary and hysterical, demanding Colin in Frances Hodgson Burnett's *The Secret Garden* is a paradigm. Of course, there are often unpleasant minor juvenile characters who give the protagonist a lot of trouble and are defeated or evaded rather than reeducated. But on occasion even the angry bully and the lying sneak can be reformed and forgiven. Richard Hughes's *A High Wind in Jamaica*, though most of its characters are children, never appears on lists of recommended juvenile fiction; not so much because of the elaborations of its diction (which is no more complex than that of, say, *Treasure Island*), but because in it children are irretrievably damaged and corrupted.

F Adults in most children's books, on the other hand, are usually stuck with their characters and incapable of alteration or growth. If they are really unpleasant, the only thing that can rescue them is the natural goodness of a child. Here again, Mrs. Burnett provides the classic example, in *Little Lord Fauntleroy*. (Scrooge's somewhat similar change of heart in Dickens's *A Christmas Carol*, however, is due mainly to regret for his past and terror of the future. This is one of the things that makes the book a family rather than a juvenile romance; another is the helpless passivity of the principal child character, Tiny Tim.).

G Of the three principal preoccupations of adult fiction – sex, money and death – the first is

IELTS
TEST 1

Exam Essentials

LISTENING MODULE   **READING MODULE**   WRITING MODULE   SPEAKING MODULE

PASSAGE 1
PASSAGE 2
PASSAGE 3

absent from classic children's literature and the other two either absent or much muted. Money is a motive in children's literature, in the sense that many stories deal with a search for treasure of some sort. These quests, unlike real-life ones, are almost always successful, though occasionally what is found in the end is some form of family happiness, which is declared by the author and the characters to be a 'real treasure'. Simple economic survival, however, is almost never the problem; what is sought, rather, is a magical (sometimes literally magical) surplus of wealth. Death, which was a common theme in nineteenth-century fiction for children, was almost banished during the first half of the twentieth century. Since then it has begun to reappear; the breakthrough book was E.B. White's *Charlotte's Web*. Today not only animals but people die, notably in the sort of books that get awards and are recommended by librarians and psychologists for children who have lost a relative. But even today the characters who die tend to be of another generation; the protagonist and his or her friends survive. Though there are some interesting exceptions, even the most subversive of contemporary children's books usually follow these conventions. They portray an ideal world of perfectible beings, free of the necessity for survival.

Matching headings to paragraphs

Task guide

▸ This task requires you to select the most suitable headings for the paragraphs of a reading passage.

▸ In the list of possible headings that you select from, some of the headings are not suitable for any of the paragraphs of the reading passage.

▸ This task requires you to decide what the main topic or point of each paragraph is. An option may refer to something that is mentioned in a certain paragraph of the text, but it may not be the correct answer because it is not the main point or topic of that paragraph.

▸ Beware of 'word spotting'. Do not choose a heading as your answer simply because it contains a word that also appears in a particular paragraph of the text. It is likely that the same word will also appear in other paragraphs.

▸ See also pages 28 and 74 for other types of matching tasks.

Step-by-step guide

The best approach to this task is to read each paragraph of the text one by one, and then look at the list of headings each time to select the appropriate one.

Question 14

▸ **Step 1 – Read the paragraph**

Read paragraph A carefully and identify the main topic.

▸ **Step 2 – Consider each option**

Look at each option and decide whether it matches the main topic of the paragraph. You will need to ask yourself the questions below in order to answer the question. Questions i–x refer to the corresponding options i–x.

i   Is the paragraph mainly about what the writers of children's books believe?

ii   Does the paragraph focus on what certain adults think of children's literature?

iii   Does the paragraph mainly talk about what features of children's literature make it attractive?

iv   Does the paragraph focus on a difference between two things?

v   Is the paragraph mainly about something that people incorrectly believe about children's literature?

vi   Does the paragraph focus on what people normally say about children's literature?

vii   Does the paragraph mainly compare different features of children's literature?

viii   Is the paragraph mainly about what causes a book to be classified as children's literature?

ix   Is the paragraph mainly about the way various subjects are dealt with in children's literature?

x   Does the paragraph focus on a different view of children's literature from one already mentioned?

▸ **Step 3 – Choose the correct option**

When you have chosen your answer for paragraph A, check that it is correct by answering this question:

Which word in the heading you have chosen means the same as 'standard' in paragraph A?

....

Question 15

▸ **Step 1 – Read the paragraph**

Repeat step 1 above for paragraph B.

▸ **Step 2 – Consider each option**

Repeat step 2 above.

▸ **Step 3– Choose the correct option**

When you have chosen your answer for paragraph B, check that it is correct by answering this question:

Which word in paragraph B indicates that a point is being made that is additional to a point previously made?

....

Questions 16–20

Now follow the same process to decide on your answers for *Questions 16–20* (Paragraphs C–G):

• Read each paragraph carefully.

• Use the questions in step 2 above to help you choose the correct heading.

IELTS TEST 1

Exam Essentials

LISTENING MODULE   **READING MODULE**   WRITING MODULE   SPEAKING MODULE

PASSAGE 1
PASSAGE 2
PASSAGE 3

Questions 21–26

Do the following statements agree with the views of the writer in Reading Passage 2?

In boxes 21–26 on your answer sheet write

YES	*if the statement agrees with the views of the writer*
NO	*if the statement contradicts the views of the writer*
NOT GIVEN	*if it is impossible to say what the writer thinks about this*

21   Adults often fail to recognise the subversive elements in books their children read.

22   In publishing, the definition of certain genres has become inconsistent.

23   Characters in *The Secret Garden* are a good example of the norm in children's literature.

24   Despite the language used in *A High Wind in Jamaica*, it should be considered a children's book.

25   The character of Tiny Tim contrasts with that of the child in *Little Lord Fauntleroy*.

26   A more realistic view of money should be given in children's books.

Yes/No/Not Given

Task guide

▸ This task requires you to understand views expressed or claims made by the writer of the text.

▸ To answer each question, you will need to ask yourself three questions:
(a) Is the same view expressed in the text?
(b) Is the opposite view expressed in the text?
(c) Is there no view on this particular matter in the text?

▸ For an answer to be 'No', the writer must directly state something that makes the statement in the question incorrect.

▸ Questions to which the answer is 'Not Given' involve the writer saying something related to the statement in the question, but not expressing a view or making a claim on the specific point mentioned in the question.

▸ This task requires you to look very closely at what the writer does say, with regard to each of the questions.

▸ The questions follow the order in which the relevant issues are discussed or points mentioned in the text.

Step-by-step guide

The best way to approach this task is to:

- look at each question one by one
- locate the relevant part of the text
- study the question and that part of the text carefully and
- then decide on your answer.

Question 21

▸ **Step 1 – Locate the relevant section of the text**

Which section or sections of the text describe children's literature as subversive?

....

▸ **Step 2 – Study the question carefully**

Focus on the place(s) in the text you identified in step 1. Look carefully at the question and decide exactly what it means.

1 What does 'subversive' mean in the context?
   A criticising what is considered to be normal
   B done only for entertainment
   C difficult for some people to understand

2 The question is asking if the author says that adults
   A pretend that the books don't have subversive elements.
   B are annoyed that the books have subversive elements.
   C don't realise that the books have subversive elements.

▸ **Step 3 – Find the answer**

Using your answers in step 2, read the relevant part of the text carefully and answer these questions:

1 Does the writer say that children's literature presents a view of life that is different from that of adults?

....

2 Does the writer say that adults think that a different view of life is presented in the books their children read?

....

3 Does the writer say that adults read the books their children read?

....

Now use your answers for steps 2 and 3 to decide on the answer to *Question 21*.

Question 22

▸ **Step 1 – Locate the relevant section of the text**

1 Which section of the text refers to the publishing world and the people involved in it?

....

2 Which people involved in the publishing world are mentioned there?

....

3 What two kinds of literature are mentioned there?

....

▸ **Step 2 – Study the question carefully**

Focus on the place(s) in the text you identified in step 1. Look carefully at the question and decide exactly what it means.

1 Which word in the relevant part of the text means 'genre'?

....

2 The question is asking whether the writer states that something
   A isn't always correct.
   B has become unfashionable.
   C doesn't always follow the same pattern.

▸ **Step 3 – Find the answer**

Using your answers in step 2, read the relevant part of the text carefully and answer these questions:

1 Does the writer say that children's books and adult books are still considered to be totally separate types of book?

....

2 Does the writer say that people find it difficult to decide what category some books belong to?

....

3 Does the writer suggest that different people categorise books differently?

....

Now use your answers for steps 1 and 2 to decide on the answer to *Question 22*.

Questions 23–26

Now answer *Questions 23–26*, using the same process:

- Locate the relevant part of the text.
- Study the question and the relevant part of the text carefully.
- Ask yourself the three questions listed in the **Task guide** on page 36.

IELTS
TEST 1

Exam Essentials

| LISTENING MODULE | READING MODULE | WRITING MODULE | SPEAKING MODULE |

PASSAGE 1
PASSAGE 2
PASSAGE 3

*You should spend about 20 minutes on **Questions 27–40** which are based on Reading Passage 3 below.*

The birth of our modern minds

When did we begin to use symbols to communicate? Roger Highfield reports on a challenge to prevailing ideas

Anyone who doubts the importance of art need do no more than refer to the current account of human evolution, where the emergence of modern people is not so much marked by Stone Age technology as a creative explosion that rocked Europe 40,000 years ago. Our ancestors began to adorn their bodies with beads and pendants, even tattoos; they painted representations of animals, people and magical hybrids on cave walls in Lascaux, France and Altamira in Spain. They sculpted voluptuous stone figures, such as the Venus of Willendorf. This cultural Big Bang, which coincided with the period when modern humans reached Europe after they set out, via the Near East, from Africa, marked a decisive point in our story, when man took a critical step beyond the limitations of his hairy ancestors and began to use symbols. The modern mind was born.

Or was it? Britain's leading archaeologist questions the dogma that the modern human mind originated in Europe and, instead, argues that its birth was much more recent, around 10,000 years ago, and took place in the Middle East. Lord Renfrew, professor of archaeology at Cambridge University, is troubled by what he calls the 'sapient behaviour paradox': genetic findings, based on the diversity of modern humans, suggest that our big brains emerged 150,000 years ago, when *Homo sapiens* evolved from *Homo erectus*, and

were fully developed about 60,000 years ago. But this hardware, though necessary, was not sufficient for modern behaviour: software (culture) is also required to run a mind and for this to be honed took tens of millennia. There is something unsatisfactory about the genetic argument that rests on the 'potential' for change emerging, he argues. Ultimately, little happened – or at least not for another 30,000 years.

Although there is no doubt that genes shaped the hardware of the modern brain, genetics does not tell the whole story. 'It is doubtful whether molecular sequences will give us any clear insights,' said Lord Renfrew, adding that the current account of our origins has also become sidetracked by placing too much emphasis on one cultural event. Either side of the boundary between the Middle and Upper Palaeolithic, 40,000 years ago, people lived much the same way. To the casual observer, the archaeological record for *Homo sapiens* does not look much different from *Homo erectus's*, or even our beetle browed European cousins, the Neanderthals. 'There are detailed changes in tools and so on but the only one that really strikes you is cave art.'

And this artistic revolution was patchy: the best examples are in Spain and France. In Britain, the oldest known cave art consists of 12,000-year-old engravings in Creswell Crags. Indeed, was there an artistic revolution 40,000 years ago at all? Two pieces of ochre engraved with geometrical patterns 70,000 years ago were recently found at Blombos Cave, 180 miles east of Cape Town, South Africa. This means people were able to think abstractly and behave as modern humans much earlier than previously thought. Lord Renfrew argues that art, like genetics, does not tell the whole story of our origins. For him, the real revolution occurred 10,000 years ago with the first permanent villages. That is when the effects of new software kicked in, allowing our ancestors to work together in a more settled way. That is when plants and animals were domesticated and agriculture born.

'First there were nests of skulls and unusual burial practices, cult centres and shrines. Then you have the first villages, the first towns, like Jericho in Jordan (around 8000 BC) and Catalhöyük in Turkey (est 6500 BC), then the spread of farming to Europe. Before long, you are accelerating towards the first cities in Mesopotamia, and then other civilisations in Mexico, China and beyond.'

Living in timber and mud brick houses led to a very different engagement between our ancestors and the material world. 'I don't think it was until settled village communities developed that you had the concept of property, or that "I own these things that have been handed down to me".' This in turn could have introduced the need for mathematics, to keep a tally of possessions, and written language to describe them. In the Near East, primitive counters date back to the early farming period and this could have marked the first stages of writing, said Lord Renfrew. 'We have not solved anything about the origins of modern humans until we understand what happened 10,000 years ago,' he said. He is excited by excavations now under way in Anatolia, a potential birthplace of the modern mind, in Catalhöyük, one of the earliest places where close-knit communities were born, and Göbekli Tepe, a shrine that predates village life. These spiritual sites may have seeded the first human settled communities by encouraging the domestication of plants and animals.

IELTS TEST 1

Exam Essentials

LISTENING MODULE   **READING MODULE**   WRITING MODULE   SPEAKING MODULE

PASSAGE 1
PASSAGE 2
PASSAGE 3

Questions 27–32

Answer the questions below using **NO MORE THAN THREE WORDS** *for each answer.*

Write your answers in boxes 27–32 on your answer sheet.

27   According to the current view, what does NOT indicate the first appearance of the modern human?

28   What type of evidence does Lord Renfrew question in general?

29   What, apart from art, were the developments in the creation of 40,000 years ago?

30   What kind of cave art in Britain is referred to?

31   What TWO things does Lord Renfrew believe to have been established 10,000 years ago?

32   What TWO things did the notion of personal possessions lead to?

Short-answer questions

Task guide

▸ This task requires you to write answers for questions, using pieces of information that are given in the reading passage.

▸ Read the instructions carefully. Notice how many words you can use to answer each question. The number of words may vary; you may be asked to write one, two or three words in each question. The instructions will also tell you if you need to use a number in one or more answers.

▸ All the questions can be answered using actual words and phrases that appear in the reading passage. You are not required to think of words that have the same meaning as words in the text, and if you do this, you may make unnecessary mistakes.

▸ The questions follow the same order as the relevant information in the text.

Step-by-step guide

The best way to approach this task is to:

- look at each question one by one
- locate the relevant part of the text and
- look for the information that relates to each question.

For some questions, you may find words and phrases in the text that mean the same as words and phrases in the question. For some questions, this will not be the case, and you will have to look for information that matches the content of the question but is expressed in a different way.

Question 27

▸ Step 1 – Locate the question in the text

1 Find a sentence in the text that mentions the current view concerning the development of the modern human being. Which sentence is it and in which paragraph is it?

....

2 Which word in that sentence means 'first appearance'?

....

3 Which word in that sentence means 'indicated'?

....

▸ Step 2 – Find the answer

The sentence in the text you identified in step 1 refers to something that does indicate the first appearance of the modern human being, and something that does not.

Find these two things and choose one of them as your answer for *Question 27*.

Question 28

▸ Step 1 – Locate the question in the text

1 If you 'question' something, you have doubts about it or think it may not be right. In which paragraphs are there references to Lord Renfrew having doubts about something?

....

2 Which word in the relevant part of the text means 'worried' or 'concerned'?

....

3 Which word in the relevant part of the text means 'not right' or 'not good enough'?

....

▸ Step 2 – Find the answer

1 In the paragraph you identified in questions 2 and 3 of step 1, Lord Renfrew is said to have doubts about certain evidence. Which word in that paragraph means 'evidence' or 'discoveries'?

....

2 In the same paragraph, Lord Renfrew is also said to consider a certain opinion not to be right. Which word means 'opinion' or 'view' in this context?

....

3 Find a word in the text that is connected with the two words you identified in questions 1 and 2 above and write it as your answer for *Question 28*.

....

Questions 29–32

Now answer *Questions 29–32*, using the same process:

- Locate the question in the text.
- Look for sentences and phrases that relate to the content of the question.
- Remember that all the answers can be actual words and phrases that you find in the text.

IELTS TEST 1

Exam Essentials

| LISTENING MODULE | READING MODULE | WRITING MODULE | SPEAKING MODULE |

PASSAGE 1
PASSAGE 2
PASSAGE 3

Questions 33–40

Classify the following statements as referring to the period

A   10,000 years ago
B   40,000 years ago
C   60,000 years ago
D   70,000 years ago

Write the correct letter **A–D** *in boxes 33–40 on your answer sheet.*

33   The brain was completely formed physically but was not capable of all the functions of the modern mind.

34   There was a major change in the attitude of humans to each other.

35   A huge amount of art in different forms began to appear.

36   Development of the human mind occurred at the same time as a migration.

37   Art from the period casts doubt on the conventional view of the development of the human mind.

38   The modern mind developed in a different location from the one normally assumed.

39   The only significant change in the development of man is shown in the art produced.

40   Further research into the period is essential for accurate conclusions to be drawn on human development.

Classification

Task guide

▸ This task requires you to match pieces of information with the categories they belong in according to the text.

▸ Make sure that there is something in the text connected with the option you choose that matches exactly the statement in the question. Often, more than one option will have a connection with the statement in the question, but only one option will match it exactly.

▸ The categories will be listed in a logical order, for example, chronologically or in alphabetical order. Therefore, they may not match the order in which they are mentioned in the text. Make sure you do not get confused and accidentally write the wrong letter for an answer.

Step-by-step guide

The best way to approach this task is to first identify the parts of the text in which the categories are mentioned. If you locate the categories in the beginning, you will only need to keep looking at those parts of the text, rather than constantly having to look through the whole text for each question.

▶ **Step 1 – Locate the categories in the text**

Look through the text and find where the time periods A–D are mentioned.

In which paragraphs and where in those paragraphs are they mentioned?

A 10,000 years ago

....

B 40,000 years ago

....

C 60,000 years ago

....

D 70,000 years ago

....

▶ **Step 2 – Find the answers**

For some questions, there may be words and phrases in the text which mean the same as words and phrases used in the question.

However, classification tasks involve more than simply matching words and phrases of similar meaning. For many questions, you will have to understand ideas that are presented in the text and match them to the ideas contained in the questions.

Question 33

1 Look at the parts of the text you identified in step 1 and find the place that relates to *Question 33*. You are looking for references to the brain being completely formed and to something it lacked. In which paragraph are these references?

....

When you have found the right part of the text, you will be able to answer these questions.

2 Which phrase in the text means 'completely formed'?

....

3 What is the modern mind said to require that it did not have at that time?

....

4 How long did it take for the mind to become capable of this?

....

Now identify which time period (A–D) this part of the text relates to. Write your answer for *Question 33*.

Question 34

1 Look at the parts of the text you identified in step 1 and find the place that relates to *Question 34*. You are looking for references to a big change and to relationships between humans. In which paragraph are these references?

....

When you have found the right part of the text, you will be able to answer these questions.

2 Which word in the text that means 'major change'?

....

3 The text refers to something having a big effect. Which phrase in the text means 'started to have a big effect'?

....

4 What did humans start to do that represented a major change?

....

Now identify which time period (A–D) this part of the text relates to. Write your answer for *Question 34*.

Questions 35–40

Now answer *Questions 35–40* using the same process:

• Read the question and look through the parts of the text you identified in step 1.

• Find information in the text that matches the content of the question.

• Identify which time period (A–D) this information relates to.

You should spend about 20 minutes on this task.

The charts below show the number of French adults whose parents spoke a French regional language to them when they were children and the number who speak a French regional language to their own children.

Write a report for a university lecturer describing the information below.

Write at least 150 words.

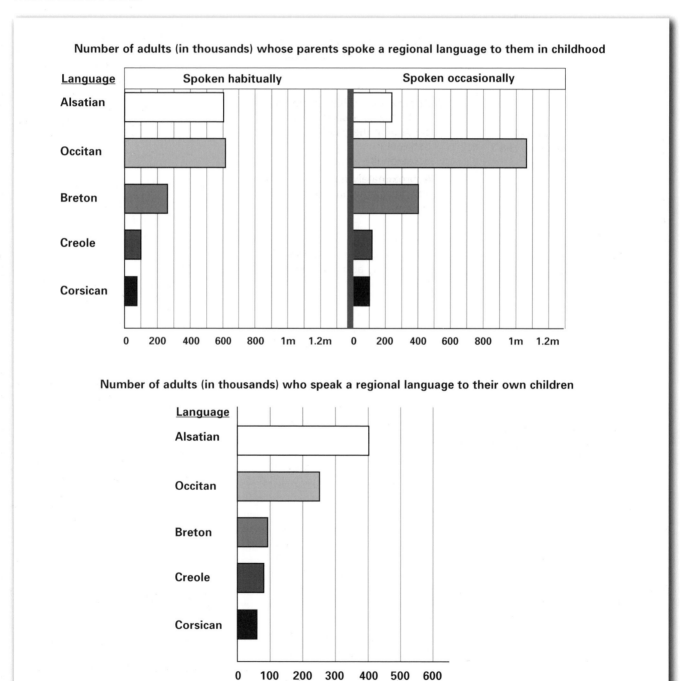

Number of adults (in thousands) whose parents spoke a regional language to them in childhood

Number of adults (in thousands) who speak a regional language to their own children

Describing charts and graphs

Task guide

▶ Tasks in the Writing Module will be marked according to the criteria described on page 84 – **content**, **organisation** and **use of language**.

▶ Many Task 1 questions involve statistical information in the form of bar charts, graphs or pie charts. Some tasks may involve a single chart or graph, others may involve more than one, and some may involve a combination of elements (for example, a graph and a bar chart).

▶ This task involves bar charts. You will find graphs, pie charts and combinations in the other tests in this book.

▶ You are required to **select the most important information and summarise it**. You should therefore begin by looking for the main points, the general trends or the overall message.

▶ **Do not list every fact and figure in your answer.** Include only the relevant main points, with relevant examples from the data. Do not include less important details.

▶ Do not become confused if there seems to be a lot of data. Even if there is more than one chart, graph, etc., there will usually be only one or two main points. Focus on finding these main points. Then decide which parts of the data best illustrate the main point or points.

▶ You are not required to do any mathematics for this task. Do not waste time adding and subtracting numbers. Concentrate on the general idea.

▶ If precise figures are not given in a chart or graph, do not waste time trying to decide what the precise figure is. Use words and phrases like: *approximately, about, roughly, (just) over, (just) under, nearly*, etc.

▶ Make sure that you write at least the minimum number of words specified in the instructions. Short answers will lose marks.

▶ On the other hand, do not write too much. If you write a very long answer, you may make mistakes and lose marks.

Step-by-step guide

▶ **Step 1 – Find the main point(s)**

1 Compare the third bar chart with the first two. What do you notice?
  A Some languages are spoken more by parents today than they used to be.
  B The numbers of people in the third chart are lower.
  C There has been little change for any of the languages.

2 a Which language was spoken to children the most in the past?

  ....

  b Approximately how many parents spoke this language to their children in the past?
  habitually ....
  occasionally ....

  c Approximately how many people now speak that language to their children?

  ....

3 a Which language is now spoken the most by adults to their children?

  ....

  b Approximately how many parents spoke that language to their children in the past?
  habitually ....
  occasionally ....

  c How many people now speak that language to their children?

  ....

4 Which language was spoken the least by parents to their children?

  ....

5 Is the number of parents speaking that language to their children now higher than the number whose parents spoke that language to them?

  ....

▶ **Step 2 – Organise your answer**

1 What should you begin your answer with?
  A a sentence about one of the languages
  B a sentence comparing two or more of the languages
  C a sentence comparing the tables in general

2 What should come next?
  A comparisons between the numbers who spoke each language habitually and the numbers who spoke each language occasionally
  B comparisons between each of the languages to indicate which were the most widely spoken in the past and which are the most widely spoken now
  C comparisons between how widely spoken languages were in the past and how widely spoken they are now

▶ **Step 3 – Language to use**

Write a sentence based on the information in the bar charts, using one word or phrase from each of these lists:

Linking phrases

although, even though, while, in the case of, as for, with regard to

....

....

Grammatical structures: comparison

a great deal lower than, not as many as, even greater than, far fewer than, not as high as

....

....

Vocabulary: increase and decrease

a rise in, a fall in, an increase in, a decrease in, rise, fall, go up, go down, drop, decline, be unchanged

....

....

Use your answers for steps 1, 2 and 3 to plan your answer.

Now write your answer for Task 1.

There is a sample answer on page 199.

You should spend about 40 minutes on this task.

Present a written argument or case to an educated reader with no specialist knowledge of the following topic.

In some societies, stress is now regarded as a major problem, and it is thought that people suffer from more stress than they did in the past.

However, others feel that the amount of stress people have today is exaggerated. They say that previous generations were under more pressure, but the idea of suffering from stress did not exist.

Discuss both these views and give your own opinion.

You should use your own ideas, knowledge and experience and support your arguments with examples and relevant evidence.

Write at least 250 words.

Giving your opinion (1)

Task guide

▸ Tasks in the Writing Module will be marked according to the criteria described on page 86 – **content**, **organisation** and **use of language**.

▸ Task 2 requires you to give your opinion on an issue.

▸ The task consists of a statement or statements, followed by a question asking for your point of view.

▸ The instructions you are given are not always the same, and you must read them very carefully to make sure that you do exactly what you are asked to do.

▸ Some tasks focus on whether you agree or disagree with a statement. In tasks of this type, you may be asked the following questions:
(a) Discuss both these views and give your opinion.
(b) Do you agree or disagree?
(c) To what extent do you agree or disagree with this statement?
In this case, Task 2 is an example of (a). There are examples of (b) and (c) in other tests in this book.

▸ You must concentrate on presenting a clear and logical argument that the reader can follow easily.

▸ Divide your answer into paragraphs. Start a new paragraph for each new topic.

▸ Make sure that your answer is not too short (minimum 250 words), but also do not write a very long answer.

Step-by-step guide

▸ **Step 1 – Read the question carefully**

Look at Task 2. Which FIVE of the following should you do in your answer?

1 Give examples of types of people who suffer from stress today.

2 Discuss reasons why people suffer from stress today.

3 Suggest ways of dealing with stress.

4 Compare the amount of stress people have today with the amount of stress people had in the past.

5 Give examples of what life was like in the past.

6 Compare stress with other problems that people have today.

7 Give an opinion on whether too much attention is paid to stress today.

8 Give an opinion on whether stress will become a bigger problem.

▸ **Step 2 – Organise your answer**

Using your answers for step 1, make a plan for your answer:

• Make a note of which points you will include in your answer.

• Think of examples that can illustrate each point.

• Think about your conclusion.

Now write your notes:

Point 1: Stress today – types of people

....

Example(s)

....

Point 2: Stress today: reasons

....

Example(s)

....

Point 3: The situation in the past compared with today

....

Example(s)

....

Point 4: Life in the past: examples

....

Example(s)

....

Point 5: Opinion – attention paid to stress today

....

▸ **Step 3 – Language to use**

Using your notes for step 2, write a sentence using one word or phrase from each of these lists:

Linking words and phrases

• *in my opinion, in my view, The impression I have is..., It seems to me that...*

• *like, such as*

• *these days, nowadays*

....

....

Grammatical structures

• *used to do, be used to doing*

• *have to*

• *passive voice*

....

....

Vocabulary

• *under pressure, suffer from, stressful*

• *pace, hurry, rush, speed*

• *accept, complain, take for granted*

....

....

Now write your answer for Task 2.

There is a sample answer on page 199.

IELTS TEST 1

Exam Essentials

LISTENING MODULE   READING MODULE   WRITING MODULE   **SPEAKING MODULE**

PART 1
PART 2
PART 3

Part 1: Introduction and interview

Task guide

▸ In this part of the Speaking module, the examiner will ask you a series of questions about yourself.

▸ You are expected to give more than 'yes' or 'no' answers. You are not expected to speak at great length in answer to any of the questions.

▸ There are no 'right' or 'wrong' answers; the examiner will ask you questions about things that you do, your likes and dislikes, and so on.

Step-by-step guide

▸ Step 1 – Take the right approach

The examiner's questions are designed to give you the opportunity to show that you can use your English to describe and explain things about yourself and familiar subjects, such as your country.

For example, the examiner may ask you about reading. You might be asked if you spend a lot of time reading. You are not being tested on how much reading you do, but on how well you explain how much reading you do (or don't).

In this part of the test, try to behave as if you were having a normal conversation with people you know.

▸ Step 2 – How much should I say?

A good principle here is 'answer plus one'. Try to be generous, and offer a little extra information on the topic.

For example, if the examiner asks you how much time you spend reading, a basic answer is 'a lot' or 'not much'. Short answers, however, do not help a conversation develop very easily.

Look at these examples of 'answer plus one':

'A lot. I really enjoy reading, and I read every evening.'

'Not much. I don't have much free time, and I prefer to watch TV in the evenings.'

Part 1 – Example questions

Friends
a How much time do you spend with friends?
b What kinds of things do you like to do with your friends?
c What kinds of work or studies do your friends do?
d What does being a good friend mean to you?

▸ Step 3 – Write your answers

Look at the answers below. Then write your own answer to each question.

A How much time do you spend with friends?

Only a little. My studies take up most of my time.

....

....

B What kinds of things do you like to do with your friends?

It depends. In the winter, we go to the cinema. In the summer, it's nice just to sit in the park together, chatting.

....

....

C What kinds of work or studies do your friends do?

All sorts. Most of my friends are students like me, studying different subjects. One of my friends is a doctor, another one works for her father's business.

....

....

D What does being a good friend mean to you?

Oh, many things. I suppose the most important thing is trust. You must be able to trust each other.

....

....

Part 2: Individual long turn

Task guide

▶ In this part of the Speaking module, the examiner will ask you to give a short talk, or 'long turn', based on a task card that you will be given.

▶ The topic on the card will be a general and straightforward one.

▶ You are expected to speak continuously for about one minute. The examiner will not ask you questions during your long turn.

▶ The examiner may ask you one or two short, easy questions when you have finished your long turn.

▶ The card you are given describes what you must talk about. It is important that you talk about this topic.

▶ The card includes three suggested points within the general topic. These are designed to help you decide what to say. If you do not talk about all of them, you will not lose marks.

Step-by-step guide

▶ **Step 1 – Take the right approach**

The long turn is designed to give you the opportunity to show how well you can speak in English on a subject that you are familiar with.

A minute can seem like quite a long time, when you are the only person speaking.

Give yourself as much practice as you can for this task. You can practise speaking to yourself.

Because a minute is quite a long time, you should use the opportunity to make notes before you start speaking. If you make a few notes, you will be able to structure your long turn.

▶ **Step 2 – How should I organise what I say?**

Making notes will help you organise what you say.

The notes you make may remind you of useful vocabulary and expressions to use, or of facts and points that you want to include in your long turn.

Part 2 – Example task

Read the topic card below carefully. You will have to talk about the topic for 1 to 2 minutes.
You have one minute to think about what you are going to say.
You can make notes to help you if you wish.

> **Describe a party you went to which you enjoyed.**
> **You should say:**
>   **where the party was**
>   **why the party happened**
>   **who was at the party**
> **and explain why you enjoyed the party.**

▶ **Step 3 – Make notes**

Look at the notes and candidate's answer for each of the suggested points. Then write your own note and answer for the same points.

where the party was
Note: *parents' house*

....

Candidate: *I remember one party very well. It took place at my parents' house.*

....

why the party happened
Note: *brother's 21st*

....

Candidate: *The party was held to celebrate my brother David's twenty-first birthday.*

....

who was at the party
Note: *all family, D's friends*

....

Candidate: *Everybody in my family came. Some of them travelled from abroad to be there. And, of course, David had invited a lot of friends, too.*

....

why you enjoyed the party
Note: *seeing everybody, David adult*

....

Candidate: *I enjoyed this party because it made me feel wonderful to be surrounded by all my family, and also because it meant that my brother was now a real adult.*

....

IELTS
TEST **1**

Exam Essentials

LISTENING MODULE   READING MODULE   WRITING MODULE   **SPEAKING MODULE**

PART 1
PART 2
PART 3

Part 3: Two-way discussion

Task guide

▶ In this part of the Speaking module, the examiner will ask you a series of questions related to the general topic of your 'long turn' in Part 2.

▶ These questions will be more demanding than the questions in Part 1. They will require you to give opinions, rather than simply explain facts.

▶ The questions will not test your general knowledge, but the way you express your ideas in English.

▶ It is important to give more than 'yes' or 'no' answers.

Step-by-step guide

▶ **Step 1 – Take the right approach**

The questions in this part of the test are designed to allow you to show that you can discuss things in English.

Part 1 and 2 focus on your own life and experiences. Part 3 encourages you to show you can express ideas that go beyond personal details.

The examiners assess your language abilities, not your opinions. Express your opinion freely and try to offer as much information on the topic as you can.

▶ **Step 2 – What should I say?**

In most of your answers to the examiner's questions, you will be expressing an opinion or giving some kind of interpretation.

You will not be stating simple facts.

You should try to introduce what you say with appropriate phrases for the kind of answer you give.

Part 3 – Example questions

A What kinds of social events are most popular in your country?

B What are the differences between the social events that older and younger people enjoy?

C Do you think it is a good idea for colleagues at work to spend time socially together?

D What changes have there been recently in social life in your country?

E Would you agree that technology can have negative effects on the way people spend their leisure time?

▶ **Step 3 – Complete the answers**

Match 1–5 with a–e to form complete answers.

1 I think it's difficult to judge. On the one hand, it gives us access to new kinds of entertainment

2 Well, I think it very much depends on people's different interests

3 It's become very different. Many people have a lot more money these days

4 I suppose that it is. It makes them enjoy their jobs more

5 I've noticed that older people prefer to spend their social time in each other's houses

a although of course they should also spend enough time with their families.

b and they like to spend it by going out in the evenings, much more than we used to.

c but, on the other, it means we spend a lot of time just sitting around, becoming unfit.

d while younger people want to go out to clubs, bars, and so on.

e but eating together is certainly very popular with everyone.

Now match the complete answers with the example questions A–E above.

Step-by-step guide

(continued)

▶ **Step 4 – Write your own answers**

Now write your own answers to questions A–E.
You can use expressions from the sample answers
in step 3.

A ....

....

B ....

....

C ....

....

D ....

....

E ....

....

LISTENING MODULE	READING MODULE	WRITING MODULE	SPEAKING MODULE

SECTION 1
SECTION 2
SECTION 3
SECTION 4

▶ **Questions 1–10**

Questions 1–10

Complete the form below.

Write **NO MORE THAN TWO WORDS AND/OR A NUMBER** *for each answer.*

COMPLAINT RECORD FORM

Holiday booked in name of:	1 First name .... Last name .... Shah ....
Address:	Flat 4
	2 ....
	Winchester SO2 4ER
Daytime telephone number:	3 ....
Booking reference:	4 ....
Special offer?	Yes, from 5 .... company
Insurance?	Yes, had 6 .... Policy
Type of holiday booked:	7 .... Break
Date holiday commenced:	8 ....
Details of complaint:	• no 9 .... at station
	• a 10 .... was missing

Form completion

Task guide

▶ This task requires you to complete a form by writing words and numbers that you hear on the recording.

▶ Read the instructions carefully. Notice how many words you can use to answer each question. The number of words may vary; you may be asked to write one, two or three words in each question. The instructions will also tell you if you need to use a number for your answer.

▶ Look at the form and think who might complete this form. When you listen to the recording, you will be able to follow which of the two speakers is actually completing the form.

▶ Do not change the words or numbers you hear. Write down exactly what you hear.

▶ The questions follow the order in which you hear the information on the recording.

▶ Form completion tasks in this section may ask you to write names of people or addresses that you have never heard before. These will usually be spelt out for you. Names, which are reasonably common English words, however, will not be spelt out for you.

Step-by-step guide

▶ **Step 1 – Think first**

Read through the form carefully. What sort of answer is required in each gap?

Remember that in the task here, you are told to write no more than two words and/or a number for each answer.

Decide if the gap will require:

A a word or two words

B a number

C a word or two words and a number

D a combination of numbers and letters

1 .... **2** .... **3** .... **4** .... **5** ....

6 .... **7** .... **8** .... **9** .... **10** ....

If you prepare yourself like this, you will find it easier to hear the answers on the recording.

▶ **Step 2 – Check what you hear**

Look at this part of the tapescript. The answers for *Questions 1–3* are in **bold**.

Tapescript

Man: Oh no – let me just get a form ready ... First, the name, please. Of the person who booked the holiday.
Woman: Well, our surname's **Sharpe. S–H** ...
Man: Like a knife?
Woman: Yes, but with an E on the end.
Man: And a first name?
Woman: I'm Alice, but I think it was my husband who actually booked the trip – his name's **Andrew.**
Man: Fine. And then the address, please.
Woman: It's Flat 4, **Beaconsfield – that's B-E-A-C-O-N-S-F-I-E-L-D – House.** That's Winchester, and it's S-O-2, er, 4-E-R.
Man: Thank you. And could I take a telephone number?
Woman: We're on 0374 56561 at home, or – do you mean during the day? – then my work number's **0374 double-5 793.**
Man: I'll put the work one down, assuming that's normal office hours?
Woman: Oh yes.

It is important to make sure that you follow the requirements of the form as you listen.

For *Question 1*, the form asks for the 'first' name first, then the 'surname'. The woman, however, gives the surname first and the first name second.

Notice that because 'sharp' is a common word, you are expected to be able to spell it, and to add the 'E' at the end of the word. You are also expected to know the common first name, Andrew.

However, you are not expected to know 'Beaconsfield', and so this is spelt out for you. You are expected to know the word 'house'.

For the telephone number, it is again important to follow the requirements of the form. Have a look at *Question 3*. You are listening for a daytime telephone number. You should not simply write down any telephone number you hear.

▶ **Step 3 – Listen and do the task**

LISTENING MODULE	READING MODULE	WRITING MODULE	SPEAKING MODULE

> SECTION 1
> **SECTION 2**
> SECTION 3
> SECTION 4

▸ **Questions 11–20**

Questions 11–15

Complete the table below.

Choose your answers from the box and write the appropriate letters **A–H** *next to questions 11–15.*

> A driving licence
> B flexible working week
> C free meals
> D heavy lifting
> E late shifts
> F training certificate
> G travel allowance
> H website maintenance

TEMPORARY HOTEL JOBS

JOB	EMPLOYER	NOTES
Reception Assistant	Park Hotel	• 11 ...... • foreign languages • 12 ......
General Assistant	Avenue Hotel	• low pay • 13 ...... • 14 ......
Catering Assistant	Hotel 56	• free uniform • 15 ...... • outside city

Table completion (with choices)

Task guide

▸ This task requires you to complete a table by selecting from a list of possible answers.

▸ Some of the information in the table will already be filled in. You can use the location of this information to help you follow the information on the recording.

▸ You should read the list of possible answers carefully. Some of the options are likely to be similar, and you will need to make sure you choose correctly.

▸ Do not choose an options simply because it contains one or more words you may hear on the recording. Select your answer according to the meaning of what you hear.

▸ Write only the letter of the option you choose. Do not copy out the words of the option.

▸ Sometimes, a gap may have other words before and/or after it. If this is the case, make sure the answer you choose fits grammatically into the gap.

▸ Possible answers may also be provided for forms and other tasks.

▸ See also page 12 for another type of table completion task.

Step-by-step guide

▶ **Step 1 – Think first**

You don't have to write anything except letters in this task.

There are twice as many possible answers here as there are questions. Therefore, the challenge is to select from more than one likely seeming answers.

You can prepare for this by checking which options may be rather similar to each other. For example, options A and G refer to transport, and options B and E refer to the time of working.

▶ **Step 2 – Check what you read and hear**

Reading the table carefully will help you follow the recording. You know that after 'Reception Assistant' and 'Park Hotel' are mentioned, you must be ready to answer *Question 11*. You also know that you must answer *Question 11* before you hear 'foreign languages' on the recording.

Look at the tapescript for *Question 11*.

Tapescript

The first job is Reception Assistant, and there are three vacancies for this position at the Park Hotel. This is quite a varied job, and in fact I should point out that at certain times of the day, it will involve heavy lifting when guests' luggage arrives, or perhaps deliveries come in, so bear that in mind when deciding whether to apply for this post.

Now look at options A–H. The job is described as 'varied', which might relate to 'flexible' in option B. 'Certain times of day' might be leading to 'late shifts' in option E. There is a clear reference to the job involving 'heavy lifting when guests' luggage arrives, or perhaps deliveries come in', which means that option D is the correct answer. Option D fully connects with what the speaker says, while options B and E only connect with part of what the speaker says.

▶ **Step 3 – Listen and do the task**

| LISTENING MODULE | READING MODULE | WRITING MODULE | SPEAKING MODULE |

SECTION 1
SECTION 2
SECTION 3
SECTION 4

Questions 16–20

Complete the flow chart below.

Write **NO MORE THAN TWO WORDS** *for each answer.*

RECRUITMENT PROCESS

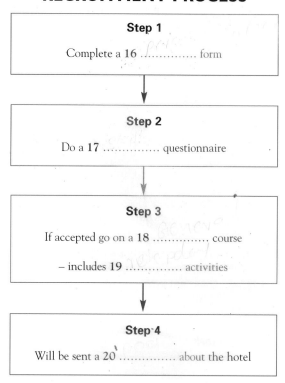

Step 1

Complete a **16** .... form

Step 2

Do a **17** .... questionnaire

Step 3

If accepted go on a **18** .... course

– includes **19** .... activities

Step 4

Will be sent a **20** .... about the hotel

Flow chart completion

Task guide

▸ This task requires you to complete a flow chart by writing answers that are pieces of information you hear on the recording.

▸ The flow chart is used to represent a process, so it is important that you follow the different stages or steps of the process described on the recording.

▸ Read the instructions carefully. Notice how many words you can use to answer each question.

▸ Make sure that the word(s) you write fit grammatically with the words around the gap.

▸ Write exactly the word(s) and/or numbers that you hear. Do not try to change them in any way – your answer will be wrong if you do.

▸ It is likely that you will hear more than one piece of information that could seem possible for each gap. Only one will in fact be correct, so listen very carefully.

Step-by-step guide

> ▶ **Step 1 – Think first**

The task asks you to write a word or two words in each gap. Make sure you are ready to write the word or words as soon as you hear the information on the recording.

Think about what you might hear in relation to the flow chart.

1 How might 'Step 1' or 'Step 2' be expressed?

2 How might 'complete' be said?

Remember, it is unlikely that the speaker will use exactly the same words in the same order as in the flow chart. However, your task is to write in the words you hear for the gaps.

> ▶ **Step 2 – Check what you hear**

Look at this part of the tapescript. The answers for *Questions 16* and *17* are in **bold**.

Tapescript

So the first thing you'll need to do is fill in one of these, a **personal information** form. It's pretty straightforward and should only take you a few minutes. Once you've done that and handed it in, we'll give you a questionnaire about your **skills** to do. Again, I don't expect this to take you very long.

'The first thing you'll need to do' refers to 'Step 1' on the flow chart. 'Complete' is 'fill in'.

'Step 2' is expressed as 'once you've done that'.

'Personal information' comes immediately before 'form' in the tapescript and in the flow chart.

'Skills', however, comes after 'questionnaire' in the tapescript, but before 'questionnaire' in the flow chart.

> ▶ **Step 3 – Listen and do the task**

SECTION 1
SECTION 2
SECTION 3
SECTION 4

▸ *Questions 21–30*

Questions 21 –26

Complete the sentences below.

Write **NO MORE THAN THREE WORDS** *for each answer.*

21   David feels that progress on the project has been slow because other members
     of the group are not ……………………………………….. .

22   Jane thinks that ……..…………………………….. were not clearly established.

23   Dr Wilson suggests that the group use the ……………………………….. available
     from the Resource Centre.

24   David doubts that the research will include an adequate …………………………… .

25   According to Dr Wilson, the ………………………….. is now the most important thing
     to focus on.

26   Jane believes the group could make more use of some ……………………………. .

Sentence completion

Task guide

▸ This task requires you to complete sentences by writing in information you hear on
   the recording.

▸ Read the sentences carefully so that you are ready for the information when it
   occurs on the recording.

▸ The questions follow the order of the recording.

▸ The order of information within each sentence may be different from that on the
   recording.

▸ The words used in the sentences will usually be synonyms or paraphrases of the
   words that you hear on the recording – the words will be different, but the meaning
   will be the same.

▸ Read the instructions carefully. Notice how many words you can use to answer each
   question. If you use more words, your answer will be wrong.

▸ For each gap, write the exact words that you hear – do not change their form in any
   way.

▸ After you have filled in the gap, check that the sentence is grammatically correct and
   makes sense.

Step-by-step guide

▸ **Step 1 – Think first**

Firstly, make sure you are clear which speaker each sentence refers to.

Then, prepare for this task by thinking about how the wording of the sentences might be expressed on the recording.

▸ **Step 2 – Check what you hear**

Look at the tapescript for *Question 21*.

Tapescript

David: Well, we anticipated problems of various kinds. None of the group has much experience of collaborating on projects. But we spent some time discussing how to go about it, and thrashed out what seemed a useful approach, but it seems that Jane and I are the only ones actually following the plan. That's meant that the whole project has been lacking coordination and so we've fallen behind our schedule.

1 What is the correct answer to *Question 21*?

....

2 What words and/or phrases might you write for *Question 21* if you didn't listen carefully?

....

3 How is 'progress on the project has been slow' represented in the tapescript?

....

4 Why should you not write 'actually' as part of your answer to *Question 21*?

....

▸ **Step 3 – Listen and do the task**

IELTS
TEST 2

Exam Essentials

LISTENING MODULE   READING MODULE   WRITING MODULE   SPEAKING MODULE

SECTION 1
SECTION 2
SECTION 3
SECTION 4

Questions 27–30

Complete the timetable below.

Choose your answers from the box and write the letters **A–H** *next to questions 27–30.*

> A   Compare photographs at newspaper offices.
> B   Interview a local historian.
> C   Listen to tapes in the City Library.
> D   Study records of shop ownership.
> E   Take photographs of the castle area.
> F   Talk to the archivist at the City Library.
> G   Tour city centre using copies of old maps.
> H   Visit an exhibition at the University Library.

MON – WED: FIELD TRIP TO CAMBRIDGE

Mon 22nd	am	arrive at hotel
	pm	27 ....
Tues 23rd	am	28 ....
	pm	free time
Wed 24th	am	29 ....
	pm	30 ....

Timetable completion

Task guide

▸ This task requires you to complete a timetable by choosing from a list of possible answers.

▸ 'Timetable' can be any kind of timetable, diary, agenda, programme, etc.

▸ The speaker(s) on the recording will talk about the events in the timetable in the same order as the timetable you are given to complete.

▸ Write only the letter of the option you choose. Do not copy out the words of the option.

▸ Read and check the list of possible answers carefully. The possible answers are usually similar, and you need to choose between them.

▸ The possible answers are usually listed alphabetically.

▸ Sometimes, there may be some discussion among the speakers about exactly what will happen when. If this is the case, make sure that you choose the answer that is the one the speakers agree about, not just one that one of the speakers mentions.

▸ You may also encounter a timetable completion task in which you are not given a list of possible answers. In this case, you will have to write in the answers in words and/or numbers, as in table or notes completion tasks.

Step-by-step guide

▸ **Step 1 – Think first**

There are eight possible answers, but only four questions.

You need to read the possible answers very carefully, so that you are ready to choose between them quickly and correctly at the relevant points on the recording.

Try to be ready to distinguish between very similar possibilities. For example, there are three options with reference to libraries, but there's reference to two libraries in the tapescript.

▸ **Step 2 – Check what you hear**

Look at the tapescript for *Question 27*.

Tapescript

I've arranged for you to have a look at some useful visual material, especially photographs and old magazines and newspapers, which is included in an exhibition at the library in the university.

The word 'visual' might refer to option A ('photographs'), option E ('photographs'), option G ('old maps') and option H ('exhibition').

Which options might these words on the recording relate to?

1 photographs: ....

2 newspapers: ....

3 exhibition: ....

4 library: ....

5 university: ....

Which is the correct answer to *Question 27*?

▸ **Step 3 – Listen and do the task**

IELTS
TEST 2

Exam Essentials

| LISTENING MODULE | READING MODULE | WRITING MODULE | SPEAKING MODULE |

SECTION 1
SECTION 2
SECTION 3
SECTION 4

▶ *Questions 31–40*

Questions 31–35

Complete the summary below.

Write **NO MORE THAN TWO WORDS** *for each answer.*

THE LONDON EYE

The architects who designed the London Eye originally drew it for a **31** .... in 1993.

Subsequently, they formed a partnership with **32** .... to develop the project. As the biggest

observation wheel ever built, its construction involved 1,700 people in five countries. Most of its components had

to be **33** .... , and delivering them had to be coordinated with the **34** .... in the

River Thames. On average, 350 hours a week are spent on maintenance of the Eye, and only

35 .... is used to clean the glass.

Summary completion

Task guide

▶ This task requires you to complete a summary by writing words you hear on the recording.

▶ You should read the summary through before the recording starts so that you have a general understanding.

▶ Read the instructions carefully. Notice how many words you can use to answer each question. If you use more words, your answer will be wrong.

▶ The questions follow the order of the recording.

▶ You can use the information provided in the summary to help you follow the recording.

▶ The words used in the given text of the summary will not be the same words as in the recording, but they will have the same meaning.

▶ When you complete the summary, don't change the form of the words you hear on the recording.

▶ When you read the summary through before listening, you may feel that you can answer some questions from your general knowledge. If this is the case, you must still listen very carefully to check if these are the correct answers on the recording.

Step-by-step guide

▶ **Step 1 – Think first**

To complete this task successfully:

• You must understand the meaning of the summary and the meaning of the recording.

• You must write the right number of correctly spelt words in the gaps.

• You must understand that the recording will contain more information than the summary, and to be able to identify the relevant information on the recording.

▶ **Step 2 – Check what you hear**

Look at the tapescript for *Questions 31* and *32*.

Tapescript

Its <u>creators</u> are husband and wife, <u>architects</u> David Marks and Julia Barfield. It was on their *kitchen table* in South London in 1993 that the <u>first drawings for the London Eye were made</u>, as the couple, who usually worked directly for *clients*, were entering **a competition**, the brief of which was to design *millennium landmarks* for the *capital*.

In fact, nobody won, and the whole idea was scrapped, but the couple remained convinced that their dream should be pursued. They started to piece the project together, and were soon attracting the attention of *the press*, and it wasn't long before **British Airways** had started to show an interest and then <u>became a partner</u>.

The words which lead you to the correct answers are <u>underlined</u>.

The correct answers are in **bold**.

Words which you might wrongly think could be the answers are in *italics*.

Notice that the words leading you to the correct answer may not be next to the actual answer on the recording.

After you have filled in a gap, check that the answer makes sense and is grammatically correct.

▶ **Step 3 – Listen and do the task**

LISTENING MODULE	READING MODULE	WRITING MODULE	SPEAKING MODULE

SECTION 1
SECTION 2
SECTION 3
SECTION 4

Questions 36–40

Label the diagram below.

Write **NO MORE THAN TWO WORDS** *for each answer.*

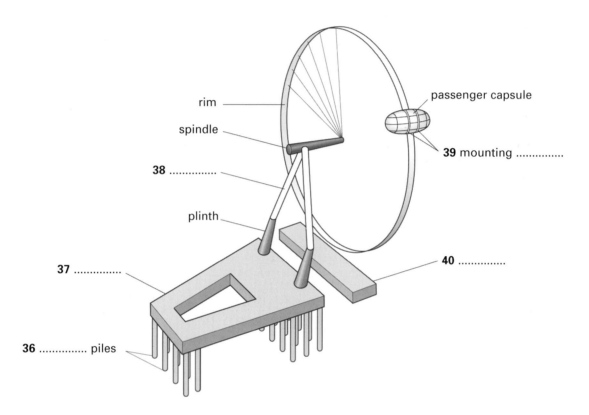

rim

spindle

38 ....

plinth

passenger capsule

39 mounting ....

37 ....

40 ....

36 .... piles

Labelling a map/plan/diagram (3)

Task guide

▶ This task requires you to complete the labelling of a diagram by writing words you hear on the recording.

▶ If the words needed for the answers are very technical, they will be provided for you in a list of possible answers.

▶ Read the instructions carefully. Notice how many words you can use to answer each question. If you use more words, your answer will be wrong.

▶ You may need to write the whole of a label or part of a label.

▶ The questions follow the order of the recording.

▶ Write the exact word(s) that you hear on the recording. Do not change them in any way.

▶ See also pages 8 and 14 for other types of labelling tasks.

Step-by-step guide

▸ **Step 1 – Put yourself in the picture**

Look carefully at the diagram before you listen.

Try to form an independent understanding of what the diagram represents. Think about how this might be presented on the recording. For example, notice which parts are above or below other parts.

If the diagram shows an object that you are familiar with, you might think that you can answer some of the questions. However, remember that the task is to label the diagram according to what you hear on the recording, not according to your general knowledge.

▸ **Step 2 – Check what you hear**

Look at the tapescript for *Questions 36, 37* and *38*.

Tapescript

The starting point was, of course, the ground, and while parts of the wheel itself were still being constructed in various countries, **tension** piles were being driven into the *ground* beside the River Thames. This was the first *step*, and once these were securely in place, a **base cap** was installed over them as a kind of *lock*, with two giant plinths pointing up, onto which an **A-frame** was attached, like a giant *letter*.

The correct answers are in **bold**. Words which you might wrongly think could be the answers are in *italics*.

Notice how the speaker guides you around the diagram, mentioning the 'starting point', the 'ground', explaining that the 'base cap was installed over them (tension piles)', and so on.

If you realise you have missed one question, focus carefully for the next one. It should be possible to find each answer independently of the other(s).

▸ **Step 3 – Listen and do the task**

IELTS TEST 2

Exam Essentials

LISTENING MODULE | **READING MODULE** | WRITING MODULE | SPEAKING MODULE
PASSAGE 1
PASSAGE 2
PASSAGE 3

*You should spend about 20 minutes on **Questions 1–13** which are based on Reading Passage 1 below.*

Emigration to the US

American history has been largely the story of migrations. That of the hundred years or so between the Battle of Waterloo and the outbreak of the First World War must certainly be reckoned the largest peaceful migration in recorded history; probably the largest of any kind, ever. It is reckoned that some thirty-five million persons entered the United States during that period, not to mention the large numbers who were also moving to Argentina and Australia. Historians may come to discern that in the twentieth and later centuries this movement was dwarfed when Africa, Asia and South America began to send out their peoples; but if so, they will be observing a pattern, of a whole continent in motion, that was first laid down in nineteenth-century Europe. Only the French seemed to be substantially immune to the virus. Otherwise, all caught it, and all travelled. English, Irish, Welsh, Scots, Germans, Scandinavians, Spaniards, Italians, Poles, Greeks, Jews, Portuguese, Dutch, Hungarians, Czechs, Croats, Slovenes, Serbs, Slovaks, Ukrainians, Lithuanians, Russians, Basques. There were general and particular causes.

As regards the general causes, the rise in population meant that more and more people were trying to earn their living on the same amount of land; inevitably, some were squeezed off it. The increasing cost of the huge armies and navies, with their need for up-to-date equipment, that every great European power maintained, implied heavier and heavier taxes which many found difficult or impossible to pay, and mass conscription, which quite as many naturally wanted to avoid. The opening up of new, superbly productive lands in the United States, Canada, Australia and New Zealand, coupled with the availability of steamers and steam trains to distribute their produce, meant that European peasants could not compete effectively in the world market: they would always be undersold, especially as the arrival of free trade was casting down the old mercantilist barriers everywhere. Steam was important in other ways too. It became a comparatively easy matter to cross land and sea, and to get news from distant parts. The invention of the electric telegraph also speeded up the diffusion of news, especially after a cable was successfully laid across the Atlantic in 1866. New printing and paper-making machines and a rapidly spreading literacy made large-circulation newspapers possible for the first time. In short, horizons widened, even for the stay-at-home. Most important of all, the dislocations in society brought about by the French Revolution, the Industrial Revolution and the various wars and tumults of nineteenth-century Europe shattered the old ways. New states came into being, old ones disappeared, frontiers were recast, the laws of land-tenure were radically altered, internal customs barriers and feudal dues both disappeared, payment in money replaced payment in kind, new industries stimulated new wants and destroyed the self-sufficiency of peasant households and the saleability of peasant products. The basic structure of rural Europe was transformed. Bad times pushed, good times pulled

(American factories were usually clamouring for workers): small wonder that the peoples moved.

Particular reasons were just as important as these general ones. For example: between 1845 and 1848 Ireland suffered the terrible potato famine. A million people died of starvation or disease, a million more emigrated (1846-51). Matters were not much better when the Great Famine was over: it was followed by lesser ones, and the basic weaknesses of the Irish economy made the outlook hopeless anyway. Mass emigration was a natural resort, at first to America, then, in the twentieth century, increasingly, to England and Scotland. Emigration was encouraged, in the Irish case as in many others, by letters sent home and by remittances of money. The first adventurers thus helped to pay the expenses of their successors. Political reasons could sometimes drive Europeans across the Atlantic too. In 1848 some thousands of Germans fled the failure of the liberal revolution of that year (but many thousands emigrated for purely economic reasons).

If such external stimuli faltered, American enterprise was more than willing to fill the gap. The high cost of labour had been a constant in American history since the first settlements; now, as the Industrial Revolution made itself felt, the need for workers was greater than ever. The supply of Americans was too small to meet the demand: while times were good on the family farm, as they were on the whole until the 1880s, or while there was new land to be taken up in the West, the drift out of agriculture (which was becoming a permanent feature of America, as of all industrialized, society) would not be large enough to fill the factories. So employers looked for the hands they needed in Europe, whether skilled, like Cornish miners, or unskilled, like Irish navvies. Then, the transcontinental railroads badly needed settlers on their Western land grants, as well as labourers: they could not make regular profits until the lands their tracks crossed were regularly producing crops that needed carrying to market. Soon every port in Europe knew the activities of American shipping lines and their agents, competing with each other to offer advantageous terms to possible emigrants. They stuck up posters, they advertised in the press, they patiently asnwered inquiries, and they shepherded their clients from their native villages, by train, to the dockside, and then made sure they were safely stowed in the steerage.

IELTS
TEST 2

Exam Essentials

LISTENING MODULE   **READING MODULE**   WRITING MODULE   SPEAKING MODULE

PASSAGE 1
PASSAGE 2
PASSAGE 3

Question 1

Choose the correct letter **A**, **B**, **C** *or* **D**. *Write it in box 1 on your answer sheet.*

1   Which of the following does the writer state in the first paragraph?

   A   The extent of emigration in the nineteenth century is unlikely to be repeated.

   B   Doubts may be cast on how much emigration there really was in the nineteenth century.

   C   It is possible that emigration from Europe may be exceeded by emigration from outside Europe.

   D   Emigration can prove to be a better experience for some nationalities than for others.

Multiple-choice with single answer

Task guide

▸ This task normally consists of questions which each focus on a particular section of the text, rather than on information spread throughout the text.

▸ The exception to this is a 'global' question, which asks about the text as a whole (for example, the writer's purpose in the whole text). A global question is always the last question on a text.

▸ If there are several multiple-choice questions, these follow the order of the relevant information in the text.

▸ Multiple-choice questions often test your understanding of complex information or opinions, and require you to read the relevant section of the text very carefully.

▸ Make sure that the option you choose correctly answers the question you have been asked. Sometimes an option may be true according to the text, but not answer the actual question that has been asked.

▸ See also page 30 for another type of multiple-choice task.

Step-by-step guide

▸ **Step 1 – Locate the question in the text**

Read the question carefully and locate the relevant section of the text. In this case, you don't have to locate the section because the question tells you where to look ('first paragraph'). If it does not, it will normally refer to something that can easily be located in the text.

▸ **Step 2 – Find the answer**

Read the first paragraph carefully and answer the questions about options A–D.

Option A

1 Does the writer say that this particular migration may be the largest until now?

....

2 Does the writer say that such large-scale emigration will not happen again?

....

Option B

1 Does the writer say how many people are believed to have emigrated to the US in this period?

....

2 Does the writer question any statistics?

....

Option C

1 Does the writer make any predictions concerning emigration?

....

2 If something is 'dwarfed' by something else, is it bigger or smaller than that?

....

Option D

1 Does the writer compare any nationalities?

....

2 Does the writer refer to what happened to people when they had emigrated?

....

Now answer *Question 1*.

IELTS TEST 2

Exam Essentials

LISTENING MODULE   **READING MODULE**   WRITING MODULE   SPEAKING MODULE

PASSAGE 1
PASSAGE 2
PASSAGE 3

Questions 2–9

Complete the sentences below with words taken from Reading Passage 1.

Use **NO MORE THAN THREE WORDS** *for each answer.*

Write your answers in boxes 2–9 on your answer sheet.

GENERAL CAUSES OF EMIGRATION TO THE US

- Population increases made it impossible for some to live from agriculture.

- In Europe, countries kept 2 .... that were both big, and this resulted in increases in 3 .... and in 4 .... , which a lot of people wanted to escape.

- It became impossible for 5 .... in Europe to earn a living because of developments in other countries and the introduction of 6 ....

- People knew more about the world beyond their own countries because there was greater 7 ....

- 8 .... had been formed because of major historical events.

- The creation of 9 .... caused changes in demand.

Sentence completion (1)

Task guide

- ▶ This task requires you to complete individual sentences with pieces of information in the text.

- ▶ This task is very similar to the summary, notes, table and flow chart completion tasks (see page 26). The difference is that each sentence is separate and there may be little or no connection between the topic of each question – the task may focus on completely separate pieces of information.

- ▶ Remember that your answers must be actual words and phrases that appear in the text. Do not try to think of different words and phrases that have the same meaning, because if you do this, your answer will be marked wrong, and you will lose marks unnecessarily.

- ▶ Read the instructions carefully. Notice how many words you can use to answer each question. The number of words may vary; you may be asked to write one, two or three words in each question. If you use more words, your answer will be wrong.

- ▶ The information required for this task may be in one specific section of the text or it may be spread throughout the text.

- ▶ See also page 71 for another type of sentence completion task.

Step-by-step guide

▶ **Step 1 – Locate the task in the text**

In this task, the title is very helpful. It tells you that the whole task is about a single topic discussed in the text, rather than about different topics spread throughout the text.

1 The title of the task refers to 'general causes'. In which paragraph of the text are 'general causes' described?

....

2 Does the next paragraph deal with 'general causes'? If not, what topic does it deal with?

....

▶ **Step 2 – Find the answers**

Look carefully at each sentence in the task and at the part of the text you identified in step 1.

Questions 2, 3 and *4* are all in one sentence in the task, and so it is likely that the answers to them will be quite close together in the text.

IELTS
TEST 2

Exam Essentials

LISTENING MODULE   **READING MODULE**   WRITING MODULE   SPEAKING MODULE

PASSAGE 1
PASSAGE 2
PASSAGE 3

Step-by-step guide

(continued)

Question 2

The word 'both' after the gap indicates that the answer must have two parts.

1 The sentence in the task says that European countries 'kept' something. Which word in the text means 'kept' in this context?

....

2 Which word in the text means 'big'?

....

Now answer *Question 2*.

Question 3

The sentence in the task refers to something increasing. Which word in the text means 'increased' or 'higher' in the context?

....

Now answer *Question 3*.

Question 4

The sentence in the task indicates that the gap must be filled with something that people wanted to escape. Which word in the text means 'escape'?

....

Now answer *Question 4*.

Questions 5–9

Answer *Questions 5–9*, using the same process:

• Look at words and phrases before and after the gaps.

• Find words and phrases in the text that have similar meanings or express the same ideas in different ways.

• Find the exact word or phrase in the text that you must use as your answer.

Questions 10–13

Complete each sentence with the correct ending **A–H** *from the box below.*

Write the correct letter **A–H** *in boxes 10–13 on your answer sheet.*

10 The end of the potato famine in Ireland

11 People who had emigrated from Ireland

12 Movement off the land in the US

13 The arrival of railroad companies in the West of the US

A   made people reluctant to move elsewhere.

B   resulted in a need for more agricultural workers.

C   provided evidence of the advantages of emigration.

D   created a false impression of the advantages of moving elsewhere.

E   did little to improve the position of much of the population.

F   took a long time to have any real effect.

G   failed to satisfy employment requirements.

H   created a surplus of people who had emigrated.

Sentence completion (2)

Task guide

▶ This task requires you to choose which of the listed options correctly completes each sentence according to the information given in the text.

▶ This task may focus on a specific section or sections of the text or the information required for the question may be spread throughout the text.

▶ Questions in this task follow the order in which the relevant information appears in the text. For example, you will find the information required for *Question 13* after the information for *Question 12*.

▶ Some of the options do not correctly complete any of the sentences.

▶ Do not answer a question too quickly. It is very likely that more than one option will relate to the information required to complete a sentence, but only one option will match precisely what is stated in the text.

▶ See also page 69 for another type of sentence completion task.

Step-by-step guide

The best approach to this task is to:

• Look at the beginning of each sentence.
• Find the specific section of the text that relates to it.
• Read this section carefully and look through the options (A–H).
• Decide which one correctly matches the information in the text.

Question 10

▶ **Step 1 – Locate the question in the text**

1 Which paragraph mentions the potato famine in Ireland?

....

2 Find the sentence in that paragraph that refers to the end of the famine. Which phrase in that sentence means 'ended' or 'finished'?

....

▶ **Step 2 – Find the answer**

Look at the paragraph you identified in step 1. What does the writer say about the end of the famine?

A It made people want to stay in Ireland.

B It didn't really change the situation in Ireland.

C It eventually led to improvements in Ireland.

Look through the options (A–H) and choose the one that most closely matches your answer to this question.

Question 11

▶ **Step 1 – Locate the question in the text**

1 Which paragraph mentions people who had emigrated from Ireland?

....

2 In that paragraph, what word does the writer use to describe these people?

....

▶ **Step 2 – Find the answer**

Look at the sentence you identified in step 1. What does the writer say about people who had emigrated from Ireland?

A They told people at home about problems they were experiencing.

B They sent things home that indicated that their lives were good.

C They said their lives abroad were better than they really were.

Look through the options (A–H) and choose the one that most closely matches your answer to this question.

Questions 12–13

Answer *Questions 12–13*, using the same process:

• Find the part of the text that relates to the subject of the question.
• Consider carefully what is said in that part of the text.
• Find the option that matches what is said in the text.

IELTS TEST 2

Exam Essentials

| LISTENING MODULE | READING MODULE | WRITING MODULE | SPEAKING MODULE |

PASSAGE 1
PASSAGE 2
PASSAGE 3

*You should spend about 20 minutes on **Questions 14–26** which are based on Reading Passage 2 below.*

How bugs hitch-hike across the galaxy

Mankind's search for alien life could be jeopardised by ultra-resilient bacteria from Earth. David Derbyshire reports

What was the most important discovery of the Apollo programme? Some have argued that it was the rocks that explained how the Moon was formed. Others believe it was the technological spin-offs. But according to Captain Peter Conrad, who led the 1969 Apollo 12 mission, it was life.

On the apparently dead lunar surface, a colony of bacteria was thriving. The organisms were not native to the Moon, but were visitors from Earth who had hitch-hiked a ride on board one of Nasa's five Surveyor probes from the 1960s. To the astonishment of biologists, between 50 and 100 Streptococcus bacteria survived the journey across space, at an average temperature 20 degrees above absolute zero with no source of energy or water, and stayed alive on the Moon in a camera for three years. Captain Conrad, who returned the bacteria to Earth, was later to confess: 'I always thought the most significant thing we ever found on the whole Moon was the little bacteria that came back and lived.'

The ability of life to survive, adapt and evolve never fails to astonish. Over the past three decades, bacteria and archaea have been found in some of the most inhospitable places on Earth. Known as extremophiles, these organisms have coped with life in a vacuum, pressure as high as 70 tons per square inch, depths of four miles beneath the surface and scorching waters around deep-sea volcanic vents. They have also survived 25 million years inside a bee preserved in resin. Their resilience has renewed enthusiasm for the search for alien life – a quest that many had assumed had been banished to fantasy fiction. Mars and the moons Titan, Europa and Callisto are once again plausible candidates for extraterrestrials.

As interest in alien life has grown, so have concerns that mankind could spread its own microscopic bugs, contaminating the places we want to explore. In 2003, Nasa ended the Galileo probe's mission by smashing it into Jupiter. The fear was that it could be carrying bacteria that might contaminate Europa's oceans.

The team behind Beagle 2 – the British probe that went to search for life on Mars in 2003 – was forced to take contamination particularly seriously. If Beagle carried to Mars life or dead spores picked up during the manufacture of the spacecraft, its science would be jeopardised. Prof Colin Pillinger, the Open University scientist who headed the Beagle project, said: 'What we've learnt since the Apollo missions and the Viking Mars missions of the 1970s is that bugs are far more tenacious than we ever imagined. They seem to be very tolerant of high temperatures, they lie dormant at low temperatures for long periods, they are immune to salt, acid and alkali, they seem to survive on substrate that are not what people expect. Extremophiles are extremely adapted to hanging on to life.'

Beagle had to be assembled in a 'clean room' – and one was specially put together in a converted BBC outside broadcast van garage in Milton Keynes. It had enough room to include an enormous set of fans that circulated and filtered the air 500 times an hour. Only a handful of trained researchers were allowed inside. 'I wasn't allowed in,' says Prof Pillinger.

'There was special training for people going in there and special conditions. There was a ban on beards and a limit of four people at any one time. The team kept samples of everything that could have contaminated the craft and monitored every stage of assembly.'

To reduce the workload, the idea was to build as much as possible before sterilising it and banishing it to the difficult working conditions inside the clean room. The easy stuff was heated to 115C for 52 hours, more than enough to kill off bugs. Electronic equipment can't cope with those sorts of temperatures, so the team used a hydrogen peroxide plasma, created in a microwave, to kill off bugs at low temperatures. Parachutes and gas bags were zapped with gamma radiation. It wasn't just facial hair that was banned. 'You've heard of the paperless office,' says Prof Pillinger. 'We had the paperless assembly line. The guys normally go in armed with loads of papers and diagrams, but we didn't allow any of that. They were given information through a glass wall, over mikes and monitors. And sometimes on a piece of paper stuck to the glass with sticky tape.'

Beagle's heat shield doubled as its biological shield. So once the instruments were encased and sealed, the craft could be brought back into the real world. The shield heated up to 1,700 degrees on its descent through the Martian atmosphere, so bugs on the casing were not a worry. Mars Express – the craft carrying Beagle – did not need sterilising. Its trajectory was designed so that if something went wrong, the craft would not simply crash into the planet. Its course could be corrected en route.

Eventually, space scientists hope to return samples of Mars to Earth. While the risks of alien bacteria proving hazardous on Earth may be remote, the rocks will still need to be quarantined. Moon rocks from Apollo were analysed in vacuum glove boxes for the first two missions. Later, researchers stored rocks in nitrogen. Prof Pillinger believed the first Mars rocks should be sterilised before they are studied on Earth. 'For security purposes it would be the most sensible thing to do. You don't have to sterilise it all, you can contain some of it and then sterilise the sample you want to look at, but it would lower the risk and make it easier to analyse.'

IELTS TEST 2

Exam Essentials

LISTENING MODULE   **READING MODULE**   WRITING MODULE   SPEAKING MODULE

PASSAGE 1
PASSAGE 2
PASSAGE 3

Questions 14–20

*Look at the statements (**Questions 14–20**) and the list of spacecraft below.*

Match each statement with the spacecraft it applies to.

*Write the correct letter **A–E** in boxes 14–20 on your answer sheet.*

14   provided transport from Earth for bacteria

15   led to realisation of how tenacious bacteria are

16   was created so that there could be no bacteria on the outer structure

17   was capable of changing direction in the event of a problem

18   brought material which was kept in more than one kind of container

19   required action because of the possibility of the introduction of harmful bacteria

20   resulted in disagreement as to the relative value of what was found

List of Spacecraft
A   Apollo craft
B   Surveyor probe
C   Galileo probe
D   Beagle 2
E   Mars Express

Matching statements to options

Task guide

▶ This task requires you to match statements with the people or things in the text that they apply to. For example, you may be required to decide which people in the text express the views presented in the questions, or you may be required to decide which thing, place, creature, etc. in a text each statement is true of.

▶ Make sure that the option you choose matches precisely what is stated in the text. Sometimes a statement may relate in some way to more than one option, but it will only match one option precisely.

▶ This task is very similar to classification tasks (see page 42). The difference is that in this task the options are people or things, whereas in classification tasks the options are categories.

▶ See also pages 28 and 34 for other types of matching tasks.

Step-by-step guide

The best approach to this task is to:

• identify the section where each of the options is mentioned
• focus on these parts of the text, rather than constantly looking through the whole text and
• look at each question one by one and find the relevant part of the text.

▸ **Step 1 – Locate the options in the text**

In which paragraphs of the text are there references to each of the options (A–E)?

A Apollo ....
B Surveyor ....
C Galileo ....
D Beagle ....
E Mars Express ....

▸ **Step 2 – Find the answers**

This task involves more than simply matching words and phrases in the statements with words and phrases that mean the same in the text. Some questions involve finding the part of the text which presents the same idea as that contained in the question.

Question 14

Look through the parts of the text you identified in step 1. You are looking for a reference to bacteria being transported from Earth.

1 Which paragraph contains this reference?

....

Look at the paragraph you identified and answer this question.

2 Which phrase in this paragraph means 'was given a lift'?

....

Decide which spacecraft (A–E) this applies to and answer *Question 14*.

Question 15

Look through the parts of the text you identified in Step 1. You are looking for a reference to bacteria being tenacious.

1 What does 'tenacious' mean in this context?
   A moving quickly
   B very strong
   C easy to destroy

2 Which paragraph contains a reference to this characteristic?

....

Look at the paragraph you identified above and answer these questions:

3 What kind of bacteria was it?

....

4 Who was on the spacecaft which found it?

....

Decide which spacecraft (A–E) this person was on and answer *Question 15*.

Questions 16–20

Now answer *Questions 16–20*, using the same process:

• Look at each question and look through the parts of the text you identified in step 1 to find the place in the text that relates to each statement.
• When you have found that place, identify which spacecraft is referred to.

IELTS TEST 2

Exam Essentials

LISTENING MODULE   **READING MODULE**   WRITING MODULE   SPEAKING MODULE

PASSAGE 1
PASSAGE 2
PASSAGE 3

Questions 21–26

Label the diagram below.

Choose **NO MORE THAN THREE WORDS** *from the reading passage for each answer.*

Write your answers in boxes 21–26 on your answer sheet.

THE ASSEMBLY OF BEAGLE 2

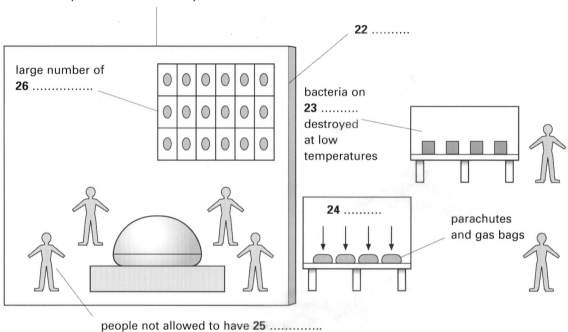

spacecraft built in newly created **21** ....

22 ....

large number of **26** ....

bacteria on **23** .... destroyed at low temperatures

24 ....

parachutes and gas bags

people not allowed to have **25** ....

Labelling a diagram

Task guide

▶ This task requires you to complete descriptions of a diagram using words that appear in the text. Remember to use words and phrases that actually appear in the text. Do not try to think of different words or phrases with the same meaning.

▶ The information you require will normally appear in one specific part of the text.

▶ Within that part of the text, the information may not appear in the same order as the question numbers in the diagram. The questions usually begin at the top left of the diagram and go round in a clockwise direction. It is therefore essential to keep looking carefully at the diagram and the parts that you need to label so that you do not get confused about the order.

Step-by-step guide

▶ **Step 1 – Locate the task in the text**

Look for clues in the title of the diagram (if there is one) or in the questions on the diagram. In this case, the title ('The Assembly of Beagle 2') points you to the relevant part of the text.

1 The relevant part of the text begins with a reference to Beagle being 'assembled'. In which paragraph and in which sentence in that paragraph is this reference?

....

2 Where does the description of the assembly of Beagle end in the text?

....

▶ **Step 2 – Find the answers**

The best approach is to look at each question in number order and then find the relevant information in the text.

Remember that the order of the questions may not be the same as the order in which the information appears in the text. If you try to take a different approach, beginning with what is said in the text and then finding which question it refers to, you may become confused and put answers into the wrong gaps.

Before looking through the text, make sure that you are clear about exactly what is being labelled.

Question 21

The arrow indicates that it refers to the whole place where Beagle was assembled.

The question tells you that you are looking for a place that was 'newly created', not one that previously existed.

Read the parts of the text you identified in step 1. Which phrase in the text means 'newly created'?

....

Identify the place that was newly created and answer *Question 21*.

Question 22

The arrow indicates that something that separated one place from another must be labelled.

Look through the parts of the text you identified in step 1. Communication took place from one side of this object to the other. What three things are mentioned as methods of communication?

....

Identify this dividing object and answer *Question 22*.

Questions 23–25

Now answer *Questions 23–25*, using the same process:

• Look at each question in number order.

• Make sure you are clear as to exactly what is being labelled.

• Look for the relevant information in the text.

• Use any other words in the label to help you find the relevant information in the text.

IELTS TEST 2

Exam Essentials

| LISTENING MODULE | READING MODULE | WRITING MODULE | SPEAKING MODULE |

PASSAGE 1
PASSAGE 2
PASSAGE 3

*You should spend about 20 minutes on **Questions 27–40** which are based on Reading Passage 3 below.*

Finding out about the world from television news

In *The Ideological Octopus* (1991), Justin Lewis points to an important issue concerning the formal structure of television news. As he notes, television news lacks the narrative element which, in other genres, serves to capture viewer interest and thus motivate viewing. Lewis posits this as one of the key reasons why television news often fails to interest people and why, when they do watch it, people often cannot understand it. Lewis argues that one fundamental problem with watching television news is that its narrative structure means that the viewer is offered the punchline before the joke – because the main point (the headline) comes right at the beginning, after which the programme, by definition, deals with less and less important things. Thus, in television news our interest is not awakened by an enigma which is then gradually solved, to provide a gratifying solution – as so often happens in fictional narratives. In Lewis's terms, in television news there is no enigma, the solution of which will motivate the viewing process. As he

baldly states, 'If we decided to try to design a television programme with a structure that would completely fail to capture an audience's interest, we might (finally) come up with the format of the average television news show' (Lewis 1991).

What Lewis also does is offer an interesting contrast, in this respect, between the high-status phenomenon of television news and the low-status genre of soap opera. The latter, he observes, offers the most highly developed use of effective narrative codes. To that extent soap opera, with its multiple narratives, could be seen, in formal terms, as the most effective type of television for the cultivation of viewer interest, and certainly as a far more effective form than that of television news for this purpose. Clearly, some of Lewis's speculation here is problematic. There are counter-examples of his arguments (e.g. instances of programmes such as sports news which share the problematic formal features he points to but which are nonetheless popular – at least among certain

types of viewers). Moreover, he may perhaps overstress the importance of structure as against content relevance in providing the basis for programme appeal. Nonetheless, I would suggest that his argument, in this respect, is of considerable interest.

Lewis argues not only that soap opera is more narratively interesting than television news, in formal terms, but, moreover, that the world of television fiction in general is much closer to most people's lives than that presented in the news. This, he claims, is because the world of television fiction often feels to people like their own lives. They can, for example, readily identify with the moral issues and personal dilemmas faced by the characters in a favourite soap opera. Conversely, the world of television news is much more remote in all senses; it is a socially distant world populated by another race of special or 'elite' persons, the world of 'them' not 'us'. This is also why 'most people feel more able to evaluate TV fiction than TV news ... because it seems closer to their own lives and to the world they live in ... [whereas] the world of television news ... might almost be beamed in from another planet' (Lewis 1991). It is as if the distant world of 'the news' is so disconnected from popular experience that it is beyond critical judgement for many viewers. Hence, however alienated they feel from it, they nonetheless lack any alternative perspective on the events it portrays.

One consequence of this, Lewis argues, is that precisely, because of this distance, people who feel this kind of alienation from the 'world of news' nonetheless use frameworks to understand news items which come from within the news themselves. This, he argues, is because in the absence of any other source of information or perspective they are forced back on using the media's own framework. Many viewers are simply unable to place the media's portrayal of events in any other critical framework (where would they get it from?). To this extent, Lewis argues, Gerbner and his colleagues (see Gerbner et al. 1986; Signorielli and Morgan 1990) may perhaps be right in thinking that the dominant perspectives and 'associative logics' offered by the media may often simply be soaked up by audiences by sheer dint of their repetition. This is not to suggest that such viewers necessarily believe, or explicitly accept, these perspectives, but simply to note that they have no other place to start from, however cynical they may be, at a general level, about 'not believing what you see on television', and they may thus tend, in the end, to fall back on 'what it said on TV'. In one sense, this could be said to be the converse of Hall's 'negotiated code' (1980), as taken over from Parkin (1973). Parkin had argued that many working-class people display a 'split consciousness', whereby they accept propositions from the 'dominant ideology' at an abstract level, but then 'negotiate' or 'discount' the application of these ideological propositions to the particular circumstances of their own situation. Here, by contrast, we confront a situation where people often express cynicism in general (so that 'not believing what you see in the media' is no more than common sense), but then in any particular case they often find themselves pushed back into reliance on the mainstream media's account of anything beyond the realm of their direct personal experience, simply for lack of any alternative perspective.

IELTS TEST 2

Exam Essentials

LISTENING MODULE   **READING MODULE**   WRITING MODULE   SPEAKING MODULE

PASSAGE 1
PASSAGE 2
PASSAGE 3

Questions 27–34

Complete the summary below using words from the box.

Write your answers in boxes 27–34 on your answer sheet.

The structure of television news

Justin Lewis says that television news does not have the **27** .... feature that other types of programme have.

As a result, many viewers do not find it interesting and may find it **28** .... . This is because the **29** ....

information comes first and after that **30** .... matters are covered. In television news, there is no **31** ....

progress towards a conclusion and nothing **32** .... to find out about. In fact, he believes that television news

is an example of how the **33** .... process in the field of television could result in something that is **34** .... to

what constitutes an interesting programme.

upsetting	creative	secondary	controversial	fast-moving
contrary	opinionated	routine	step-by-step	informal
crucial	story-telling	additional	overwhelming	mysterious
repetitive	informative	related	confusing	diverse

Summary completion (with choices)

Task guide

▸ This task requires you to fill in gaps in a summary with the correct words that appear in the box.

▸ This task usually, but not always, focusses on one particular part or section of the text, rather than on information that is spread throughout the text.

▸ The words in the box will normally all belong to the same part of speech (adjectives, nouns, etc.). You are therefore required to decide on the word with the correct meaning for each gap, not what kind of word fits grammatically.

▸ The words you need to choose have the same or very similar meanings to words and phrases used in the text, or they express the same ideas as what is stated in the text.

▸ The questions follow the same order as the relevant information in the text.

▸ There are significantly more words to choose from in the box than there are answers. Be careful. Several words in the box may be connected in meaning, but only one will have the precise meaning required to match what is stated in the text.

▸ See also page 26 for another type of summary completion task.

Step-by-step guide

First of all, you need to identify which words and phrases in the text relate to each gap. Then you need to find the word in the box that has the same meaning as those words or phrases, or expresses the same idea as what is stated in the text.

▶ **Step 1 – Locate the task in the text**

In this case, the title and the reference to Justin Lewis at the beginning of the summary can help you locate the task in the text.

Which sentence in the text contains a reference to the structure of television news and Justin Lewis?

....

▶ **Step 2 – Find the answers**

As with the summary task that does not have a box of choices (see page 26), the summary in this task presents the information and ideas in the text in different words and phrases from those in the text. You will need to understand the ideas that are contained in the text and see how they relate to the content of the summary.

The box contains words that mean the same as words or ideas that appear in the text. To answer each question, you first need to identify which part of the text relates to the gap in the summary. Then you must identify the word in the box that has the same meaning as the relevant word or idea in the text.

Question 27

1 Look at the words before and after the gap, and look at the part of the text you identified in step 1. Which word in the text means 'feature' in this context?

....

2 The summary refers to other types of programme. Which word in the text means 'types'?

....

3 You are looking for a feature that television news doesn't have, but other types of programme do have. Which word in the text means 'doesn't have'?

....

4 Which word in the text could fill the gap in the summary?

....

Now look at the words in the box and find the word that has the same meaning as this word from the text.

Now write your answer for *Question 27*.

Question 28

Look at the paragraph you identified in step 1.

The sentence containing the gap in the summary refers to two reactions that viewers have to television news. One is that they don't find it interesting. What other problem does the text say that they have?

....

Question 28 relates to the phrase you have just identified. Now look at the words in the box and find the word that expresses the same idea.

Now write your answer for *Question 28*.

Questions 29–34

Answer *Questions 29–34*, using the same process:

• Look at the words before and after each gap and find the part of the text that relates to them.

• Find a word in the text that could fill the gap or identify a phrase in the text that expresses the idea of the word that fills the gap.

• Look through the box of choices and identify the word that matches the meaning of the word in the text or expresses the same idea as the phrase in the text.

IELTS TEST 2

Exam Essentials

| LISTENING MODULE | READING MODULE | WRITING MODULE | SPEAKING MODULE |

PASSAGE 1
PASSAGE 2
PASSAGE 3

Questions 35–40

Do the following statements agree with the information given in Reading Passage 3?

In boxes 35–40 on your answer sheet write

TRUE	*if the statement agrees with the information*
FALSE	*if the statement contradicts the information*
NOT GIVEN	*if there is no information on this*

35 Lewis concentrates more on the structure of programmes than on what is actually in them.

36 Lewis regrets viewers' preference for soap operas over television news.

37 Lewis suggests that viewers sometimes find that television news contradicts their knowledge of the world.

38 Lewis believes that viewers have an inconsistent attitude towards the reliability of television news.

39 Parkin states that many working class people see themselves as exceptions to general beliefs.

40 The writer of the text believes that viewers should have a less passive attitude towards what they are told by the media.

True/False/Not Given

Task guide

▶ This task, which is very similar to the Yes/No/Not Given task (see page 36), tests you on the detailed understanding of complex pieces of information in the text.

▶ For an answer to be 'False', there must be something in the text that makes the statement in the question definitely incorrect.

▶ Questions to which the answer is 'Not Given' involve something being stated in the text that relates to the statement in the question, but which does not actually match the statement or directly show it to be correct or incorrect.

▶ The questions follow the order in which the relevant information appears in the text.

▶ This task may focus on one specific part of the text, but it is more likely that the information relevant to it will be spread throughout the text or large parts of it.

Step-by-step guide

The best approach to this task is to:
- look at each question one by one
- find the relevant part of the text
- study the question and that part of the text carefully and
- decide on your answer.

Remember that you will have to understand the ideas presented in the text, and that you may not find words and phrases in the text that mean the same as those in the question.

▶ **Step 1 – Locate the task in the text**

This is a very difficult text. Before starting the task, it is a good idea to locate the task in the text.

1 *Question 35* refers to 'structure'. Which paragraph(s) of the text mention the structure of programmes?

....

2 *Question 36* mentions 'soap operas'. Which paragraph(s) of the text refer to soap operas?

....

3 *Question 39* refers to Parkin. In which paragraph is Parkin mentioned?

....

4 Where do you think you will find the answers to this task?
   A in one specific part of the text
   B spread throughout the text

▶ **Step 2 – Find the answers**

As with the Yes/No/Not Given task (see page 36), to answer the questions you will need to find the relevant part of the text, read it carefully and ask yourself three questions:
- Is the same thing stated in the text?
- Is the opposite stated in the text?
- Is there no information on this particular matter in the text?

Question 35

1 Find a sentence in the text that mentions that Lewis concentrates more on one thing than another. What is the first word of that sentence?

....

2 Which phrase in that sentence means 'concentrate too much on' or 'put too much emphasis on'?

....

3 In that sentence, which word means 'what is in something'?

....

Now answer *Question 35*.

Question 36

1 Find a paragraph that deals with why people prefer soap operas but doesn't deal with the differences in structure between soap operas and television news.

....

2 Read this paragraph carefully. Does Lewis say that he can understand why people prefer soap operas?

....

3 Does Lewis say that he also prefers soap operas to television news?

....

4 Does Lewis say that he prefers television news to soap operas?

....

Now answer *Question 36*.

Questions 37–40

Answer *Questions 37–40*, using the same process:
- Find the part of the text that relates to the question.
- Read carefully what is stated in that part of the text and in the question.
- Ask yourself the three questions at the beginning of step 2.

IELTS
TEST 2

Exam Essentials

LISTENING MODULE   READING MODULE   **WRITING MODULE**   SPEAKING MODULE

Task 1
Task 2

You should spend about 20 minutes on this task.

> *The table below gives information about the five small companies in Britain that came top in a survey of staff conducted by a national newspaper to find out which companies are the best to work for.*

> *Write a report for a university lecturer describing the information below.*

Write at least 150 words.

THE FIVE BEST SMALL COMPANIES TO WORK FOR

POSITION IN SURVEY	1ST	2ND	3RD	4TH	5TH
staff numbers	56	79	72	76	190
male:female ratio	30:70	47:53	74:26	13:87	51:49
under 35s / over 55s	77% / 0%	59% / 1%	82% / 0%	26% / 8%	93% / 0%
staff turnover	5%	18%	8%	13%	33%
staff in high income bracket	34%	48%	74%	5%	2%

Describing tables

Task guide

▶ Many Task 1 questions involve tables presented in columns, according to categories, etc.

▶ A task may involve a single table, more than one table, or a table together with a bar chart or graph.

▶ This task involves a single table with data on five companies in five categories.

▶ For this kind of task, you must select important information and summarise it. Do not list all the data presented in the table.

▶ Make sure that you include all relevant points. If important information is missing from your answer, you may lose marks.

▶ Look for overall patterns or trends. It is possible, however, that there are no simple patterns or obvious general trends. If this is the case, you could say this in your answer.

▶ Remember that your answer must not be too short or too long. It is better to write just over 150 words and check that your answer flows well and logically, and that the English is accurate, than to write a longer answer.

▶ Remember that tasks in the Writing module will be marked according to certain criteria:
Content: Have you included all the relevant information?
Organisation: Does your answer flow well and is it clear and easy to read?
Use of language: Have you used appropriate linking words and phrases? Have you used a range of grammatical structures? Is the vocabulary used accurately?

Step-by-step guide

▸ **Step 1 – Find the main point(s)**

1 Look carefully through the table. What do you notice?

A The company that came first is different from all the others in every category.

B There are differences between the five companies in every category.

C None of the companies have anything in common with each other.

2

a What is the highest number of staff and which company has it?

....

b What is the lowest number of staff and which company has it?

....

3

a How many companies have more male than female staff?

....

b Which company has the highest proportion of female staff?

....

4

a What is the highest percentage of staff aged under 35 and which company has it?

....

b What is the highest percentage of staff aged over 55 among the five companies and which company has it?

....

5 How many companies have a staff turnover rate of over 10%?

....

6 How many companies have fewer than 10% of staff earning high incomes?

....

▸ **Step 2 – Organise your answer**

1 What should you begin your answer with?

A a description of the company that came first

B a reference to whether there is a general pattern or not

C a comparison of the staff numbers in the various companies

2 What should come next?

A a sentence or sentences about each category

B a sentence or sentences about each company

C a comment on each one of the figures

▸ **Step 3 – Language to use**

Write a sentence based on the information in the table, using one word or phrase from each of these lists:

Linking phrases

• *apart from, except for*
• *as for, with regard to*

....
....

Grammatical structures: adverbs

greatly, fairly, comparatively, far, extremely

....
....

Vocabulary: difference and similarity

have in common with, differ from, be similar to, difference between

....
....

Use your answers for step 1, 2 and 3 to plan your answer.

Now write your answer for Task 1.

There is a sample answer on page 200.

Task 1
Task 2

You should spend about 40 minutes on this task.
Present a written argument or case to an educated reader with no specialist knowledge of the following topic.

> *The ease of international travel and the spread of various kinds of mass media all over the world have made it more possible than ever for people to know how other people live in other countries.*

> *Do the advantages of this development outweigh the disadvantages?*

You should use your own ideas, knowledge and experience and support your arguments with examples and relevant evidence. Write at least 250 words.

Giving your opinion (2)

Task guide

▶ Remember to read the statement(s) and the question very carefully, so that you do exactly what you are asked to do in your answer.

▶ Some tasks ask you to discuss the advantages and disadvantages of something, while others ask you to discuss the causes of a problem and suggest possible solutions to it. In tasks of this type, you may be asked the following questions:
  (a) *Do the advantages of this outweigh the disadvantages?*
  (b) *Do you think this is a positive or negative development?*
  (c) *What do you think are the causes of this problem and what measures could be taken to solve/reduce it?*

  In this case, Task 2 is an example of (a). There are examples of (b) and (c) in other tests in this book.

▶ Remember to concentrate on presenting a clear and logical argument that the reader can follow easily.

▶ Remember to divide your answer into paragraphs appropriately.

▶ Remember that your answer must not be too short or too long.

▶ Remember that tasks in the Writing module will be assessed according to certain criteria:

  Content: Have you included all the relevant information?
  Organisation: Does your answer flow well and is it clear and easy to read?
  Use of language: Have you used appropriate linking words and phrases? Have you used a range of grammatical structures? Is the vocabulary used accurately?

Step-by-step guide

▶ **Step 1 – Read the question carefully**

Look at Task 2. Which FIVE of the following should you do in your answer?

1 Compare international travel now and in the past.

2 Discuss the effect of international travel on local economies and the environment.

3 Discuss relationships between visitors and local people.

4 Compare the quality of different types of mass media.

5 Give examples of types of mass media that have spread.

6 Discuss the reactions people have when seeing programmes about other countries.

7 Give examples of political events that have been covered by media all over the world.

8 Give an opinion on whether developments in travel and mass media have been beneficial in life in general.

9 Give an opinion on whether developments in travel and mass media have affected relationships between different nationalities.

▶ **Step 2 – Organise your answer**

Using your answers for step 1, make a plan for your answer:

• Deal with each of the two topics – international travel and mass media – separately.

• Discuss the developments and advantages of each separately.

• Then discuss the disadvantages of both of them together.

• Finally, present a conclusion.

This is a suggested plan only. You could decide to organise your answer in a different way.

Now write your notes:

International travel

Developments: ....
....
Advantages: ....
....

Mass media

Developments: ....
....
Advantages: ....
....

International travel – disadvantages

....

Mass media – disadvantages

....

Conclusion

....

▶ **Step 3 – Language to use**

Using your notes for step 2, write a sentence using one word or phrase from each of these lists:

Linking words and phrases

• *first of all, in addition, in conclusion, on the whole*

• *because, as, since, as a result*

• *although, though, whereas*

....
....
....

Grammatical structures

• comparison: *more ... than, less ... han*

• clauses beginning with *what* and *how*

• reflexives: *themselves, each other, one another*

....
....
....

Vocabulary

• *affordable, accessible*

• *envy, envious, sympathy, sympathetic, understanding*

• *cause, lead to, create, produce*

....
....

Now write your answer for Task 2.

There is a sample answer on page 200.

IELTS
TEST 2

Exam Essentials

LISTENING MODULE   READING MODULE   WRITING MODULE   **SPEAKING MODULE**

PART 1
PART 2
PART 3

Assessment guide

In the Speaking module, the examiner will assess your performance on the basis of:

- Fluency and coherence
- Lexical resource
- Grammatical range and accuracy
- Pronunciation

The examiner will be applying these four criteria at all times in all three parts of the Speaking module.

Fluency and coherence
This refers to how much and quickly you speak, and to how organised what you say is. If you pause a lot, or repeat yourself, you do not communicate very effectively. If you talk reasonably continuously, and present what you say in a logical and organised way, you communicate well.

Lexical resource
This refers to the vocabulary you use. If you understand what you are asked, you will be able to answer the examiner's questions effectively. If you are able to use a variety of words and expressions to say what you want, you will be interesting to listen to.

Grammatical range and accuracy
This refers to the grammar you use. If you only use simple structures and do not vary them, you will not be very interesting to listen to. But if you do not make a large number of mistakes, and you also use different structures, then you will be able to communicate what you want to say effectively.

Pronunciation
This refers to the way you pronounce individual sounds, words, phrases and complete sections of talk. For example, if you do not pronounce certain sounds distinctly, or if you don't use the intonation patterns of the English language, it can be difficult for the examiner to understand what you are saying. If all aspects of your pronunciation are clear and correct, the examiner will be able to understand what you want to say easily.

Part 1 – Example questions

What journeys do you make every day?
What do you do during journeys?
Do you sometimes have problems with transport?
What is your favourite form of transport?

Step-by-step guide

▸ **Step 1 – Check your grammar**
Look at this candidate's answer for this task.

Examiner: What journeys do you make every day?
Candidate: I go college every day. I go by foot to underground station and take a train for about 15 minutes.
Examiner: What do you do during journeys?
Candidate: Sometimes I reading a newspaper, but if I travel with my friend we will talk a lot.
Examiner: Do you sometimes have problems with transport?
Candidate: The trains have crowded, and sometimes are delay and I arrive to college late.
Examiner: What is your favourite form of transport?
Candidate: I like planes best. They are very fast and convenient, despite expensive.

How would you assess this candidate's grammar? Has the candidate used a good range of structures? Can you find any mistakes?

▸ **Step 2 – Improve your answer**
Look at the candidate's answer again. Correct the mistakes by filling in some of the gaps with words from the box.

are	at	being	delayed	on	read	the	to

I go **1** .... college every day. I go **2** .... foot to **3** .... underground station and take a train for about 15 minutes.

Sometimes I **4** .... a newspaper, but if I travel with my friend, we **5** .... talk a lot.

The trains **6** .... crowded, and sometimes are **7** ...., and I arrive **8** .... college late.

I like **9** .... planes best. They are very fast and convenient, despite **10** .... expensive.

Part 2 – Example questions

Read the topic card below carefully. You will have to talk about the topic for 1 to 2 minutes.

You have one minute to think about what you are going to say.

You can make notes to help you if you wish.

> **Describe a conversation you had which was important to you.**
>
> **You should say:**
>   **when the conversation took place**
>   **who you had the conversation with**
>   **what the conversation was about**
> **and explain why the conversation was important to you.**

Step-by-step guide

▶ **Step 1 – Check for fluency and coherence**

Look at the candidate's notes and answer for this task.

- 3 years ago – visiting my parents

- George – my uncle

- going to England

- changed my life

I remember one conversation that was important to me. It was about three years ago, and it had a big impact on my life. What happened was that my uncle – George, he is my mother's brother, and lives in London – he has a business – talked to me. He was visiting us in my country. I was bored with my life, and I was complaining about how I didn't know what to do – there aren't many opportunities in my small town, you see. My uncle said that I should come to London. He could help me to find work and meet people. Then I could study and get qualifications. I did it and I came to London. Now I have a job and I study part–time. This conversation changed my life. Without this conversation, I would still be bored at home.

How would you assess this candidate's fluency and coherence? Can you find any areas that need improvement?

▶ **Step 2 – Improve your answer**

Look at the candidate's answer again. Improve the fluency and coherence by filling in the gaps with words from the box.

a at the time
b in particular
c so
d this was because
e what he suggested
f where
g who
h would be able to

I remember one conversation **1** .... that was important to me. It was about three years ago, and it had a big impact on my life. What happened was that my uncle – George, **2** .... is my mother's brother, and lives in London **3** .... he has a business – talked to me. He was visiting us in my country. **4** .... I was bored with my life, and I was complaining about how I didn't know what to do – **5** .... there aren't many opportunities in my small town, you see. My uncle said that I should come to London. He could help me to find work and meet people. Then I **6** .... study and get qualifications. I did **7** .... and **8** .... I came to London. Now I have a job and I study part-time. This conversation changed my life. Without this conversation, I would still be bored at home.

IELTS TEST 2

Exam Essentials

LISTENING MODULE	READING MODULE	WRITING MODULE	**SPEAKING MODULE**

PART 1
PART 2
PART 3

Part 3 – Example questions

A   What differences are there when using channels of communication (face-to-face, telephone, writing)?

B   To what extent do you think films and TV influence how people communicate with each other?

C   Do you think that there are differences in the way men and women communicate?

D   Do you agree that education has a strong and positive effect on people's ability to communicate effectively?

E   What impact do you think the growth of technology might have on communication in the future?

Step-by-step guide

> ▶ **Step 1 – Check your vocabulary**

Look at this candidate's answer for this task.

Examiner: What factors need to be considered when using different channels of communication (face-to-face, telephone, writing)?
Candidate: Well, for example, when you're talking on the telephone, you can't see the other person so you have to depend on your voice. When you're writing, you have more time to think about what you want to say, but on the other hand, if the other person doesn't understand, they can't ask you to say what you mean.
Examiner: To what extent do you think films and TV influence how people communicate with each other?
Candidate: I think that's something that's very hard to know. But we watch a large amount of TV from the US, for example, and people tend to copy expressions and attitudes of the actors.
Examiner: Do you think that there are differences in the way men and women communicate?
Candidate: I'm not sure ... people say there are. Personally, I think that there might be more important differences, across cultures, for example. Or generations – the way old and young people communicate.
Examiner: Do you agree that education has a strong and positive effect on people's ability to communicate effectively?
Candidate: I would say that it can do, that it should do. It can increase your awareness of things beyond your own direct experience, and so make you better at communicating. On the other hand, a lot of education is very specialised and separate from daily life.
Examiner: What impact do you think the growth of technology might have on communication in the future?
Candidate: I'm afraid that it won't be good. We are likely to become more and more isolated, sitting over computers, sending emails rather than meeting and talking together properly.

How would you assess the candidate's vocabulary? Has the candidate used a range of different words and expressions? Are they used correctly?

Step-by-step guide

(continued)

▸ **Step 2 – Use alternatives**

Look at the candidate's answer again. There are gaps and there are possible answers. Choose the word from the box for each gap that will fit in with what the candidate says.

beneficial	calculate	claim	clarify	considerable
consider	develop	hunched	imitate	increasingly
immediate	rely	remote	significant	suspect

A Well, for example, when you're talking on the telephone, you can't see the other person so you have to **1** …….. on your voice. When you're writing, you have more time to **2** …….. what you want to say, but on the other hand, if the other person doesn't understand, they can't ask you to **3** …….. what you mean.

B I think that's something that's very hard to **1** …….. . But we watch a **2** …….. amount of TV from the US, for example, and people tend to **3** …….. expressions and attitudes of the actors.

C I'm not sure – people **1** …….. there are. Personally, I **2** …….. that there might be more **3** …….. differences, across cultures, for example. Or generations – the way old and young people communicate.

D I would say that it can do, that it should do. It can **1** …….. your awareness of things beyond your own **2** …….. experience, and so make you better at communicating. On the other hand, a lot of education is very specialised and **3** …….. from daily life.

E I'm afraid that it won't be **1** …….. . We are likely to become **2** …….. isolated, **3**…….. over computers, sending emails rather than meeting and talking together properly.

IELTS
TEST 3

Exam Essentials

| LISTENING MODULE | READING MODULE | WRITING MODULE | SPEAKING MODULE |

SECTION 1
SECTION 2
SECTION 3
SECTION 4

▶ **Questions 1–10**

Answer the questions below.

Write **NO MORE THAN THREE WORDS AND/OR A NUMBER** *for each answer.*

1 How many members does the cycling club have currently?

   ....

2 How much does Youth Membership cost?

   ....

3 From whom must you get a signature when applying to join?

   ....

4 How long does it take to process a membership application?

   ....

5 How often do family rides take place?

   ....

6 How long are the Saturday rides usually?

   ....

7 What must you get for your bike?

   ....

8 When is the next camping tour?

   ....

9 What is happening on May 5th?

   ....

10 How much discount do members get at Wheels Bike Shop?

    ....

▸ **Questions 11–20**

Complete the timetable below.

Write **NO MORE THAN THREE WORDS AND/OR A NUMBER** *for each answer.*

PARK ARTS CENTRE

DATES	TIMES	EVENT	NOTES
18 – 24 Feb	**11** .... and	Folk music concert	Can get a **12** .... in shop
1 – 8 March	See the **13**	Annual **14**	Groups from **15** ....
16	8pm	Film: **17** ' .... '	Talk by the **18** ....
2 April	To be confirmed	**19**	It will be **20** ....

IELTS TEST 3

Exam Essentials

| LISTENING MODULE | READING MODULE | WRITING MODULE | SPEAKING MODULE |

SECTION 1
SECTION 2
SECTION 3
SECTION 4

▸ **Questions 21–30**

Questions 21–25

What opinion is expressed about each dissertation?

*Choose your answers from the box and write the letters **A–I** next to questions 21–25.*

> **A** It has an inadequate index.
> **B** It contains unusual illustrations.
> **C** It is too detailed in places.
> **D** It presents clear arguments.
> **E** It contains diagrams which are not clear.
> **F** It omits important historical facts.
> **G** It is poorly translated.
> **H** It contains useful background information.
> **I** It is not suitable for new students.

21 Twentieth Century Architecture ....
22 Modern Construction ....
23 Steel, Glass and Concrete ....
24 The Space We Make ....
25 Change and Tradition ....

Questions 26–30

Complete the flow chart below.

*Write **NO MORE THAN THREE WORDS** for each answer.*

BEN'S PROGRAMME

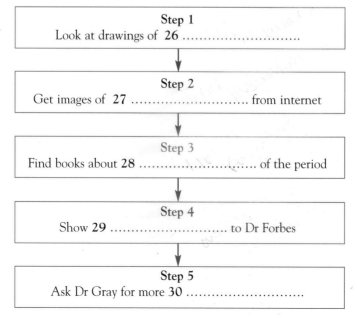

Step 1
Look at drawings of **26** ....

Step 2
Get images of **27** .... from internet

Step 3
Find books about **28** .... of the period

Step 4
Show **29** .... to Dr Forbes

Step 5
Ask Dr Gray for more **30** ....

▶ **Questions 31–40**

Complete the sentences below.

Write **NO MORE THAN TWO WORDS** *for each answer.*

31 Rival cameras were claimed to .... less than the Cinématographe.

32 In Russia, on one occasion, the Cinématographe was suspected of being a ....

33 Early filming in Russia led to the creation of a new approach to ....

34 One problem for historians is not knowing whether early equipment .... as it was claimed.

35 Marey encountered difficulties achieving the .... of strips of photographic paper.

36 The .... of the comic strip influenced the way films were planned.

37 Documentaries used .... shots before fiction films did.

38 The popularity of .... films led to increased numbers of shots.

39 When filming ...., the screen might be divided.

40 As films became more complex, ... became an important part of film-making.

IELTS
TEST 3

Exam Essentials

LISTENING MODULE   **READING MODULE**   WRITING MODULE   SPEAKING MODULE

PASSAGE 1
PASSAGE 2
PASSAGE 3

*You should spend about 20 minutes on **Questions 1–13** which are based on Reading Passage 1 on pages 96 and 97.*

Working in the movies

When people ask French translator Virginie Verdier what she does for a living, it must be tempting to say enigmatically: 'Oh me? I'm in the movies'. It's strictly true, but her starring role is behind the scenes. As translating goes, it doesn't get more entertaining or glamorous than subtitling films. If you're very lucky, you get to work on the new blockbuster films before they're in the cinema, and if you're just plain lucky, you get to work on the blockbuster movies that are going to video or DVD.

Virginie is quick to point out that this is as exacting as any translating job. 'You work hard. It's not all entertainment as you are doing the translating. You need all the skills of a good translator and those of a top-notch editor. You have to be precise and, of course, much more concise than in traditional translation work.'

The process starts when you get the original script and a tape. 'We would start with translating and adapting the film script. The next step is what we call 'timing', which means synchronising the subtitles to the dialogue and pictures.' This task requires discipline. 'You play the film, listen to the voice and the subtitles are up on your screen ready to be timed. You insert your subtitle when you hear the corresponding dialogue and delete it when the dialogue finishes. The video tape carries a time code which runs in hours, minutes, seconds and frames. Think of it as a clock. The subtitling unit has an insert key to capture the time code where you want the subtitle to appear. When you press the delete key, it captures the time code where you want the subtitle to disappear. So each subtitle would

> **Subtitling is an exacting part of the translation profession. Melanie Leyshon talks to Virginie Verdier of London translation company VSI about the glamour and the grind**

have an 'in' point and an 'out' point which represent the exact time when the subtitle comes in and goes out. This process is then followed by a manual review, subtitle by subtitle, and time-codes are adjusted to improve synchronisation and respect shot changes. This process involves playing the film literally frame by frame as it is essential the subtitles respect the visual rhythm of the film.'

Different subtitlers use different techniques. 'I would go through the film and do the whole translation and then go right back from the beginning and start the timing process. But you could do it in different stages, translate let's say 20 minutes of the film, then time this section and translate the next 20 minutes, and so on. It's just a different method.'

For multi-lingual projects, the timing is done first to create what is called a 'spotting list', a subtitle template, which is in effect a list of English subtitles pre-timed and edited for translation purposes. This is then translated and the timing is adapted to the target language with the help of the translator for quality control.

'Like any translation work, you can't hurry subtitling,' says Virginie. 'If subtitles are translated and timed in a rush, the quality will be affected and it will show.' Mistakes usually occur when the translator does not master the source language and misunderstands the original dialogue. 'Our work also involves checking and reworking subtitles when the translation is not up to standard. However, the reason for redoing subtitles is not just because of poor quality translation. We may need to adapt subtitles to a new version of the film: the time code may be different, the film may have been edited or the subtitles may have been created for the cinema rather than video. If subtitles were done for cinema on 35mm, we would need to reformat the timing for video, as subtitles could be out of synch or too fast. If the translation is good, we would obviously respect the work of the original translator.'

On a more practical level, there are general subtitling rules to follow, says Virginie. 'Subtitles should appear at the bottom of the screen and usually in the centre.' She says that different countries use different standards and rules. 'In Scandinavian countries and Holland, for example, subtitles are traditionally left justified. Characters usually appear in white with a thin black border for easy reading against a white or light background. We can also use different colours for each speaker when subtitling for the hearing impaired. Subtitles should have a maximum of two lines and the maximum number of characters on each line should be between 32 and 39. Our company standard is 37 (different companies and countries have different standards).'

Translators often have a favourite genre, whether it's war films, musicals, comedies (one of the most difficult because of the subtleties and nuances of comedy in different countries), drama or corporate programmes. Each requires a certain tone and style. 'VSI employs American subtitlers, which is incredibly useful as many of the films we subtitle are American,' says Virginie. 'For an English person, it would not be so easy to understand the meaning behind typically American expressions, and vice-versa.'

IELTS TEST 3

Exam Essentials

LISTENING MODULE   **READING MODULE**   WRITING MODULE   SPEAKING MODULE

PASSAGE 1
PASSAGE 2
PASSAGE 3

Questions 1–5

Complete the flow chart below.

Use **NO MORE THAN THREE WORDS** *from the passage for each answer.*

Write your answers in boxes 1–5 on your answer sheet.

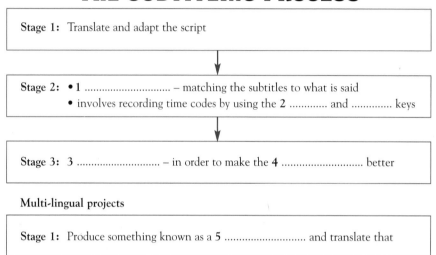

THE SUBTITLING PROCESS

Stage 1: Translate and adapt the script

Stage 2: • **1** .... – matching the subtitles to what is said
      • involves recording time codes by using the **2** .... and .... keys

Stage 3: **3** .... – in order to make the **4** .... better

Multi-lingual projects

Stage 1: Produce something known as a **5** .... and translate that

Questions 6–9

Do the following statements agree with the information given in Reading Passage 1?

In boxes 6–9 on your answer sheet write

TRUE   *if the statement agrees with the information*
FALSE   *if the statement contradicts the information*
NOT GIVEN *if there is no information on this*

6   For translators, all subtitling work on films is desirable.

7   Subtitling work involves a requirement that does not apply to other translation work.

8   Some subtitling techniques work better than others.

9   Few people are completely successful at subtitling comedies.

Questions 10–13

Complete the sentences below with words from Reading Passage 1.

Use **NO MORE THAN THREE WORDS** *for each answer.*

Write your answers in boxes 10–13 on your answer sheet.

10 Poor subtitling can be a result of the subtitler not being excellent at ....

11 To create subtitles for a video version of a film, it may be necessary to ....

12 Subtitles usually have a .... around them.

13 Speakers can be distinguished from each other for the benefit of ....

IELTS
TEST 3
Exam Essentials

LISTENING MODULE   READING MODULE   WRITING MODULE   SPEAKING MODULE

PASSAGE 1
PASSAGE 2
PASSAGE 3

*You should spend about 20 minutes on **Questions 14–26** which are based on Reading Passage 2 on pages 100 and 101.*

Complementary and alternative medicine

WHAT DO SCIENTISTS IN BRITAIN THINK ABOUT 'ALTERNATIVE' THERAPIES? ORLA KENNEDY READS A SURPRISING SURVEY

Is complementary medicine hocus-pocus or does it warrant large-scale scientific investigation? Should science range beyond conventional medicine and conduct research on alternative medicine and the supposed growing links between mind and body? This will be hotly debated at the British Association for the Advancement of Science.

One Briton in five uses complementary medicine, and according to the most recent Mintel survey, one in ten uses herbalism or homoeopathy. Around £130 million is spent on oils, potions and pills every year in Britain, and the complementary and alternative medicine industry is estimated to be worth £1.6 billion. With the help of Professor Edzard Ernst, Laing chair of complementary medicine at The Peninsula Medical School, Universities of Exeter and Plymouth, we asked scientists their views on complementary and alternative medicine. Seventy-five scientists, in fields ranging from molecular biology to neuroscience, replied.

Surprisingly, our sample of scientists was twice as likely as the public to use some form of complementary medicine, at around four in 10 compared with two in 10 of the general population. Three quarters of scientific users believed they were effective. Acupuncture, chiropractic and osteopathy were the most commonly used complementary treatments among scientists and more than 55 per cent believed these were more effective than a placebo and should be available to all on the National Health Service.

Scientists appear to place more trust in the more established areas of complementary and alternative medicine, such as acupuncture, chiropractic and osteopathy, for which there are professional bodies and recognised training, than therapies such as aromatherapy and spiritual healing. 'Osteopathy is now a registered profession requiring a certified four-year degree before you can advertise and practise,' said one neuroscientist who used the therapy.

Nearly two thirds of the scientists who replied to our survey believed that aromatherapy and homoeopathy were no better than placebos, with almost a half thinking the same of herbalism and spiritual thinking. Some of the comments we received were scathing, even though one in ten of our respondents had used homoeopathy. 'Aromatherapy and homoeopathy are scientifically nonsensical,' said one molecular biologist from the University of Bristol. Dr Romke Bron, a molecular biologist at the Medical Research Council Centre at King's College London, added: 'Homoeopathy is a big scam and I am convinced that if someone sneaked into a homoeopathic pharmacy and swapped labels, nobody would notice anything.'

Two centuries after homeopathy was introduced, it still lacks a watertight demonstration that it works. Scientists are happy that the resulting solutions and sugar pills have no side effects, but are baffled by how they can do anything.

Both complementary and conventional medicine should be used in routine health care, according to followers of the 'integrated health approach', who want to treat an individual 'as a whole'. But the scientists who responded to our survey expressed serious concerns about this approach, with more than half believing that integrated medicine was an attempt to bypass rigorous scientific testing. Dr Bron said: 'There is an awful lot of bad science going on in alternative medicine and the general public has a hard time to distinguish between scientific myth and fact. It is absolutely paramount to maintain rigorous quality control in health care. Although the majority of alternative health workers mean well, there are just too many frauds out there preying on vulnerable people.'

One molecular biologist from the University of Warwick admitted that 'by doing this poll I have realised how shamefully little I understand about alternative therapy. Not enough scientific research has been performed. There is enough anecdotal evidence to suggest that at least some of the alternative therapies are effective for some people, suggesting this is an area ripe for research.'

When asked if complementary and alternative medicine should get more research funding, scientists believed the top three (acupuncture, chiropractic and osteopathy) should get money, as should herbalism. It seems that therapies based on physical manipulation or a known action – like the active ingredients in a herb on a receptor in the body – are the ones that the scientific community has faith in. Less than a quarter thought that therapies such as aromatherapy, homoeopathy and spiritual healing should get any funding.

Scientists believed that the 'feelgood' counselling effect of complementary medicine and the time taken to listen to patients' problems was what worked, rather than any medicinal effect. In contrast, the average visit to

the doctor lasts only eight minutes, says the British Medical Association. Dr Stephen Nurrish, a molecular biologist at University College London, said: 'Much of the benefit people get from complementary medicine is the time to talk to someone and be listened to sympathetically, something that is now lacking from medicine in general.'

But an anonymous neuroscientist at King's College London had a more withering view of this benefit: 'On the validity of complementary and alternative medicines, no one would dispute that 'feeling good' is good for your health, but why discriminate between museum-trip therapy, patting-a-dog therapy and aromatherapy? Is it because only the latter has a cadre of professional 'practitioners'?'

There are other hardline scientists who argue that there should be no such thing as complementary and alternative medicine. As Professor David Moore, director of the Medical Research Council's Institute for Hearing Research, said: 'Either a treatment works or it doesn't. The only way to determine if it works is to test it against appropriate controls (that is, scientifically).'

IELTS TEST 3

Exam Essentials

LISTENING MODULE   **READING MODULE**   WRITING MODULE   SPEAKING MODULE

PASSAGE 1
PASSAGE 2
PASSAGE 3

Questions 14–19

*Look at the following views (**Questions 14–19**) and the list of people below them.*

Match each view with the person expressing it in the passage.

*Write the correct letter **A–E** in boxes 14–19 on your answer sheet.*

NB *You may use any letter more than once.*

14 Complementary medicine provides something that conventional medicine no longer does.

15 It is hard for people to know whether they are being told the truth or not.

16 Certain kinds of complementary and alternative medicine are taken seriously because of the number of people making money from them.

17 Nothing can be considered a form of medicine unless it has been proved effective.

18 It seems likely that some forms of alternative medicine do work.

19 One particular kind of alternative medicine is a deliberate attempt to cheat the public.

> **List of People**
> **A** Dr Romke Bron
> **B** a molecular biologist from the University of Warwick
> **C** Dr Stephen Nurrish
> **D** a neuroscientist at King's College London
> **E** Professor David Moore

Questions 20–22

*Complete each sentence with the correct ending **A–F** from the box below.*

*Write the correct letter **A–F** in boxes 20–22 on your answer sheet.*

20 The British Association for the Advancement of Science will be discussing the issue of

21 A recent survey conducted by a certain organisation addressed the issue of

22 The survey in which the writer of the article was involved gave information on

> **A**   what makes people use complementary rather than conventional medicine.
> **B**   how many scientists themselves use complementary and alternative medicine.
> **C**   whether alternative medicine should be investigated scientifically.
> **D**   research into the use of complementary and conventional medicine together.
> **E**   how many people use various kinds of complementary medicine.
> **F**   the extent to which attitudes to alternative medicine are changing.

Questions 23–26

Classify the following information as being given about

A	acupuncture
B	aromatherapy
C	herbalism
D	homoeopathy

*Write the correct letter, **A**, **B**, **C** or **D** in boxes 23–26 on your answer sheet.*

23 Scientists believe that it is ineffective but harmless.

24 Scientists felt that it could be added to the group of therapies that deserved to be provided with resources for further investigation.

25 Scientists felt that it deserved to be taken seriously because of the organised way in which it has developed.

26 A number of scientists had used it, but harsh criticism was expressed about it.

IELTS
TEST 3

Exam Essentials

LISTENING MODULE   **READING MODULE**   WRITING MODULE   SPEAKING MODULE

PASSAGE 1
PASSAGE 2
PASSAGE 3

▶ **Questions 27–40**

You should spend about 20 minutes on **Questions 27–40** *which are based on Reading Passage 3 on the following pages.*

Questions 27–32

Reading Passage 3 has six paragraphs **A–F**.

Choose the correct heading for each paragraph from the list of headings below.

Write the correct number ***i–x*** *in boxes 27–32 on your answer sheet.*

List of Headings

i	An easily understood system
ii	Doubts dismissed
iii	Not a totally unconventional view
iv	Theories compared
v	A momentous occasion
vi	A controversial use of terminology
vii	Initial confusion
viii	Previous beliefs replaced
ix	More straightforward than expected
x	An obvious thing to do

27   Paragraph **A**

28   Paragraph **B**

29   Paragraph **C**

30   Paragraph **D**

31   Paragraph **E**

32   Paragraph **F**

THE CLOUD MESSENGER

At six o'clock one evening in December 1802, in a dank and cavernous laboratory in London, an unknown young amateur meteorologist gave the lecture that was to make him famous

A Luke Howard had been speaking for nearly an hour, during which time his audience had found itself in a state of gradually mounting excitement. By the time that he reached the concluding words of his address, the Plough Court laboratory was in an uproar. Everyone in the audience had recognized the importance of what they had just heard, and all were in a mood to have it confirmed aloud by their friends and neighbours in the room. Over the course of the past hour, they had been introduced not only to new explanations of the formation and lifespan of clouds, but also to a poetic new terminology: 'Cirrus', 'Stratus', 'Cumulus', 'Nimbus', and the other names, too, the names of intermediate compounds and modified forms, whose differences were based on altitude, air temperature and the shaping powers of upward radiation. There was much that needed to be taken on board.

B Clouds, as everyone in the room would already have known, were staging posts in the rise and fall of water as it made its way on endless compensating journeys between the earth and the fruitful sky. Yet the nature of the means of their exact construction remained a mystery to most observers who, on the whole, were still in thrall to the vesicular or 'bubble' theory that had dominated meteorological thinking for the better part of a century. The earlier speculations, in all their strangeness, had mostly been forgotten or were treated as historical curiosities to be glanced at, derided and then abandoned. Howard, however, was adamant that clouds were formed from actual solid drops of water and ice, condensed from their vaporous forms by the fall in temperature which they encountered as they ascended through the rapidly cooling lower atmosphere. Balloon pioneers during the 1780s had confirmed just how cold it could get up in the realm of the clouds: the temperature fell some 6.5°C for every thousand metres they ascended. By the time the middle of a major cumulus cloud had been reached, the temperature would have dropped to below freezing, while the oxygen concentration of the air would be starting to thin quite dangerously. That was what the balloonists meant by 'dizzy heights'.

C Howard was not, of course, the first to insist that clouds were best understood as entities with physical properties of their own, obeying the same essential laws which governed the rest of the natural world (with one or two interesting anomalies: water, after all, is a very strange material). It had long been accepted by many of the more scientifically minded that clouds, despite their distance and their seeming intangibility, should be studied and apprehended like any other objects in creation.

D There was more, however, and better. Luke Howard also claimed that there was a fixed and constant number of basic cloud types,

IELTS
TEST 3

Exam Essentials

LISTENING MODULE   READING MODULE   WRITING MODULE   SPEAKING MODULE

PASSAGE 1
PASSAGE 2
PASSAGE 3

and this number was not (as the audience might have anticipated) in the hundreds or the thousands, like the teeming clouds themselves, with each as individual as a thumbprint. Had this been the case, it would render them both unclassifiable and unaccountable; just so many stains upon the sky. Howard's claim, on the contrary, was that there were just three basic families of cloud, into which every one of the thousands of ambiguous forms could be categorized with certainty. The clouds obeyed a system and, once recognized in outline, their basic forms would be 'as distinguishable from each other as a tree from a hill, or the latter from a lake', for each displayed the simplest possible visual characteristics.

E The names which Howard devised for them were designed to convey a descriptive sense of each cloud type's outward characteristics (a practice derived from the usual procedures of natural history classification), and were taken from the Latin, for ease of adoption 'by the learned of different nations': Cirrus (from the Latin for fibre or hair), Cumulus (from the Latin for heap or pile) and Stratus (from the Latin for layer or sheet). Clouds were thus divided into tendrils, heaps and layers: the three formations at the heart of their design. Howard then went on to name four other cloud types, all of which were either modifications or aggregates of the three major families of formation. Clouds continually unite, pass into one another and disperse, but always in recognizable stages. The rain cloud Nimbus, for example (from the Latin for cloud), was, according to Howard, a rainy combination of all three types, although Nimbus was reclassified as nimbostratus by meteorologists in 1932, by which time the science of rain had developed beyond all recognition.

F The modification of clouds was a major new idea, and what struck the audience most vividly about it was its elegant and powerful fittingness. All of what they had just heard seemed so clear and so self-evident. Some must have wondered how it was that no one – not even in antiquity – had named or graded the clouds before, or if they had, why their efforts had left no trace in the language. How could it be that the task had been waiting for Howard, who had succeeded in wringing a kind of exactitude from out of the vaporous clouds? Their forms, though shapeless and unresolved, had at last, it seemed, been securely grasped. Howard had given a set of names to a radical fluidity and impermanence that seemed every bit as magical, to that first audience, as the Eskimo's fabled vocabulary of snow.

Questions 33–36

Label the diagram below.

Choose **NO MORE THAN THREE WORDS AND/OR A NUMBER** *from the passage for each answer.*

Write your answers in boxes 33–36 on your answer sheet.

Reaching situation known as the **33** ....

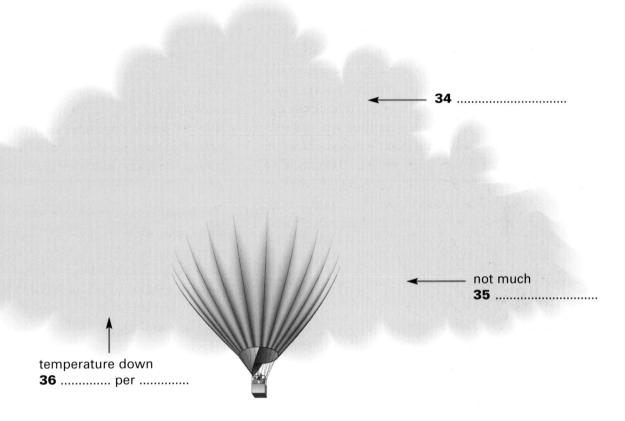

34 ....

not much
35 ....

temperature down
36 .... per ....

Questions 37–40

*Reading Passage 3 has six paragraphs labelled **A–F**.*

Which paragraph contains the following information?

*Write the correct letter **A–F** in boxes 37–40 on your answer sheet.*

NB *You may use any letter more than once.*

37 an example of a modification made to work done by Howard

38 a comparison between Howard's work and another classification system

39 a reference to the fact that Howard presented a very large amount of information

40 an assumption that the audience asked themselves a question

You should spend about 20 minutes on this task.

The graphs below show the number of drivers in Britain who have been caught driving too fast by speed cameras placed on roads, and the number of people killed in road accidents, over an eight-year period since the introduction of speed cameras. The tables show the results of a survey on people's opinions on speed cameras.

Write a report for a university lecturer describing the information below.

Write at least 150 words.

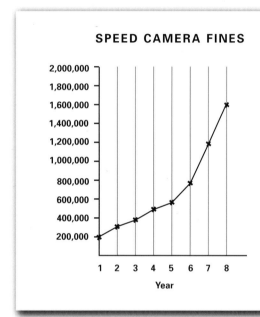

SPEED CAMERA FINES

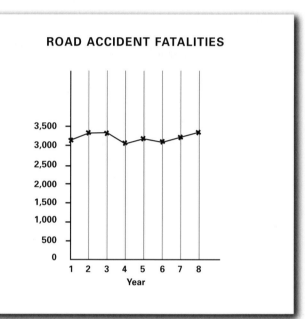

ROAD ACCIDENT FATALITIES

Do you think speed cameras reduce the number of accidents on the roads?

Yes	32%
No	60%
Don't know	8%

What do you think is the main reason for the installation of speed cameras?

To improve road safety	26%
To raise revenue	71%
Don't know	3%

What do you think about the number of speed cameras on the roads?

Too many	56%
Too few	19%
About right	17%
Don't know	8%

There is a sample answer on page 201.

You should spend about 40 minutes on this task.

Present a written argument or case to an educated reader with no specialist knowledge of the following topic.

> *In some countries today, there is an attitude that 'anyone can do it' in the arts – music, literature, acting, art, etc. As a result, people with no talent become rich and famous and genuine talent is not valued or appreciated.*
>
> *Do you agree or disagree?*

You should use your own ideas, knowledge and experience and support your arguments with examples and relevant evidence.

Write at least 250 words.

There is a sample answer on page 201.

▶ PART 1

Example questions

- What subject did you find most interesting when you were at school?
- Apart from classes, what else did you enjoy at school?
- Do you think that you will stay friends with people from your school?
- What study or training would you like to do in the future?

▶ PART 2

Example task

Read the topic card below carefully.

You will have to talk about the topic for 1 to 2 minutes.

You have one minute to think about what you're going to say.

You can make notes to help you if you wish.

> Describe a holiday you would like to go on.
> You should say:
>> what place you would like to go to
>>
>> how you would like to get there
>>
>> what you would like to do while you were there
>
> and explain why you would like to go on this holiday.

▶ PART 3

Example questions

- Which places in your country do you think visitors would enjoy visiting most?
- What are the benefits of going away on holiday?
- What kinds of benefits might a significant increase in tourist numbers bring to a location?
- What developments affecting international travel might there be in the future?

IELTS TEST 4

Exam Essentials

| LISTENING MODULE | READING MODULE | WRITING MODULE | SPEAKING MODULE |

SECTION 1
SECTION 2
SECTION 3
SECTION 4

▸ **Questions 1–10**

Complete the form below.

Write **NO MORE THAN THREE WORDS AND/OR A NUMBER** *for each answer.*

ABLE EMPLOYMENT AGENCY

APPLICATION FORM

Full name: 1 ....

Address: 2 ....
                      Melford MF4 5JB

Contact number: 3 ....

Qualifications: (a) A levels
                      (b) 4 ....
                      (c) 5 ....

Previous experience: (a) general work in a 6 .... (3 months)
                      (b) part-time job as a 7 ....

Interests: (a) member of a 8 ....
                      (b) enjoys 9 .... (10 years)

Date available: 10 ....

IELTS TEST 4

Exam Essentials

LISTENING MODULE	READING MODULE	WRITING MODULE	SPEAKING MODULE

SECTION 1
SECTION 2
SECTION 3
SECTION 4

▶ **Questions 11–20**

Questions 11–16

Complete the sentences below.

Write **NO MORE THAN TWO WORDS** *for each answer.*

The hotel

11 You must book .... in advance.

12 There are some interesting .... in the lounge.

Activities

13 The visit to the .... has been cancelled.

14 There will be a talk about .... from the area on Saturday.

15 The visit to the .... will take place on Sunday.

16 There is a collection of .... in the art gallery.

Questions 17–20

Label the map below.

Write the correct letter **A–I** *next to questions 17–20.*

Where are the following places situated?

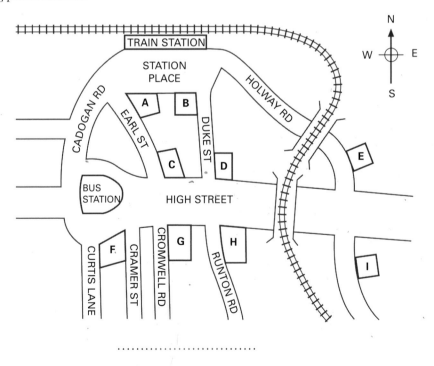

17 Park Hotel   ....

18 Internet Café   ....

19 Tourist Information Office   ....

20 Royal House Restaurant   ....

▸ **Questions 21–30**

Questions 21–26

*Write the correct letter, **A**, **B** or **C** next to questions 21–26.*

At which college are the following features recommended?

A   at Forth College
B   at Haines College
C   at both Forth and Haines Colleges

21   student support services
22   residential accommodation
23   on-line resources
24   libraries
25   teaching staff
26   research record

Questions 27–30

*Choose the correct letter, **A**, **B** or **C**.*

27   David is concerned that he may feel
    A   unmotivated.
    B   isolated.
    C   competitive.

28   In the future, Dr Smith thinks David should aim to
    A   do further research.
    B   publish articles.
    C   get teaching work.

29   What does Dr Smith think has improved masters' study in recent years?
    A   the development of the internet
    B   the growth of flexible courses
    C   the introduction of changes in assessment

30   David would like to improve the way he
    A   takes notes in lectures.
    B   writes up assignments.
    C   manages his time.

SECTION 1
SECTION 2
SECTION 3
SECTION 4

▶ **Questions 31–40**

Questions 31–37

Complete the table below.

Write **NO MORE THAN TWO WORDS** *for each answer.*

Type of writing	Notes	Tips
Short stories	3 basic styles	start with a 31 ....
Non-fiction	biographies often popular	tell publishers about your 32 ....
Articles	advice articles work well	write for a 33 ....
Poetry	meaning shouldn't be too 34	read your poems aloud
Plays	movements usually decided by the 35	learn about acting
Radio	BBC publishes Handbook	try 36 .... first
Children's literature	illustrations important	decide on an 37 ....

Questions 38–40

*Choose the correct letter, **A**, **B** or **C**.*

38 What is a disadvantage of first person narration in novels?
   A It makes it harder for the main character to be interesting.
   B It is difficult for beginners to do well.
   C It limits what can be described.

39 What is a mistake when writing novels?
   A failing to include enough detail
   B trying to explain ironic effects
   C including too many characters

40 In order to make dialogue seem natural, writers should
   A make recordings of real conversations.
   B include unfinished sentences.
   C break up long speeches.

You should spend about 20 minutes on **Questions 1–13** *which are based on Reading Passage 1 on pages 116 and 117.*

Groucho Marx & Arthur Sheekman

In a show-business career that spanned over seventy years, Groucho Marx successfully conquered every entertainment medium, becoming a star of the vaudeville stage, Broadway, motion pictures, radio and television. But, as the author of seven books, a play, two film screenplays and over one hundred magazine articles and essays, Groucho quietly conquered another medium, one in which he was as proud to work as any of the others. His writing is often overlooked in studies of his career, perhaps due to the quantity and variety of his other work.

Throughout his literary career, Groucho was dogged by the incorrect and unfair assumption by many critics and even by his biographer that he used a ghost writer. Most Hollywood celebrities who wrote books had professional writers do the actual work. The fact that Groucho publicly stated on many occasions that he abhorred ghost writers is clouded by his relationship with Arthur Sheekman. Friends for many years, Groucho and Sheekman had an unusual literary relationship. They worked in collaboration and each offered the other editorial help. For a brief time in the early 1940s, Groucho fronted for Sheekman, who was having trouble selling his work. By thus lending his name to another writer's work, Groucho subjected all of his literary endeavors to suspicion from critics who simply refused to believe that an entertainer could write.

That some of Sheekman's magazine pieces got into print under Groucho's byline becomes apparent from reading the unedited correspondence between the two of them. The letters indicate that Groucho's essays from this period fall into three categories: first, pieces written by Groucho with no input from Sheekman at all. In a July 1, 1940, letter to Sheekman, Groucho asked, 'Did you see that little piece

I wrote for *Reader's Digest?*' On March 17, 1941, he wrote, 'My drool is coming out in next week's issue of *This Week* so cancel your subscription now.' Clearly Sheekman could not have had anything to do with a piece that he was told to look for.

The second and probably largest category of Groucho's essays of this period consists of those written by Groucho and sent to Sheekman for editorial assistance. On July 20, 1940, Groucho wrote: 'I'm enclosing a copy of the piece I wrote. Probably another page or so is needed to complete it, but our starting date [for filming *Go West*] came and I just haven't had time to finish it. Let me know what you think of it and be honest because any other kind of opinion would be of no value to me. I won't attempt to influence you by telling you the reactions I've already had, so for the love of God tell me the truth.' Shortly thereafter, on October 10, Groucho wrote: 'I received your suggestions on my piece – I'm glad you liked it, if you did – you're probably right about the beginning. I'll do it over again.' By the time Groucho wrote to Sheekman on July 25, 1942, it appears that some sort of financial arrangement had been made regarding Sheekman's suggestions. On that date Groucho also wrote: 'I'm writing an unfunny piece on insomnia and I'll send it in a week or so, I hope, for you to read – I'd like your opinion, proofread – correcting all the glaring illiteracies and, otherwise, do a fine polishing job.'

The remainder of Groucho's essays from this period comprise the third category, Sheekman compositions with varying degrees of input from Groucho. The level of Groucho's contributions to the articles in the third category ranges from actually suggesting the topic and drawing up an outline to simply rewriting a few paragraphs for the purpose of injecting his own style into the piece. In a July 10, 1940, letter Groucho wrote: 'I think you ought to try another political piece – a campaign thing – for *This Week* or some other magazine. This will be an extremely hot topic for the next few months and I think you should take advantage of it. If you'll write to me, I'll try to jot down a few items that you could complain about.' Presumably, the chain of events would continue with Sheekman sending an essay to Groucho for his approval and whatever rewrites were needed. On May 29, 1940, Groucho wrote, 'Received your piece and looked it over.' In these letters to Sheekman, Groucho always referred to a piece as either 'my piece' or 'your piece'. The letter continued, 'I thought the piece was good ... and I'll send it to Bye and see if he can sell it ... I'll just rewrite a couple of paragraphs in your piece – not that I can improve them, but perhaps they'll sound a little more like me.' Groucho was concerned enough about this arrangement to take the care to at least make the piece somewhat his own.

Groucho really had no need for this entire enterprise. He gave the money to Sheekman and had no trouble getting his own work published. The principal reason for him submitting Sheekman's work to magazines as his own was that it made Sheekman's material easily marketable based on Groucho's celebrity. Sheekman couldn't have been altogether happy with the arrangement, but the reality was that he was periodically unemployed and the use of Groucho's name brought in occasional paychecks. So it is not quite fair to call Sheekman Groucho's ghost writer. A more apt description of their literary relationship at this time is that Groucho occasionally fronted for Sheekman and offered him the services of his literary agent, while each offered the other editorial advice. The reasons for some of their collaborative efforts not being credited as such remain unexplained, but Groucho was never shy about crediting his collaborators, and in every other case he did so.

IELTS TEST 4

Exam Essentials

LISTENING MODULE   READING MODULE   WRITING MODULE   SPEAKING MODULE

PASSAGE 1
PASSAGE 2
PASSAGE 3

Questions 1–4

Do the following statements reflect the claims of the writer of Reading Passage 1?

In boxes 1–4 on your answer sheet write

YES	*if the statement agrees with the claims of the writer*
NO	*if the statement contradicts the claims of the writer*
NOT GIVEN	*if it is impossible to say what the writer thinks about this*

1   Groucho's work as a writer was sometimes better than his work in other media.
2   Groucho's relationship with Sheekman cast doubt on his own abilities as a writer.
3   Money was occasionally a source of disagreement between Groucho and Sheekman.
4   Groucho occasionally regretted his involvement with Sheekman.

Questions 5–8

Complete the notes below.

Choose **NO MORE THAN THREE WORDS** *from the passage for each answer.*

Write your answers in boxes 5–8 on your answer sheet.

Groucho's essays in the early 1940s

Category 1	Category 2	Category 3
Sheekman had 5	Sheekman provided 6	mostly 7 .... Groucho added 8 ....

Questions 9–13

Look at the following statements (Questions 9–13) and the list of dates of letters sent by Groucho to Sheekman below.

Match each statement with the letter it relates to.

*Write the correct letter **A–G** in boxes 9–13 on your answer sheet.*

9 Groucho referred to his own inadequacy with regard to use of language.

10 Groucho explained his reason for amending an essay.

11 Groucho agreed that part of an essay needed revising.

12 Groucho drew Sheekman's attention to an essay soon to be published.

13 Groucho suggested that an essay should adopt a negative point of view.

List of Letters Sent by Groucho to Sheekman	
A	July 1, 1940
B	March 17, 1941
C	July 20, 1940
D	October 10, 1940
E	July 25, 1942
F	July 10, 1940
G	May 29, 1940

*You should spend about 20 minutes on **Questions 14–26** which are based on Reading Passage 2 on pages 120 and 121.*

An earth-shaking discovery

The discovery of sea floor spreading is earth-shaking, yet those responsible are forgotten, says Anna Grayson

In 1963, a paper appeared in the journal Nature that radically changed the way we view this planet and its resources. Its authors, Fred Vine and Drummond Matthews, did for the Earth sciences what Crick and Watson did for biology and Einstein did for physics, and new areas of scientific development are still emerging as a result.

Yet both men are largely forgotten and unrecognised. What Vine and Matthews did was to provide proof that continents really do drift across the surface of the globe. This understanding profoundly affects the way we use the planet today – it directs the way we prospect for resources such as oil and minerals; it has enabled us to predict most volcanic eruptions and to understand patterns of earthquakes. Incredibly, perhaps, an understanding of the mobile dynamic nature of the Earth is helping an understanding of long-term global climate changes. Despite the significance of their work, neither man received great honour or fame.

The idea of continental drift was first proposed in a serious way by the German meteorologist Alfred Wegener in 1915. People had noticed the neat jigsaw-like fit between South America and Africa, but Wegener found actual fossil evidence that the two continents were once joined. No one took him seriously; in fact he was ridiculed by most of the geological community. This was partly because, not being a geologist, he was perceived as an outsider. But the main reason for the hostility, according to Vine, was that Wegener was unable to come up with an explanation as to how whole continents could possibly move even an inch, let alone dance to the music of time around the globe.

In the 1920s, the Scottish geologist Arthur Holmes hypothesised that convection currents within the Earth could become sufficiently vigorous to drag the two halves of the original continent apart. In the late 1950s, an American, Harry Hess, came up with the hypothesis that new sea floor is constantly being generated at the mid-ocean ridges by hot material rising in a convection current. But neither man could find evidence to prove it. It was no more than just a hunch that it had to be right, and a hunch is not enough for science.

Vine had been fascinated by the apparent fit of the continents since the age of 14, and as a graduate student at Cambridge was assigned a project analysing one of the new magnetic surveys of the ocean floor. He found what he describes as 'parallel zebra stripes of normal and reversed magnetism' around the mid-ocean ridge. Most significantly, these stripes were symmetrical either side of the ridge crests. There had to be a reason for this. The young Vine and his supervisor Matthews proposed that the magnetic stripes were caused by new ocean floor being formed as molten rock rose at the mid-ocean ridges and spread each side of the ridge.

As the molten rock solidified, it became weakly magnetised parallel to the Earth's magnetic field. It was just becoming recognised in the early 1960s that the Earth's magnetic field flips every so often, so magnetic north becomes a magnetic south pole and visa versa. These flips in magnetic field were being recorded in the new sea floor. It was like a giant tape recording of the ocean floor's history. As new sea floor was made, it pushed the last lot aside, widening the ocean and in turn pushing the continents either side further apart. In other words, they had discovered the mechanism driving drifting continents that was missing from Wegener's work. The science of the Earth was never the same again.

By the end of the 1960s, confirmation of global sea floor spreading led to plate tectonics – the view of the outside of the Earth comprising just a few rigid plates which are shunted about by growing sea floor. There was a realisation that mountains are formed when two plates collide, and that most volcanoes and earthquakes occur on the edges of these plates. All this was accepted as fact by all but a few die-hard dinosaurs in the geological world.

It is now in the impact of shifting continents on the global environment that Vine feels the most exciting and significant research lies: 'The distribution of continents and the opening and closing of ocean gates between continents has had a profound effect on climates and has caused flips from Ice-house Earth to Green-house Earth.' The recognition that the Earth's hydrosphere, atmosphere and biosphere are all intimately linked with the drifting continents and the goings-on deep within the Earth has spawned the term 'Earth Systems Science'. It is a great oak tree of science that has grown from the acorn of truth supplied by Vine and Matthews. The holistic approach of earth systems science is very much welcomed by Vine: 'I'm rather pleased that this has come together.' He feels that the future for understanding the planet lies in an integrated approach to the sciences, rather than the isolated stance the geologists took throughout the 20th century: 'There was an incredible polarisation of science and I was caught between the boundaries. It was anathema to me – the whole of environmental science should be integrated.'

IELTS
TEST 4
Exam Essentials

LISTENING MODULE **READING MODULE** WRITING MODULE SPEAKING MODULE

PASSAGE 1
PASSAGE 2
PASSAGE 3

Questions 14–17

Complete each sentence with the correct ending **A–G** *from the box below.*

Write the correct letter **A–G** *in boxes 14–17 on your answer sheet.*

14   The work done by Vine and Matthews has had implications concerning

15   Wegener attempted to provide an explanation of

16   Wegener's conclusions were greeted as

17   The theories presented by both Holmes and Hess concerned

> **A** matters that had not received much attention for some time.
> **B** something which could not possibly be true.
> **C** something misunderstood at first but later seen as a breakthrough.
> **D** matters beyond simply the movement of continents.
> **E** something that had already been observed.
> **F** something arrived at by intuition that could not be demonstrated.
> **G** matters requiring different research techniques

Questions 18–22

Label the diagram below.

Choose **NO MORE THAN THREE WORDS** *from the passage for each answer.*

Write your answers in boxes 18–22 on your answer sheet.

THE DISCOVERIES OF VINE AND MATTHEWS
The Ocean Floor

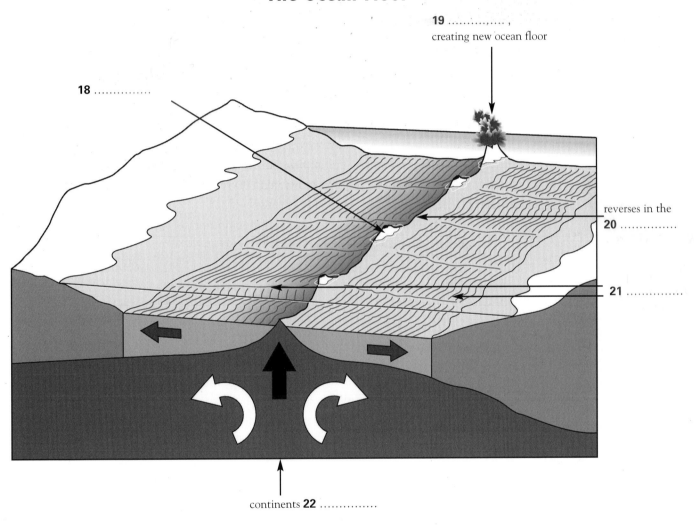

19 ....,
creating new ocean floor

18 ....

reverses in the
20 ....

21 ....

continents **22** ....

Questions 23–26

Answer the questions below using **NO MORE THAN THREE WORDS** *for each answer.*

Write your answers in boxes 23–26 on your answer sheet.

23 What is the name of the theory concerning the structure of the Earth that developed from the demonstration of sea floor spreading?

24 According to Vine, what has the movement of continents had a big influence on?

25 What branch of science has emerged as a result of the work done by Vine and Matthews?

26 Which word does Vine use to describe the way in which he believes study of the Earth should be conducted?

IELTS
TEST 4

Exam Essentials

LISTENING MODULE   READING MODULE   WRITING MODULE   SPEAKING MODULE

PASSAGE 1
PASSAGE 2
PASSAGE 3

You should spend about 20 minutes on **Questions 28–40** *which are based on Reading Passage 3 on pages 124 and 125.*

Think happy

It's no joke: even scientists at the Royal Society
are now taking the search for the source
of happiness very seriously

A What would Sir Isaac Newton have made of it? There he was, painted in oils, gazing down at one of the strangest meetings that the Royal Society, Britain's most august scientific body, has ever held. If Newton had flashed a huge grin, it would have been completely appropriate, for beneath him last week a two-day conference was unfolding on a booming new field of science: investigating what makes people happy. Distinguished professors strode up to the podium, including one eminent neurologist armed with videos of women giggling at comedy films; another was a social scientist brandishing statistics on national cheerfulness. Hundreds of other researchers sat scribbling notes on how to produce more smiles.

B The decision by the Royal Society to pick 'the science of wellbeing' from hundreds of applications for conferences on other topics is no laughing matter. It means that the investigation of what makes people happy is being taken very seriously indeed. 'Many philosophies and religions have studied this subject, but scientifically it has been ignored,' said Dr Nick Baylis, a Cambridge University psychologist and one of the conference organisers. 'For the Royal Society to give us its

countenance is vital, because that states that what we are doing deserves to be acknowledged and investigated by the best scientific minds.'

C At first sight, the mission of Baylis – and the growing number of other scientists working on happiness research – appears fanciful. They want to deploy scientifically rigorous methods to determine why some people are lastingly happy while others tend to misery. Then they envisage spreading the secret of happiness across the globe and, in short, increasing the sum of human happiness. 'If someone is happy, they are more popular and also healthier, they live longer and are more productive at work. So it is very much worth having,' he says.

D Baylis, the only 'positive psychology' lecturer in Britain, knows that the aims of happiness research might sound woolly, so he is at pains to distance himself from the brigades of non-academic self-help gurus. He refers to 'life satisfaction' and 'wellbeing' and emphasises that his work, and that of others at the conference, is grounded in solid research. So what have the scientists discovered – has a theory of happiness been defined yet?

E According to Professor Martin Seligman, probably the world's leading figure in this field, happiness could be but a train ride – and a couple of questionnaires – away. It was Seligman, a psychologist from Pennsylvania University, who kick-started the happiness science movement with a speech he made as President of the American Psychological Association (APA). Why, asked Seligman, shocking delegates at an APA conference, does science only investigate suffering? Why not look into what steps increase happiness, even for those who are not depressed, rather than simply seek to assuage pain? For a less well-known scientist, the speech could have spelt the end of a career, but instead Seligman landed funding of almost £18m to follow his hunch. He has been in regular contact with hundreds of other researchers and practising psychologists around the world, all the while conducting polls and devising strategies for increasing happiness.

F His findings have led him to believe that there are three main types of happiness. First, there is 'the pleasant life' – the kind of happiness we usually gain from sensual pleasures such as eating and drinking or watching a good film. Seligman blames Hollywood and the advertising industry for encouraging the rest of us, wrongly as he sees it, to believe that lasting happiness is to be found that way. Second, there is 'the good life', which comes from enjoying something we are good or talented at. The key to this, Seligman believes, lies in identifying our strengths and then taking part in an activity that uses them. Third, there is 'the meaningful life'. The most lasting happiness, Seligman says, comes from finding something you believe in and then putting your strengths at its service. People who are good at communicating with others might thus find long-lasting happiness through becoming involved in politics or voluntary work, while a rock star wanting to save the world might find it in organising a charity concert.

G Achieving 'the good life' and 'the meaningful life' is the secret of lasting happiness, Seligman says. For anybody unsure of how to proceed, he has an intriguing idea. To embark on the road to happiness, he suggests that you need a pen, some paper and, depending on your location, a railway ticket. First, identify a person to whom you feel a deep debt of gratitude but have never thanked properly. Next, write a 300-word essay outlining how important the help was and how much you appreciate it. Then tell them you need to visit, without saying what for, turn up at their house and read them the essay. The result: tears, hugs and deeper, longer-lasting happiness, apparently, than would come from any amount of champagne.

H Sceptics may insist that science will always remain a clumsy way of investigating and propagating happiness and say that such things are better handled by artists, writers and musicians – if they can be handled at all. And not everybody at the conference was positive about the emerging science. Lewis Wolpert, professor of biology as applied to medicine at University College London, who has written a bestseller about his battle with depression, said: 'If you were really totally happy, I'd be very suspicious. I think you wouldn't do anything, you'd just sort of sit there in a treacle of happiness. There's a whole world out there, and unless you have a bit of discomfort, you'll never actually do anything.'

IELTS
TEST 4

Exam Essentials

LISTENING MODULE   READING MODULE   WRITING MODULE   SPEAKING MODULE

PASSAGE 1
PASSAGE 2
PASSAGE 3

Questions 27–30

Complete the sentences below with words taken from Reading Passage 3.

Use **NO MORE THAN THREE WORDS** *for each answer.*

Write your answers in boxes 27–30 on your answer sheet.

27   At the conference, research into happiness was referred to as the ....

28   Baylis and others intend to use .... to find out what makes people happy or unhappy.

29   Baylis gives classes on the subject of ....

30   Baylis says he should not be categorised among the .... who do not have academic credentials.

Questions 31–36

Complete the summary below using words from the box.

Write your answers in boxes 31–36 on your answer sheet.

Seligman's categories of happiness

Seligman's first type of happiness involves the enjoyment of pleasures such as 31 .... He believes that people should not be under the 32 .... that such things lead to happiness that is not just temporary. His second type is related to 33 .... Identification of this should lead to 34 .... and the result is 'the good life'. His third type involves having a strong 35 .... and doing something about it for the benefit of others. This, according to Seligman, leads to happiness that has some 36 ....

confidence	entertainment	incentive	leadership
thrill	perseverance	illusion	effort
ability	theory	celebration	participation
ego	permanence	leadership	encouragement
exaggeration	concept	conviction	support

Questions 37–40

*Reading Passage 3 has eight paragraphs labelled **A–H**.*

Which paragraph contains the following information?

*Write the correct letter **A–H** in boxes 37–40 on your answer sheet.*

37   a view that complete happiness may not be a desirable goal

38   a reference to the potential wider outcomes of conducting research into happiness

39   an implication of the fact that the conference was held at all

40   a statement concerning the possible outcome of expressing a certain view in public

IELTS
TEST 4

Exam Essentials

LISTENING MODULE   READING MODULE   **WRITING MODULE**   SPEAKING MODULE

Task 1
Task 2

You should spend about 20 minutes on this task.

The diagram below shows the process for making a water clock.

Write a report for a university lecturer describing the information below.

Write at least 150 words.

HOW TO BUILD YOUR OWN WATER CLOCK

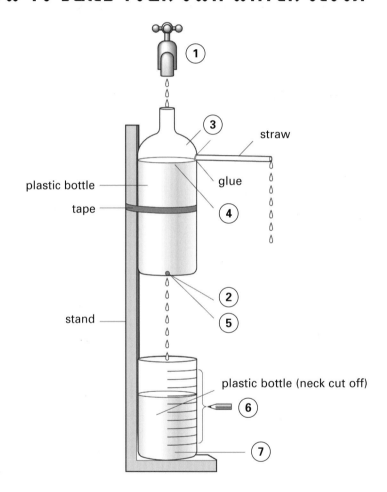

STAGES
1 tap on
2 cover hole with finger
3 fill top bottle to overflow
4 level constant
5 finger away from hole
6 levels per minute
7 empty and repeat process for timing things

There is a task guide for this task type on page 228 and a sample answer on page 202.

You should spend about 40 minutes on this task.

Present a written argument or case to an educated reader with no specialist knowledge of the following topic.

> *In some countries, it can be very difficult for people over the age of 50 to get good jobs, despite their experience.*
>
> *What do you think are the causes of this problem, and what measures could be taken to solve it?*

You should use your own ideas, knowledge and experience and support your arguments with examples and relevant evidence.

Write at least 250 words.

There is a sample answer on page 202.

▶ PART 1

Example questions

- What sorts of food do you enjoy eating most?
- Do you spend much time shopping for food?
- Which do you prefer, eating at home or eating in restaurants?
- Do you think people should be careful about what they eat?

▶ PART 2

Example task

Read the topic card below carefully.

You will have to talk about the topic for 1 to 2 minutes.

You have one minute to think about what you are going to say.

You can make notes if you want.

> **Describe a town you have enjoyed visiting.**
>
> **You should say:**
>
>   **why you went to the town**
>
>   **who you saw there**
>
>   **what you did there**
>
> **and explain why you enjoyed visiting the town.**

▶ PART 3

Example questions

- What are the kinds of things people like to do when visiting towns and cities?
- Why do many people prefer to live in cities rather than in the countryside?
- Can you identify some of the main problems of living in large cities?
- What measures could be taken to reduce problems of congestion in cities?

LISTENING MODULE   READING MODULE   WRITING MODULE   SPEAKING MODULE

SECTION 1
SECTION 2
SECTION 3
SECTION 4

▶ **Questions 1–10**

Questions 1–6

Write **NO MORE THAN TWO WORDS AND/OR A NUMBER** *for each answer.*

GROUP TRIP TO TIDBOROUGH

1 How far is it from the youth hostel to the city centre?
....
2 What is the website address of the youth hostel?
....
3 What event is taking place on March 22nd?
....
4 Who does the concert feature?
....
5 What exhibition starts on March 24th?
....
6 What will be closed in March?
....

Questions 7–10

Choose the correct letters **A–C**.

7 When does the train ride depart?
  A 9.00
  B 9.15
  C 9.30

8 Where is it recommended to buy tickets?
  A at the tourist office
  B at the station
  C at the youth hostel

9 How much is the group discount?
  A 10%
  B 15%
  C 20%

10 How long does the excursion last?
  A 3 hours
  B 3½ hours
  C 4 hours

IELTS TEST 5

Exam Essentials

| LISTENING MODULE | READING MODULE | WRITING MODULE | SPEAKING MODULE |

SECTION 1
SECTION 2
SECTION 3
SECTION 4

▸ **Questions 11–20**

Questions 11–13

Choose the correct letter, **A**, **B** *or* **C**.

11 Which chart shows the company's sales figures for the last five years?

12 Which chart shows the relationship of three departments this year?

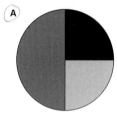 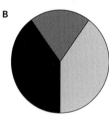 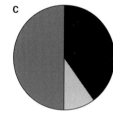

Food ▮   Clothing ▮   Electrical ▮

13 Which chart shows numbers of temporary staff in the company?

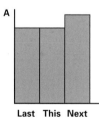 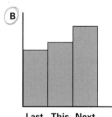 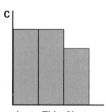

Questions 14–19

Complete the notes below.

Write **NO MORE THAN TWO WORDS** *for each answer.*

- Company's mission statement: '**14** .... for customers'

- In case of problems, always <u>ask your</u> **15** .... for help

- Important for customers to have a **16** .... <u>experience</u>

- Tell customers about **17** .... goods

- Read the **18** .... every month

- Must attend **19** .... on Thursdays

Question 20

Choose **TWO** *letters* **A–E***.*

20 Which **TWO** things must be done today?
   A complete form
   B get security pass
   C register for discount
   D show certificates
   E watch information video

IELTS
TEST 5

Exam Essentials

LISTENING MODULE   READING MODULE   WRITING MODULE   SPEAKING MODULE

SECTION 1
SECTION 2
SECTION 3
SECTION 4

▸ **Questions 21–30**

Questions 21–24

Which action does each type of penguin do?

Choose your answers **A–G** *from the box below and write them next to questions 21–24.*

> A   always hesitate before jumping
> B   avoid climbing if possible
> C   lean backwards when calling
> D   move around at night
> E   use its bill when climbing
> F   usually look twice at things
> G   walk with its flippers pointing downwards

21 Gentoo   ....

22 Rockhopper   ....

23 Magellanic   ....

24 King   ....

Questions 25–27

Write **NO MORE THAN TWO WORDS** *for each answer.*

25 How do penguins usually sleep?
....

26 What do a Rockhopper's yellow feathers do when it is angry?
....

27 What do penguins recognise in the Skua's wings?
....

Questions 28–30

Complete the summary below.

Write **NO MORE THAN TWO WORDS** *for each answer.*

Penguins prefer to swim in groups because it makes it easier to **28** ....
When they are on land, they appear to be **29** .... The majority of
species are characterised by their **30** ...., which makes them
particularly interesting for humans to study.

▶ **Questions 31–40**

Complete the sentences below.

Write **NO MORE THAN TWO WORDS** *for each answer.*

31 Governments have been mistaken to .... slums.

32 There is often a lack of .... concerning housing projects.

33 Housing policies which are based on principles of .... are particularly effective.

34 Some .... should always be provided by governments.

35 Migrants will only .... in housing if they feel secure.

36 Governments often underestimate the importance of .... to housing projects.

37 The availability of .... is the starting point for successful housing development.

38 Urbanisation can have a positive effect on the .... of individuals.

39 The population size of cities enables a range of .... to occur.

40 City living tends to raise the level of .... among people.

IELTS
TEST 5

Exam Essentials

| LISTENING MODULE | READING MODULE | WRITING MODULE | SPEAKING MODULE |

PASSAGE 1
PASSAGE 2
PASSAGE 3

*You should spend about 20 minutes on **Questions 1–13** which are based on Reading Passage 1 on pages 136 and 137.*

The birds of London

There are more than two hundred different species and sub-species of birds in the London area, ranging from the magpie to the greenfinch, but perhaps the most ubiquitous is the pigeon. It has been suggested that the swarms of feral pigeons are all descended from birds which escaped from dovecotes in the early medieval period; they found a natural habitat in the crannies and ledges of buildings as did their ancestors, the rockdoves, amid the sea-girt cliffs. 'They nest in small colonies,' one observer has written, 'usually high up and inaccessible' above the streets of London as if the streets were indeed a sea. A man fell from the belfry of St Stephen's Walbrook in 1277 while in quest of a pigeon's nest, while the Bishop of London complained in 1385 of 'malignant persons' who threw stones at the pigeons resting in the city churches. So pigeons were already a familiar presence, even if they were not treated with the same indulgence as their more recent successors. A modicum of kindness to these creatures seems to have been first shown in the late nineteenth century, when they were fed oats rather than the customary stale bread.

From the end of the nineteenth century, woodpigeons also migrated into the city; they were quickly urbanised, increasing both in numbers and in tameness. 'We have frequently seen them on the roofs of houses,' wrote the author of *Bird Life in London* in 1893, 'apparently as much at home as any dovecote pigeon.' Those who look up today may notice their 'fly-lines' in the sky, from Lincoln's Inn Fields over Kingsway and Trafalgar Square to Battersea, with other lines to Victoria Park and to Kenwood. The air of London is filled with such 'fly-lines', and to trace the paths of the birds would be to envisage the city in an entirely different form; then it would seem linked and unified by thousands of thoroughfares and small paths of energy, each with its own history of use.

The sparrows move quickly in public places, and they are now so much part of London that they have been adopted by the native population as the 'sparrer'; a friend was known to Cockneys as a 'cocksparrer' in tribute to a bird which is sweet and yet watchful, blessed with a dusky plumage similar to that of the London dust, a plucky little bird darting in and out of the city's endless uproar. They are small birds which can lose body heat very quickly, so they are perfectly adapted to the 'heat island' of London. They will live in any small cranny or cavity, behind drainpipes or ventilation shafts, or in public statues, or holes in buildings; in that sense they are perfectly suited to a London topography. An ornithologist who described the sparrow as 'peculiarly attached to man' said it 'never now breeds at any distance from an occupied building'. This sociability, bred upon the fondness of the Londoner, is manifest in many ways. One naturalist, W.H. Hudson, has described how any stranger in a green space or public garden will soon find that 'several sparrows are keeping him company ... watching his every movement, and if he sits down on a chair or a bench several of them will come close to him, and hop this way and that before him, uttering a little plaintive note of interrogation – *Have you got nothing for us?* They have also been described as the urchins of the streets –'thievish, self-assertive and pugnacious' – a condition which again may merit the attention and admiration of native Londoners. Remarkably attached to their surroundings, they rarely create 'fly-lines' across the city; where they are born, like other Londoners, they stay.

There are some birds, such as the robin and the chaffinch, which are less approachable and trustful in the city than in the country. Other species, such as the mallard, grow increasingly shyer as they leave London. There has been a severe diminution of the number of sparrows, while blackbirds are more plentiful. Swans and ducks have also increased in number. Some species, however, have all but vanished. The rooks of London are, perhaps, the most notable of the disappeared, their rookeries destroyed by building work or by tree-felling. Areas of London were continuously inhabited by rooks for many hundreds of years. The burial ground of St Dunstan's in the East and the college garden of the Ecclesiastical Court in Doctors' Commons, the turrets of the Tower of London and the gardens of Gray's Inn, were once such localities. There was a rookery in the Inner Temple dating from at least 1666, mentioned by Oliver Goldsmith in 1774. Rooks nested on Bow Church and on St Olave's. They were venerable London birds, preferring to cluster around ancient churches and the like as if they were their local guardians. Yet, in the words of the nineteenth-century song, 'Now the old rooks have lost their places'. There was a grove in Kensington Gardens devoted to the rooks; it contained some seven hundred trees forming a piece of wild nature, a matter of delight and astonishment to those who walked among them and listened to the endless cawing that blotted out the city's noise. But the trees were torn down in 1880. The rooks have never returned.

IELTS TEST 5

Exam Essentials

LISTENING MODULE   **READING MODULE**   WRITING MODULE   SPEAKING MODULE

PASSAGE 1
PASSAGE 2
PASSAGE 3

Questions 1–4

Answer the questions below using **NO MORE THAN THREE WORDS** *for each answer.*

Write your answers in boxes 1–4 on your answer sheet.

1   What kind of birds are the London pigeons descended from?

2   What were pigeons given to eat before attitudes towards them changed?

3   What are the routes taken by woodpigeons known as?

4   What **TWO** activities have contributed to the drastic reduction in the number of rooks?

Questions 5–9

Complete the notes below.

Choose **NO MORE THAN THREE WORDS** *from the passage for each answer.*

Write your answers in boxes 5–9 on your answer sheet.

SPARROWS

- word meaning 5 .... is derived from the bird's name

- suited to atmosphere of London because of tendency to rapidly
  6 ....

- always likely to reproduce close to 7 ....

- characteristic noted: 8 .... because of attitude of people in London

- make a sound that seems to be a kind of 9 ....

Questions 10–13

Classify the following as being stated of

    A pigeons
    B woodpigeons
    C sparrows
    D chaffinches
    E blackbirds
    F rooks

*Write the correct letter **A–F** in boxes 10–13 on your answer sheet.*

10 They are happier with people when they are in rural areas.

11 They rapidly became comfortable being with people.

12 They used to congregate particularly at old buildings.

13 They used to be attacked by people.

IELTS TEST 5

Exam Essentials

LISTENING MODULE   READING MODULE   WRITING MODULE   SPEAKING MODULE

PASSAGE 1
PASSAGE 2
PASSAGE 3

▶ **Questions 14–26**

You should spend about 20 minutes **on Questions 14–26** *which are based on Reading Passage 2 on the following pages.*

Questions 14–20

Reading Passage 2 has seven paragraphs **A–G***.*

Choose the correct heading for each paragraph from the list of headings below.

Write the correct number ***i–x*** *in boxes 14–20 on your answer sheet.*

List of Headings	
i	The advantage of an intuitive approach to personality assessment
ii	Overall theories of personality assessment rather than valuable guidance
iii	The consequences of poor personality assessment
iv	Differing views on the importance of personality assessment
v	Success and failure in establishing an approach to personality assessment
vi	Everyone makes personality assessments
vii	Acknowledgement of the need for improvement in personality assessment
viii	Little progress towards a widely applicable approach to personality assessment
ix	The need for personality assessments to be well-judged
x	The need for a different kind of research into personality assessment

14   Paragraph **A**

15   Paragraph **B**

16   Paragraph **C**

17   Paragraph **D**

18   Paragraph **E**

19   Paragraph **F**

20   Paragraph **G**

Psychology and personality
ASSESSMENT

A Our daily lives are largely made up of contacts with other people, during which we are constantly making judgments of their personalities and accommodating our behaviour to them in accordance with these judgments. A casual meeting of neighbours on the street, an employer giving instructions to an employee, a mother telling her children how to behave, a journey in a train where strangers eye one another without exchanging a word – all these involve mutual interpretations of personal qualities.

B Success in many vocations largely depends on skill in sizing up people. It is important not only to such professionals as the clinical psychologist, the psychiatrist or the social worker, but also to the doctor or lawyer in dealing with their clients, the businessman trying to outwit his rivals, the salesman with potential customers, the teacher with his pupils, not to speak of the pupils judging their teacher. Social life, indeed, would be impossible if we did not, to some extent, understand, and react to the motives and qualities of those we meet; and clearly we are sufficiently accurate for most practical purposes, although we also recognize that misinterpretations easily arise – particularly on the part of others who judge us!

C Errors can often be corrected as we go along. But whenever we are pinned down to a definite decision about a person, which cannot easily be revised through his 'feed-back', the inadequacies of our judgments become apparent. The hostess who wrongly thinks that the Smiths and the Joneses will get on well together can do little to retrieve the success of her party. A school or a business may be saddled for years with an undesirable member of staff, because the selection committee which interviewed him for a quarter of an hour misjudged his personality.

D Just because the process is so familiar and taken for granted, it has aroused little scientific curiosity until recently. Dramatists, writers and artists throughout the centuries have excelled in the portrayal of character, but have seldom stopped to ask how they, or we, get to know people, or how accurate is our knowledge. However, the popularity of such unscientific systems as Lavater's physiognomy in the eighteenth century, Gall's phrenology in the nineteenth, and of handwriting interpretations by graphologists, or palm-readings by gipsies, show that people are aware of weaknesses in their judgments and desirous of better methods of diagnosis. It is natural that they should turn to psychology for help, in the belief that psychologists are specialists in 'human nature'.

E This belief is hardly justified: for the primary aim of psychology had been to establish the general laws and principles underlying behaviour and thinking, rather than to apply these to concrete problems of the individual person. A great many professional psychologists still regard it as their main function to study the nature of learning, perception and motivation in the abstracted or average human being, or in lower organisms, and consider it premature to put so young a science to practical uses. They would disclaim the possession of any superior skill in judging their fellow-men. Indeed, being more aware of the difficulties than is the non-psychologist, they may be more reluctant to commit themselves to definite predictions or decisions about other people. Nevertheless, to an increasing

IELTS
TEST 5

Exam Essentials

LISTENING MODULE   **READING MODULE**   WRITING MODULE   SPEAKING MODULE

PASSAGE 1
PASSAGE 2
PASSAGE 3

extent psychologists are moving into educational, occupational, clinical and other applied fields, where they are called upon to use their expertise for such purposes as fitting the education or job to the child or adult, and the person to the job. Thus a considerable proportion of their activities consists of personality assessment.

F The success of psychologists in personality assessment has been limited, in comparison with what they have achieved in the fields of abilities and training, with the result that most people continue to rely on unscientific methods of assessment. In recent times there has been a tremendous amount of work on personality tests, and on carefully controlled experimental studies of personality. Investigations of personality by Freudian and

other 'depth' psychologists have an even longer history. And yet psychology seems to be no nearer to providing society with practicable techniques which are sufficiently reliable and accurate to win general acceptance. The soundness of the methods of psychologists in the field of personality assessment and the value of their work are under constant fire from other psychologists, and it is far from easy to prove their worth.

G The growth of psychology has probably helped responsible members of society to become more aware of the difficulties of assessment. But it is not much use telling employers, educationists and judges how inaccurately they diagnose the personalities with which they have to deal unless

psychologists are sure that they can provide something better. Even when university psychologists themselves appoint a new member of staff, they almost always resort to the traditional techniques of assessing the candidates through interviews, past records, and testimonials, and probably make at least as many bad appointments as other employers do. However, a large amount of experimental development of better methods has been carried out since 1940 by groups of psychologists in the Armed Services and in the Civil Service, and by such organizations as the (British) National Institute of Industrial Psychology and the American Institute of Research.

Question 21

Choose **THREE** *letters* **A–F**.

Write your answers in box 21 on your answer sheet.

Which **THREE** *of the following are stated about psychologists involved in personality assessment?*

A   'Depth' psychologists are better at it than some other kinds of psychologist.
B   Many of them accept that their conclusions are unreliable.
C   They receive criticism from psychologists not involved in the field.
D   They have made people realise how hard the subject is.
E   They have told people what not to do, rather than what they should do.
F   They keep changing their minds about what the best approaches are.

Questions 22–26

Do the following statements agree with the views of the writer in Reading Passage 2?

In boxes 22–26 on your answer sheet write

YES	*if the statement agrees with the views of the writer*
NO	*if the statement contradicts the views of the writer*
NOT GIVEN	*if it is impossible to say what the writer thinks about this*

22   People often feel that they have been wrongly assessed.

23   Unscientific systems of personality assessment have been of some use.

24   People make false assumptions about the expertise of psychologists.

25   It is likely that some psychologists are no better than anyone else at assessing personality.

26   Research since 1940 has been based on acceptance of previous theories.

IELTS
TEST 5
Exam Essentials

LISTENING MODULE   READING MODULE   WRITING MODULE   SPEAKING MODULE

PASSAGE 1
PASSAGE 2
PASSAGE 3

*You should spend about 20 minutes on **Questions 27–40** which are based on Reading Passage 3 on pages 144 and 145.*

TITAN of technology

Gordon Moore is one of the people who gave the world personal computers. Peter Richards spoke to him in 2003

Gordon Moore is the scientific brain behind Intel, the world's biggest maker of computer chips. Both funny and self-deprecating, he's a shrewd businessman too, but admits to being an 'accidental entrepreneur', happier in the back room trading ideas with techies than out selling the product or chatting up the stockholders. When he applied for a job at Dow Chemical after gaining his PhD, the company psychologist ruled that 'I was okay technically, but that I'd never manage anything'. This year Intel is set to turn over $28 billion.

When Moore co-founded Intel (short for Integrated Electronics) to develop integrated circuits thirty-five years ago, he provided the motive force in R&D (Research & Development) while his more extrovert partner Robert Noyce became the public face of the company. Intel's ethos was distinctively Californian: laid-back, democratic, polo shirt and chinos. Moore worked in a cubicle like everyone else, never had a designated parking space and flew Economy. None of this implied lack of ambition. Moore and Noyce shared a vision, recognising that success depended just as much on intellectual pizazz as on Intel's ability to deliver a product. Noyce himself received the first patent for an integrated circuit in 1961, while both partners were learning the business of electronics at Fairchild Semiconductor.

Fairchild's success put money in Moore and Noyce's pockets, but they were starved of R&D money. They resigned, frustrated, to found Intel in 1968. 'It was one of those rare periods when money was available,' says Moore. They put in $250,000 each and drummed up another $2.5m of venture capital 'on the strength of a one-page business plan that said essentially nothing'. Ownership was divided 50:50 between founders and backers. Three years later, Intel's first microprocessor was released: the 4004, carrying 2,250 transistors. Progress after that was rapid. By the time the competition realised what was happening, Intel had amassed a seven-year R&D lead that it was never to relinquish.

By the year 2000, Intel's Pentium®4 chip was carrying 42 million transistors. 'Now,' says Moore, 'we put a quarter of a billion transistors on a chip and are looking forward to a billion in the near future.' The performance gains have been phenomenal. The 4004 ran at 108 kilohertz (108,000 hertz), the Pentium®4 at three gigahertz (3 billion hertz). It's calculated that if automobile speed had increased similarly over the same period, you could now drive from New York to San Francisco in six seconds.

Moore's prescience in forecasting this revolution is legendary. In 1965, while still head of the R&D laboratory at Fairchild, he wrote a piece for *Electronics* magazine observing 'that over the first few years we had essentially doubled the complexity of integrated circuits every year. I blindly extrapolated for the next ten years and said we'd go from about 60 to about 60,000 transistors on a chip. It proved a much more spot-on prediction than I could ever have imagined. Up until then, integrated circuits had been expensive and had had principally military applications. But I could see that the economics were going to switch dramatically. This was going to become the cheapest way to make electronics.'

The prediction that a chip's transistor-count – and thus its performance – would keep doubling every year soon proved so accurate that Carver Mead, a friend from Caltech, dubbed it 'Moore's Law'. The name has stuck. 'Moore's Law' has become the yardstick by which the exponential growth of the computer industry has been measured ever since. When, in 1975, Moore looked around him again and saw transistor-counts slowing, he predicted that in future chip-performance would double only every two years. But that proved pessimistic. Actual growth since then has split the difference between his two predictions, with performance doubling every 18 months.

And there's a corollary, says Moore. 'If the cost of a given amount of computer power drops 50 per cent every 18 months, each time that happens the market explodes with new applications that hadn't been economical before.' He sees the microprocessor as 'almost infinitely elastic'. As prices fall, new applications keep emerging: smart light bulbs, flashing trainers or greetings cards that sing 'Happy Birthday'. Where will it all stop? Well, it's true, he says, 'that in a few more generations [of chips], the fact that materials are made of atoms starts to be a real problem. Essentially, you can't make things any smaller.' But in practice, the day of reckoning is endlessly postponed as engineers find endlessly more ingenious ways of loading more transistors on a chip. 'I suspect I shared the feelings of everybody else that when we got to the dimensions of a micron [about 1986], we wouldn't be able to continue because we were touching the wavelength of light. But as we got closer, the barriers just melted away.'

When conventional chips finally reach their limits, nanotechnology beckons. Researchers are already working on sci-fi sounding alternatives such as molecular computers, built atom by atom, that theoretically could process hundreds of thousands times more information than today's processors. Quantum computers using the state of electrons as the basis for calculation could operate still faster. On any measure, there looks to be plenty of life left in Moore's Law yet.

IELTS **TEST** 5

Exam Essentials

LISTENING MODULE   **READING MODULE**   WRITING MODULE   SPEAKING MODULE

PASSAGE 1
PASSAGE 2
PASSAGE 3

Questions 27–29

Choose the correct letter, **A**, **B**, **C** *or* **D**.

Write your answers in boxes 27–29 on your answer sheet.

27 What do we learn about Gordon Moore's personality in the first two paragraphs?
   A It has changed noticeably as his career has developed.
   B It was once considered unsuitable for the particular type of business he was in.
   C It made him more suited to producing things than to selling them.
   D It is less complicated than it may at first appear.

28 What do we learn about Intel when it was first established?
   A It was unlike any other company in its field at the time.
   B It combined a relaxed atmosphere with serious intent.
   C It attracted attention because of the unconventional way in which it was run.
   D It placed more emphasis on ingenuity than on any other aspect.

29 What is stated about the setting up of Intel in the third paragraph?
   A It was primarily motivated by the existence of funds that made it possible.
   B It involved keeping certain sensitive information secret.
   C It resulted from the founders' desire to launch a particular product.
   D It was caused by the founders' dissatisfaction with their employer's priorities.

Questions 30–34

Do the following statements agree with the information given in Reading Passage 3?

In boxes 30–34 on your answer sheet write

   TRUE   *if the statement agrees with the information*
   FALSE   *if the statement contradicts the information*
   NOT GIVEN *if there is no information on this*

30 Competitors soon came close to catching up with Intel's progress.

31 Intel's Pentium®4 chip was more successful than Moore had anticipated.

32 Moore's prediction in 1975 was based on too little evidence.

33 Flashing trainers are an example of Moore's theory about the relationship between cost and applications.

34 Moore has always been confident that problems concerning the size of components will be overcome.

Questions 35–40

Complete the summary below using words from the box.

Write your answers in boxes 35–40 on your answer sheet.

MOORE'S LAW

Gordon Moore's ability to foresee developments is well-known. In 1965, he referred to the increase in the **30** .... of integrated circuits and guessed that the number of transistors would go on rising for a decade. The **31** .... of his prediction surprised him. Previously, the **32** .... and main **33** ..... of integrated circuits had been the major **34** .... with regard to their development. But Moore observed that the **35** .... of integrated circuits was going to improve dramatically. His resulting forecasts concerning chips led to the creation of the term 'Moore's Law'.

design	use	opinion	invention
cost-effectiveness	failure	sophistication	proposition
production	influence	understanding	cost
accuracy	demand	theory	inter-dependence
familiarity	reception	appearance	reference

IELTS
TEST 5

Exam Essentials

LISTENING MODULE   READING MODULE   WRITING MODULE   SPEAKING MODULE

Task 1
Task 2

You should spend about 20 minutes on this task.

> *The bar charts and line graph below show the results of a survey conducted over a three-year period to discover what people who live in London think of the city.*

Write a report for a university lecturer describing the information below.

Write at least 150 words.

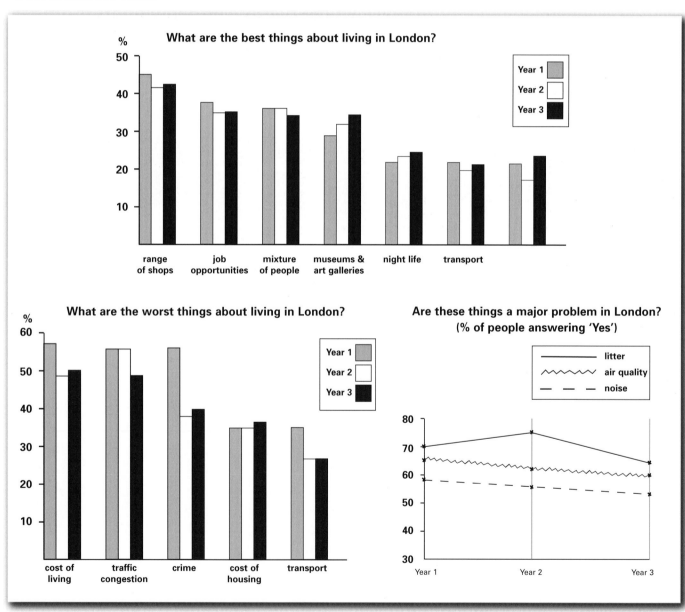

There is a sample answer on page 203.

You should spend about 40 minutes on this task.

Present a written argument or case to an educated reader with no specialist knowledge of the following topic.

> *In many countries these days, the number of people continuing their education after school has increased, and the range of courses available at universities and colleges has also increased.*
>
> *Do you think this is a positive or negative development?*

You should use your own ideas, knowledge and experience and support your arguments with examples and relevant experience.

Write at least 250 words.

There is a sample answer on page 203.

▶ PART 1

Example questions

- When did you start to learn English?
- What do you enjoy about learning languages?
- Apart from classes, what are useful ways to practise a language that you are learning?
- How do you plan to use your English in the future?

▶ PART 2

Example task

Read the topic card below carefully.

You will have to talk about the topic for 1 to 2 minutes.

You have one minute to think about what you are going to say.

You can make notes if you want.

> **Describe a film you found interesting.**
>
> **You should say:**
>
> > **when you saw this film**
> >
> > **why you decided to see this film**
> >
> > **what happened in the film**
>
> **and explain why you found this film interesting.**

▶ PART 3

Example questions

- Which do you think is more enjoyable, watching films in the cinema or watching TV programmes?
- Do you think that cinema films should have an educational value?
- Is it important for governments to support film-making in their countries?
- In what ways do you think that entertainment media may develop in the future?

SECTION 1
SECTION 2
SECTION 3
SECTION 4

▸ **Questions 1–10**

Questions 1–7

Complete the form below.

Write **NO MORE THAN TWO WORDS AND/OR A NUMBER** *for each answer.*

GO-TRAVEL

BOOKING FORM

Name:	1 [Last] .... [First] ....
Source of enquiry:	saw ad in 2 .... Magazine
Holiday reference:	3 ....
Number of people:	4 ....
Preferred departure date:	5 ....
Number of nights:	6 ....
Type of insurance:	7 ....

IELTS
TEST 6

Exam Essentials

| LISTENING MODULE | READING MODULE | WRITING MODULE | SPEAKING MODULE |

SECTION 1
SECTION 2
SECTION 3
SECTION 4

Questions 8–10

Choose **THREE** *letters* **A–H**.

Which **THREE** options does the woman want to book?

    A arts demonstration
    B dance show
    C museums trip
    D bus tour at night
    E picnic lunches
    F river trip
    G room with balcony
    H trip to mountains

8 ....

9 ....

10 ....

IELTS TEST 6

Exam Essentials

LISTENING MODULE	READING MODULE	WRITING MODULE	SPEAKING MODULE

SECTION 1
SECTION 2
SECTION 3
SECTION 4

▸ **Questions 11–20**

Questions 11–17

Complete the notes below.

Write **NO MORE THAN THREE WORDS AND/OR A NUMBER** *for each answer.*

RUN-WELL CHARITY

Background to Run-Well charity
- Set up in **11** ....
- Aim: raise money for the **12** ....

Race details
- Teams to supply own **13** ....
- Teams should **14** .... together
- Important to bring enough **15** ....
- Race will finish in the **16** ....
- Prizes given by the **17** ....

Questions 18–20.

Choose **THREE** *letters* **A–H**.

Which **THREE** ways of raising money for the charity are recommended?

- A badges
- B bread and cake stall
- C swimming event
- D concert
- E door-to-door collecting
- F picnic
- G postcards
- H quiz
- I second-hand sale

18 ....

19 ....

20 ....

IELTS TEST 6

Exam Essentials

| LISTENING MODULE | READING MODULE | WRITING MODULE | SPEAKING MODULE |

SECTION 1
SECTION 2
SECTION 3
SECTION 4

▶ *Questions 21–30*

Questions 21–26

What do the students decide about each topic for Joe's presentation?
A   Joe will definitely include this topic.
B   Joe might include this topic.
C   Joe will not include this topic.

*Write the correct letter, **A**, **B** or **C** next to questions 21–26.*

21 cultural aspects of naming people   ....

22 similarities across languages in naming practices   ....

23 meanings of first names   ....

24 place names describing geographic features   ....

25 influence of immigration on place names   ....

26 origins of names of countries   ....

Questions 27–30

Complete the summary below.

Write **NO MORE THAN TWO WORDS** *for each answer.*

Researchers showed a group of students many common nouns, brand names and 27 .... Students found it easier to identify brand names when they were shown in 28 .... Researchers think that 29 .... is important in making brand names special within the brain. Brand names create a number of 30 .... within the brain.

IELTS TEST 6

Exam Essentials

LISTENING MODULE	READING MODULE	WRITING MODULE	SPEAKING MODULE

SECTION 1
SECTION 2
SECTION 3
SECTION 4

▶ **Questions 31–40**

Complete the notes below.

Write **NO MORE THAN TWO WORDS** *for each answer.*

Gas balloons

Uses:
- instead of **31** ....
  in the US civil war

- to make **32** ....

- to **33** ....
  for research

- as part of studies of
  34 ....

Hot air balloons

Create less **35** ....
than gas balloons

Airships

Early examples had no **36**

.... for crew

To be efficient, needed a

37 ....

Development of large airships stopped because of:

- success of **38** ....

- series of **39** ....

Recent interest in use for carrying

40 ....

IELTS
TEST **6**   *Exam Essentials*

| LISTENING MODULE | READING MODULE | WRITING MODULE | SPEAKING MODULE |

PASSAGE 1
PASSAGE 2
PASSAGE 3

*You should spend about 20 minutes on **Questions 1–13** which are based on Reading Passage 1 on pages 156 and 157.*

How to run a...

Publisher and author David Harvey
on what makes a good management book

A Prior to the Second World War, all the management books ever written could be comfortably stacked on a couple of shelves. Today, you would need a sizeable library, with plenty of room for expansion, to house them. The last few decades have seen the stream of new titles swell into a flood. In 1975, 771 business books were published. By 2000, the total for the year had risen to 3,203, and the trend continues.

B The growth in pubishing activity has followed the rise and rise of management to the point where it constitutes a mini-industry in its own right. In the USA alone, the book market is worth over $1bn. Management consultancies, professional bodies and business schools were part of this new phenomenon, all sharing at least one common need: to get into print. Nor were they the only aspiring authors. Inside stories by and about business leaders balanced the more straight-laced textbooks by academics. How-to books by practising managers and business writers appeared on everything from making a presentation to developing a business strategy. With this upsurge in output, it is not really surprising that the quality is uneven.

C Few people are probably in a better position to evaluate the management canon than Carol Kennedy, a business journalist and author of *Guide to the Management Gurus*, an overview of the world's most influential management thinkers and their works. She is also the books editor of *The Director*. Of course, it is normally the best of the bunch that are reviewed in the pages of *The Director*. But from time to time, Kennedy is moved to use *The Director*'s precious column inches to warn readers off certain books. Her recent review of *The Leader's Edge* summed up her irritation with authors who over-promise and under-deliver. The banality of the treatment of core competencies for leaders, including the 'competency of paying attention', was a conceit too far in the context of a leaden text. 'Somewhere in this book,' she wrote, 'there may be an idea worth reading and taking note of, but my own competency of paying attention ran out on page 31.' Her opinion of a good proportion of the other books that never make it to the review pages is even more terse. 'Unreadable' is her verdict.

D Simon Caulkin, contributing editor of the *Observer*'s management page and former editor of *Management Today*, has formed a similar opinion. 'A lot is pretty depressing, unimpressive stuff.' Caulkin is philosophical about the inevitability of finding so much dross. Business books, he says, 'range from total drivel to the ambitious stuff. Although the confusing thing is that the really ambitious stuff can sometimes be drivel.' Which leaves the question open as to why the subject of management is such a literary wasteland. There are some possible explanations.

E Despite the attempts of Frederick Taylor, the early twentieth-century founder of scientific management, to establish a solid, rule-based foundation for the practice, management has come to be seen as just as much an art as a science. Once psychologists like Abraham Maslow, behaviouralists and social anthropologists persuaded business to look at management from a human perspective, the topic became more multi-dimensional and complex. Add to that the requirement for management to reflect the changing demands of the times, the impact of information technology and other factors, and it is easy to understand why management is in a permanent state of confusion. There is a constant requirement for reinterpretation, innovation and creative thinking: Caulkin's ambitious stuff. For their part, publishers continue to dream about finding the next big management idea, a topic given an airing in Kennedy's book, *The Next Big Idea*.

F   Indirectly, it tracks one of the phenomena of the past 20 years or so: the management blockbusters which work wonders for publishers' profits and transform authors' careers. Peters and Waterman's *In Search of Excellence: Lessons from America's Best-Run Companies* achieved spectacular success. So did Michael Hammer and James Champy's book, *Reengineering the Corporation: A Manifesto for Business Revolution*. Yet the early euphoria with which such books are greeted tends to wear off as the basis for the claims starts to look less than solid. In the case of *In Search of Excellence*, it was the rapid reversal of fortunes that turned several of the exemplar companies into basket cases. For Hammer's and Champy's readers, disillusion dawned with the realisation that their slash-and-burn prescription for reviving corporate fortunes caused more problems than it solved.

G   Yet one of the virtues of these books is that they could be understood. There is a whole class of management texts that fail this basic test. 'Some management books are stuffed with jargon,' says Kennedy. 'Consultants are among the worst offenders.' She believes there is a simple reason for this flight from plain English. 'They all use this jargon because they can't think clearly. It disguises the paucity of thought.'

H   By contrast, the management thinkers who have stood the test of time articulate their ideas in plain English. Peter Drucker, widely regarded as the doyen of management thinkers, has written a steady stream of influential books over half a century. 'Drucker writes beautiful, clear prose,' says Kennedy, 'and his thoughts come through.' He is among the handful of writers whose work, she believes, transcends the specific interests of the management community. Caulkin also agrees that Drucker reaches out to a wider readership. 'What you get is a sense of the larger cultural background,' he says. 'That's what you miss in so much management writing.' Charles Handy, perhaps the most successful UK business writer to command an international audience, is another rare example of a writer with a message for the wider world.

Questions 1–2

*Choose the correct letter, **A**, **B**, **C** or **D**.*

Write your answers in boxes 1 and 2 on your answer sheet.

1   What does the writer say about the increase in the number of management books published?
   A It took the publishing industry by surprise.
   B It is likely to continue.
   C It has produced more profit than other areas of publishing.
   D It could have been foreseen.

2   What does the writer say about the genre of management books?
   A It includes some books that cover topics of little relevance to anyone.
   B It contains a greater proportion of practical than theoretical books.
   C All sorts of people have felt that they should be represented in it.
   D The best books in the genre are written by business people.

Questions 3–7

*Reading Passage 1 has eight paragraphs **A–H**.*

Which paragraph contains the following information?

*Write the correct letter **A–H** in boxes 3–7 on your answer sheet.*

3   reasons for the deserved success of some books

4   reasons why managers feel the need for advice

5   a belief that management books are highly likely to be very poor

6   a reference to books not considered worth reviewing

7   an example of a group of people who write particularly poor books

Questions 8–13

*Look at the statements (**Questions 8–13**) and the list of books below.*

Match each statement with the book it relates to.

*Write the correct letter **A–E** in boxes 8–13 on your answer sheet.*

NB *You may use any letter more than once.*

  8 It examines the success of books in the genre.

  9 Statements made in it were later proved incorrect.

10 It fails to live up to claims made about it.

11 Advice given in it is seen to be actually harmful.

12 It examines the theories of those who have developed management thinking.

13 It states the obvious in an unappealing way.

List of Books

A *Guide to the Management Gurus*
B *The Leader's Edge*
C *The Next Big Idea*
D *In Search of Excellence*
E *Reengineering the Corporation*

IELTS
TEST 6

Exam Essentials

LISTENING MODULE   **READING MODULE**   WRITING MODULE   SPEAKING MODULE

PASSAGE 1
PASSAGE 2
PASSAGE 3

You should spend about 20 minutes on **Questions 14–26** *which are based on Reading Passage 2 on the following pages.*

Questions 14–18

Reading Passage 2 has five paragraphs **A–E**.

Choose the correct heading for each paragraph from the list of headings below.

Write the correct number **i–x** *in boxes 14–18 on your answer sheet.*

List of Headings

i	A strange combination
ii	An overall requirement
iii	A controversial decision
iv	A strong contrast
v	A special set-up
vi	A promising beginning
vii	A shift in attitudes
viii	A strongly held belief
ix	A change of plan
x	A simple choice

---

14   Paragraph **A**

15   Paragraph **B**

16   Paragraph **C**

17   Paragraph **D**

18   Paragraph **E**

STADIUM AUSTRALIA

A You might ask, why be concerned about the architecture of a stadium? Surely, as long as the action is entertaining and the building is safe and reasonably comfortable, why should the aesthetics matter? This one question has dominated my professional life, and its answer is one I find myself continually rehearsing. If one accepts that sporting endeavour is as important an outlet for human expression as, say, the theatre or cinema, fine art or music, why shouldn't the buildings in which we celebrate this outlet be as grand and as inspirational as those we would expect, and demand, in those other areas of cultural life? Indeed, one could argue that because stadiums are, in many instances, far more popular than theatres or art galleries, we should actually devote more, and not less, attention to their form. Stadiums have frequently been referred to as 'cathedrals'. Football has often been dubbed 'the opera of the people'. What better way, therefore, to raise the general public's awareness and appreciation of quality design than to offer them the very best buildings in the one area of life that seems to touch them most? Could it even be that better stadiums might just make for better citizens?

B But then maybe, as my detractors have labelled me in the past, I am a snob. Maybe I should just accept that sport, and its associated accoutrements and products, is an essentially tacky and ephemeral business, while stadium design is all too often driven by pragmatists and penny-pinchers. Certainly, when I first started writing about stadium architecture, one of the first and most uncomfortable truths I had to confront was that some of the most popular stadiums in the world were also amongst the the least attractive or innovative in architectural terms. 'Worthy and predictable' has usually won more votes than 'daring and different'. Old Trafford football ground in Manchester, the Yankee Stadium in New York, Ellis Park in Johannesburg. The list is long and is not intended to suggest that these are necessarily poor buildings. Rather, that each has derived its reputation more from the events that it has staged, from its associations, than from the actual form it takes. Equally, those stadiums whose forms have been revered – such as the Maracana in Rio, or the San Siro in Milan – have turned out to be rather poorly designed in several respects, once one analyses them not as icons but as functioning 'public assembly facilities' (to use the current jargon). Finding the balance between beauty and practicality has never been easy.

C Homebush Bay was the site of the main Olympic Games complex for the Sydney Olympics of 2000. To put it politely, I am no great admirer of the Olympics as an event, or, rather, of the insane pressures its past bidding procedures have placed upon candidate cities. Nor, as a spectator, do I much enjoy the bloated Games programme and the consequent demands this places upon the designers of stadiums. Yet in my calmer moments it would be churlish to deny that, if approached sensibly and imaginatively, the opportunity to stage the Games can yield enormous benefits in the long term (as well they should, considering the expenditure involved), if not for sport then at least for the cause of urban regeneration. Following in Barcelona's footsteps, Sydney undoubtedly set about its urban regeneration in a wholly impressive way. To an outsider, the 760-hectare site at Homebush Bay, once the home of an abattoir, a racecourse, a brickworks and light industrial units, seemed miles from anywhere – it was actually fifteen kilometres from the centre of Sydney and pretty much in the heart of the city's extensive conurbation. Some £1.3 billion worth of construction and reclamation was commissioned, all of it, crucially, with an eye to post-Olympic usage. Strict guidelines, studiously monitored

IELTS TEST 6

Exam Essentials

LISTENING MODULE   **READING MODULE**   WRITING MODULE   SPEAKING MODULE

PASSAGE 1
PASSAGE 2
PASSAGE 3

by Greenpeace, ensured that the 2000 Games would be the most environmentally friendly ever. What's more, much of the work was good-looking, distinctive and lively. 'That's a reflection of the Australian spirit,' I was told.

D At the centre of Homebush lay the main venue for the Olympics, Stadium Australia. It was funded by means of a BOOT (Build, Own, Operate and Transfer) contract, which meant that the Stadium Australia consortium, led by the contractors Multiplex and the financiers Hambros, bore the bulk of the construction costs, in return for which it was allowed to operate the facility for thirty years, and thus, it hopes, recoup its outlay, before handing the whole building over to the New South Wales government in the year 2030.

E Stadium Australia was the most environmentally friendly Olympic stadium ever built. Every single product and material used had to meet strict guidelines, even if it turned out to be more expensive. All the timber was either recycled or derived from renewable sources. In order to reduce energy costs, the design allowed for natural lighting in as many public areas as possible, supplemented by solar-powered units. Rainwater collected from the roof ran off into storage tanks, where it could be tapped for pitch irrigation. Stormwater run-off was collected for toilet flushing. Wherever possible, passive ventilation was used instead of mechanical air-conditioning. Even the steel and concrete from the two end stands due to be demolished at the end of the Olympics was to be recycled. Furthermore, no private cars were allowed on the Homebush site. Instead, every spectator was to arrive by public transport, and quite right too. If ever there was a stadium to persuade a sceptic like myself that the Olympic Games do, after all, have a useful function in at least setting design and planning trends, this was the one. I was, and still am, I freely confess, quite knocked out by Stadium Australia.

Questions 19–22

Do the following statements agree with the information given in Reading Passage 2?

In boxes 19–22 on your answer sheet write

TRUE	*if the statement agrees with the information*
FALSE	*if the statement contradicts the information*
NOT GIVEN	*if there is no information on this*

19 The public have been demanding a better quality of stadium design.

20 It is possible that stadium design has an effect on people's behaviour in life in general.

21 Some stadiums have come in for a lot more criticism than others.

22 Designers of previous Olympic stadiums could easily have produced far better designs.

Questions 23–26

Label the diagram below.

Choose **NO MORE THAN THREE WORDS** *from the reading passage for each answer.*

Write your answers in boxes 23–26 on your answer sheet.

STADIUM AUSTRALIA

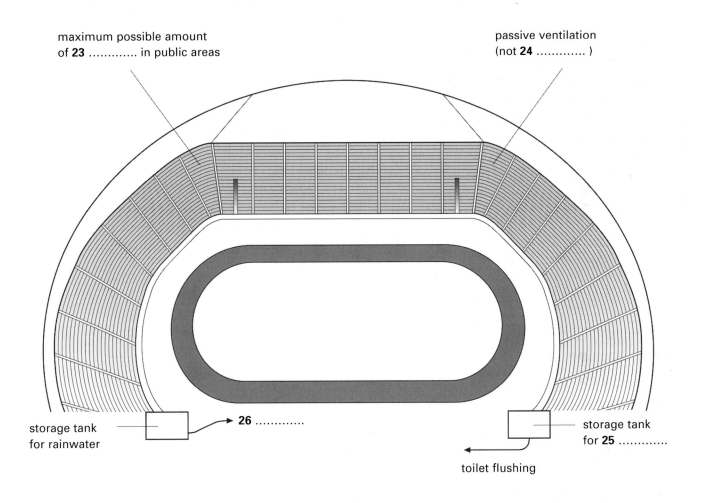

maximum possible amount
of **23** .... in public areas

passive ventilation
(not **24** ....)

storage tank
for rainwater

26 ....

storage tank
for **25** ....

toilet flushing

*You should spend about 20 minutes on **Questions 27–40** which are based on Reading Passage 3 on pages 164 and 165.*

A Theory of Shopping

For a one-year period I attempted to conduct an ethnography of shopping on and around a street in North London. This was carried out in association with Alison Clarke. I say 'attempted' because, given the absence of community and the intensely private nature of London households, this could not be an ethnography in the conventional sense. Nevertheless, through conversation, being present in the home and accompanying householders during their shopping, I tried to reach an understanding of the nature of shopping through greater or lesser exposure to 76 households.

My part of the ethnography concentrated upon shopping itself. Alison Clarke has since been working with the same households, but focusing upon other forms of provisioning such as the use of catalogues (see Clarke 1997). We generally first met these households together, but most of the material that is used within this particular essay derived from my own subsequent fieldwork. Following the completion of this essay, and a study of some related shopping centres, we hope to write a more general ethnography of provisioning. This will also examine other issues, such as the nature of community and the implications for retail and for the wider political economy. None of this, however, forms part of the present essay, which is primarily concerned with establishing the cosmological foundations of shopping.

To state that a household has been included within the study is to gloss over a wide diversity of degrees of involvement. The minimum requirement is simply that a householder has agreed to be interviewed about their shopping, which would include the local shopping parade, shopping centres and supermarkets. At the other extreme are families that we have come to know well during the course of the year. Interaction would include formal interviews, and a less formal presence within their homes, usually with a cup of tea. It also meant accompanying them on one or several 'events', which might comprise shopping trips or participation in activities associated with the area of Clarke's study, such as the meeting of a group supplying products for the home.

In analysing and writing up the experience of an ethnography of shopping in North London, I am led in two opposed directions. The tradition of anthropological relativism leads to an emphasis upon difference, and there are many ways in which shopping can help us elucidate differences. For example, there are differences in the experience of shopping based on gender, age, ethnicity and class. There are also differences based on the various genres of shopping experience, from a mall to a corner shop. By contrast, there is the tradition of anthropological generalisation about 'peoples' and comparative theory. This leads to the question as to whether there are any fundamental aspects of shopping which suggest a robust normativity that comes through the research and is not entirely dissipated by relativism. In this essay I want to emphasize the latter approach and argue that if not all, then most acts of shopping on this street exhibit a normative form which needs to be addressed. In the later discussion of the discourse of shopping I will defend the possibility that such a heterogenous group of households could be fairly represented by a series of homogenous cultural practices.

The theory that I will propose is certainly at odds with most of the literature on this topic. My premise, unlike that of most studies of consumption, whether they arise from economists, business studies or cultural studies, is that for most households in this street the act of shopping was hardly ever directed towards the person who was doing the shopping. Shopping is therefore not best understood as an individualistic or individualising act related to the subjectivity of the shopper. Rather, the act of buying goods is mainly directed at two forms of 'otherness'. The first of these expresses a relationship between the shopper and a particular other individual such as a child or partner, either present in the household, desired or imagined. The second of these is a relationship to a more general goal which transcends any immediate utility and is best understood as cosmological in that it takes the form of neither subject nor object but of the values to which people wish to dedicate themselves.

It never occurred to me at any stage when carrying out the ethnography that I should consider the topic of sacrifice as relevant to this research. In no sense then could the ethnography be regarded as a testing of the ideas presented here. The literature that seemed most relevant in the initial analysis of the London material was that on thrift discussed in chapter 3. The crucial element in opening up the potential of sacrifice for understanding shopping came through reading Bataiile. Bataille, however, was merely the catalyst, since I will argue that it is the classic works on sacrifice and, in particular, the foundation to its modern study by Hubert and Mauss (1964) that has become the primary grounds for my interpretation. It is important, however, when reading the following account to note that when I use the word 'sacrifice', I only rarely refer to the colloquial sense of the term as used in the concept of the 'self-sacrificial' housewife. Mostly the allusion is to this literature on ancient sacrifice and the detailed analysis of the complex ritual sequence involved in traditional sacrifice. The metaphorical use of the term may have its place within the subsequent discussion but this is secondary to an argument at the level of structure.

IELTS TEST 6

Exam Essentials

LISTENING MODULE   **READING MODULE**   WRITING MODULE   SPEAKING MODULE

PASSAGE 1
PASSAGE 2
PASSAGE 3

Questions 27–29

Choose **THREE** *letters A–F.*

Write your answers in boxes 27–29 on your answer sheet.

Which **THREE** *of the following are problems the writer encountered when conducting his study?*

A   uncertainty as to what the focus of the study should be

B   the difficulty of finding enough households to make the study worthwhile

C   the diverse nature of the population of the area

D   the reluctance of people to share information about their personal habits

E   the fact that he was unable to study some people's habits as much as others

F   people dropping out of the study after initially agreeing to take part

Questions 30–37

Do the following statements agree with the views of the writer in Reading Passage 3?

In boxes 30–37 on your answer sheet write

YES	*if the statement agrees with the views of the writer*
NO	*if the statement contradicts the views of the writer*
NOT GIVEN	*if it is impossible to say what the writer thinks about this*

30   Anthropological relativism is more widely applied than anthropological generalisation.

31   Shopping lends itself to analysis based on anthropological relativism.

32   Generalisations about shopping are possible.

33   The conclusions drawn from this study will confirm some of the findings of other research.

34   Shopping should be regarded as a basically unselfish activity.

35   People sometimes analyse their own motives when they are shopping.

36   The actual goods bought are the primary concern in the activity of shopping.

37   It was possible to predict the outcome of the study before embarking on it.

Questions 38–40

Complete the sentences below with words taken from Reading Passage 3.

Use **NO MORE THAN THREE WORDS** for each answer.

Write your answers in boxes 38–40 on your answer sheet.

38 The subject of written research the writer first thought was directly connected with his study was ....

39 The research the writer has been most inspired by was carried out by ....

40 The writer mostly does not use the meaning of 'sacrifice' that he regards as ....

IELTS
TEST 6

Exam Essentials

LISTENING MODULE   READING MODULE   **WRITING MODULE**   SPEAKING MODULE

Task 1
Task 2

You should spend about 20 minutes on this task.

The pie charts below show responses by teachers of foreign languages in Britain to a survey concerning why their students are learning a foreign language. The first chart shows the main reason for learning a foreign language. The second chart shows how many teachers felt that there has been a recent change in the reason.

Write a report for a university lecturer describing the information below.

Write at least 150 words.

% of teachers reporting the following as most common reason for learning:

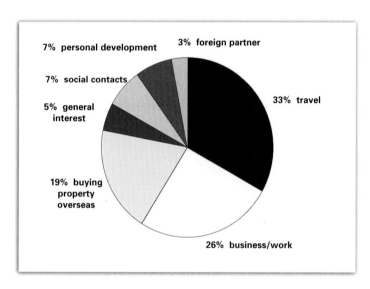

% of teachers reporting recent increase in people learning for the following reasons:

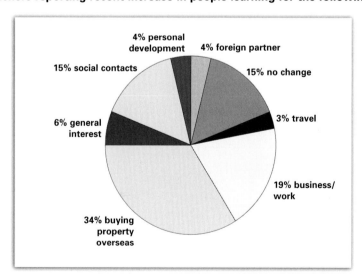

There is a sample answer on page 204.

You should spend about 40 minutes on this task.

Present a written argument or case to an educated reader with no specialist knowledge of the following topic.

> *Some people regard work as the most important thing in life and have little interest in anything else. Other people are more enthusiastic about their hobbies and leisure interests than their jobs.*
>
> **Discuss both these attitudes and give your own opinion.**

You should use your own ideas, knowledge and experience and support your arguments with examples and relevant evidence.

Write at least 250 words.

There is a sample answer on page 204.

▶ PART 1

Example questions

- What hobbies and interests are popular in your country?
- Which hobbies or interests do you enjoy?
- Which hobbies or interests did you have when you were a child?
- Do you think parents should encourage their children to have a hobby or interest?

▶ PART 2

Example task

Read the topic card below carefully.

You will have to talk about the topic for 1 to 2 minutes.

You have one minute to think about what you are going to say.

You can make notes if you want.

> **Describe the job you most like to have.**
>
> **You should say:**
>
>   **what this job would be**
>
>   **where you would work**
>
>   **which qualifications you would need**
>
> **and explain why you would like to have this job most.**

▶ PART 3

Example questions

- Which jobs are most respected in your country?
- Do you think schools provide enough advice and support about future careers?
- What changes have there been in recent years in employment in your country?
- Do you agree that pay for a job should reflect the level of contribution to community the job makes?

GENERAL TRAINING MODULE

Tests A and B

IELTS
GENERAL TRAINING TEST A

Exam Essentials

READING MODULE   WRITING MODULE

SECTION 1
SECTION 2
SECTION 3

▸ **Questions 1–14**

Questions 1–7

Look at the extract from a leaflet about London buses on the following page.

Using **NO MORE THAN THREE WORDS** *each answer the following questions.*

Write your answers in boxes 1–7 on your answer sheet.

1   How many new buses have been introduced?

2 & 3 What **TWO** features of bendy buses are mentioned?

4   When must you buy a ticket to go on a bendy bus?

5   What **TWO** kinds of Travelcard can be purchased online?

6   Which item can you buy to get a discount on bus journeys?

7   Where is it possible to buy every kind of ticket for transport in London?

LONDON BUSES

are getting better

Less time waiting at bus stops

With so many routes having more buses on them, you'll spend less time waiting at stops and more time doing the things you enjoy. There are also additional Night buses on many routes, particularly on Friday and Saturday nights.

91 routes now have more buses

Getting there faster and easier

over **300** more buses on the roads

New bendy buses have been introduced to route 507 from Waterloo to Victoria, and to route 521 from Waterloo via the City to London Bridge. These buses carry up to 60 more passengers than a double decker bus, and have three doors, allowing quick and easy access for everyone. The buses are low floor, and because you have to buy your ticket before boarding, the bus spends less time at each stop, helping you get to your destination quicker.

over **6000** buses across London every day

BUY Travelcards and Bus Passes here

Where to buy tickets

Bus Passes and Travelcards are available from most Tube stations, Travel Information centres and over 2,900 local travel ticket outlets – or wherever you see the sign above. Monthly and annual Travelcards and annual Bus Passes can also be purchased in advance by calling 0870 849 9999 or visiting www.ticket-on-line.co.uk

Travelcards:

Any valid Travelcard can be used across the entire London Bus network.

Saver tickets:

A Saver is a book of 6 single bus tickets bought in advance that can be used by anyone at any time, across the entire London bus network and can save you up to 35p per journey. Saver tickets are available from selected local ticket outlets and, like all other tickets, Travel Information centres.

For more information, visit **www.tfl.gov.uk** or phone **020 7222 1234**.

IELTS
GENERAL TRAINING TEST A

Exam Essentials

READING MODULE | WRITING MODULE

SECTION 1
SECTION 2
SECTION 3

Questions 8–14

Read the extract from a leaflet about housing on the following page.

Do the following statements agree with the information given in the leaflet on page 175.

In boxes 8–14 on your answer sheet write

TRUE	*if the statement agrees with the information*
FALSE	*if the statement contradicts the information*
NOT GIVEN	*if there is no information on this*

8   The New Start Scheme has already proved very popular.

9   The New Start Scheme has been developed because of a lack of local properties.

10   Even if you do not meet the requirements for the scheme, you may be able to get a new home.

11   If you owe rent, you have no chance of getting another home through the scheme.

12   It is easier to get properties in some areas than in others.

13   An officer will accompany you when you visit a possible new home.

14   Expenses are paid only if you accept a property that you visit.

NEW START

What is the New Start Scheme?

The council's New Start scheme has been set up to give you and your family the opportunity to move to a permanent home in a new part of the country. As you may already know, even if you have been approved by us for rehousing, you may still have to wait several years before a permanent property could be made available to you. With this new scheme, you could have the chance to move into a new home in the very near future.

Can I apply?

You can apply to be considered for the scheme if you are:

- Currently on our Housing Register and being helped to prevent homelessness

- Have been accepted as homeless

- Living in temporary accommodation provided by us

- A Council tenant

If you cannot meet any of these points, you can still contact our New Start Officer for information on how to apply directly to councils outside the area. However, the councils with which we work will not accept people who have caused a nuisance in their council home or temporary accommodation. Furthermore, if you have rent arrears, you are unlikely to be offered permanent accommodation through this scheme. If you wish to be considered for more than one area, you should state this clearly on your application form.

What help is available for me?

- If, after reading this, you make an application for the Scheme, our officer will send you a form and if you are eligible, we will arrange a trip for you to visit your chosen area.

- We will arrange for you to go and see a property only if your application is successful. We will also help you by paying your reasonable expenses when you travel to visit it; (you do not have to take the property if you do not like it).

- Should you then decide that you want to accept this offer of permanent accommodation, we will help pay for reasonable removal costs. We will also pay for your disconnection and reconnection charges (such as electricity, gas and home telephone). If you currently live in furnished temporary accommodation, we may be able to help you get some basic items of furniture.

▸ **Questions 15–27**

Questions 15–21

*Read the information about a college's different centres **A–E** on the following page.*

Write the letters of the appropriate centres in boxes 15–21 on your answer sheet.

NB *You may use any letter more than once.*

Which centre

15 is recommended as a good place for students from abroad?

16 is where courses related to subjects such as nursing are held?

17 is very near to an area where lots of people go shopping?

18 has a new facility for people aiming to work in TV or films?

19 is said to be in a pleasant and attractive area?

20 contains a part that formerly had a different use?

21 has a named area that was specially created to contain certain equipment?

COLLEGE
CENTRES

The College has five main Centres:

A Grahame Park Centre

Our Grahame Park Centre offers some of the best training opportunities in North London. It has industry-standard facilities, including hairdressing salons, a construction area, kitchens and a fully functioning training restaurant. The latest addition is a professional media make-up studio with its own photographic area. Our Grahame Park Centre also has superb sports facilities including a 20-metre pool and cardiovascular suite. Naturally, like all our Centres, Grahame Park offers state-of-the-art IT suites all running the latest software. It is also home to the Business Training & Advisory Service (BTAS).

B Montagu Road Centre

With its welcoming, community atmosphere, Montagu Road is a perfect setting for many of the College's international students. Situated in a leafy, residential area, the Centre is close to tube and mainline stations as well as local shops and eateries.

C North London Business Park Centre

The North London Business Park Centre offers a wide-ranging selection of courses, including much of the College's Business & Management and Health & Social Care provision. The Centre has domestic facilities and a horticultural centre for students with special needs. It also houses a working travel agency staffed by Travel & Tourism students. The Centre is served by regular bus routes and has plenty of car parking space.

D Stanhope Road Centre

This small and friendly Centre offers ESOL (English for Speakers of Other Languages), Art & Craft and Adult Basic Skills courses. It is just a short step from busy shopping streets and close to many public transport links.

E Wood Street Centre

Close to all local amenities and with excellent public transport links, this Centre offers courses in varying subjects, and is home to our renowned Art & Design programmes. Facilities at Wood Street include a professional multimedia suite and excellent dance and drama studios. Students have the opportunity to take advantage of the College's extensive IT facilities in the Centre's Belling Suite, a purpose-built unit housing some 50 top-of-the-range PCs. One of the earliest examples of learning in the area can be found at this Centre with the historic Tudor Hall, which was originally opened as a school by Queen Elizabeth 1 in the 16th century.

IELTS
GENERAL TRAINING TEST A

Exam Essentials

READING MODULE   WRITING MODULE

SECTION 1
SECTION 2
SECTION 3

Questions 22–27

Read the information from the college prospectus on the following page.

Complete the sentences below with words taken from the passage.

Write **NO MORE THAN THREE WORDS** *for each answer.*

Write your answers in boxes 22–27 on your answer sheet.

22 At the ...., college employees are available to give advice at all times.

23 Students should get in touch with the people who run the .... to find out about the Student Union.

24 For people who are interested in discussions, ... are organised.

25 You can visit the .... to find out about Youth & Community Team activities.

26 Paper and pens can be bought in .... at two of the Centres.

27 Students wishing to use the fitness room must do ....

FACILITIES, ACTIVITIES & SPORT

It's not all work, work, work!

We want you to enjoy your time here as well as succeed in your studies. All College Centres have pleasant atmospheres and, when you're not in class, there are plenty of ways to fill your time.

Learning centres

The state-of-the-art learning centres at all our College Centres are carefully designed to optimise self-directed study in a supportive learning environment. There are plenty of networked PCs to work at, with internet access, and a range of other computerised and paper-based resources. Our staff are always on hand to help.

Student Union

The College has an active Student Union, which organises and helps to fund a wide range of activities, represents student opinion to the College management and offers support and advice to its members. Contact the Youth Work team leaders or see the Student Guide for more information.

The Youth & Community Team

This team works with students to organise activities to make your time at the College even more enjoyable and interesting. Some activities complement course work and provide extra accreditation. A programme of actvities runs throughout the year, and usually includes: trips and visits; singing, music and comedy workshops; debates; karaoke and cabaret; yoga and self-defence. Look out for details on College notice boards, or drop into the student common rooms. The Youth Work teams at each College Centre also play a vital part in ensuring the safety and wellbeing of students when they are on College sites.

Food and refreshments

All College Centres offer a selection of refreshments. Grahame Park and Russell Lane provide freshly cooked meals and the other Centres offer a variety of lighter snacks. Grahame Park and Russell Lane also have Poppins shops, which sell a range of items from stationery to confectionery.

Sports

You can enjoy the use of the superb sports facilities at our Grahame Park Centre. There are plenty of arranged activities, and there are drop-in times for you to make use of the facilities at your convenience:

The multi-use sports hall is ideal for a range of activities and exercise classes.

The fitness room is well-equipped with a variety of different resistance and cardiovascular machines to suit most needs. Students wishing to use the equipment must complete an induction course, which can be arranged by a member of staff.

The swimming pool is 20m in length, and regular drop-in times and activities are scheduled. The pool is supervised by a qualified lifeguard. Facilities include showers and changing areas.

▶ **Questions 28–40**

Questions 28–33

*The article on pages 181 and 182 has six sections **A–F**.*

Choose the correct heading for each section from the list of headings below.

*Write the correct number **i–x** in boxes 28–33 on your answer sheet.*

List of Headings	
i	Not enough sympathy
ii	The need for action
iii	An inaccurate comparison
iv	Is it really a new phenomenon?
v	The problem gets worse
vi	Not a complete solution
vii	Progress resulting from research
viii	How common is the problem?
ix	Changing attitudes
x	A variety of attempts

28   Paragraph **A**

29   Paragraph **B**

30   Paragraph **C**

31   Paragraph **D**

32   Paragraph **E**

33   Paragraph **F**

RSI

A Pia Enoizi panicked when a specialist told her that she had repetitive strain injury (RSI) and would never be able to work with a computer. Then 19, she was studying history at Cambridge University. 'I saw my career being shot to pieces,' she says. 'What on earth was I going to do? At the time, I was thinking about an academic life.'

The first warning sign was cramp, which struck during a summer job that involved data entry and analysis. 'I sat at the computer on a plastic chair with no thought about posture or taking breaks. One evening, I was cooking pasta and was surprised when I could not lift a pan of boiling water.' The cramps recurred, but she was enjoying the work and put the discomfort out of her mind. Back at Cambridge for her final year, however, she quickly developed essay-writer's cramp. 'We handwrote essays,' says Enoizi, who is now 25. 'First, I found it a struggle to get through a full essay. Next, to my horror, the pain and cramp became so intense I could not write at all. I began to have horrific pins and needles and pains shooting up my arm.'

B More than half a million Britons suffer from RSI – or work-related upper-limb disorder, the description specialists prefer to use. However, this figure includes only reported cases, says Andrew Chadwick, the chief executive of the RSI Association. 'Students and children are not included. Nor are the thousands of stoics who struggle in silence. Many who call our helpline are desperate. They say they cannot afford to lose their jobs.'

RSI is not a diagnosis, but an umbrella term for a range of about 30 painful inflammatory disorders linked to daily overuse of a muscle. Tennis and golfer's elbow are common examples, but many more are occupational. Factory assembly workers and computer users are believed to be the most susceptible, followed by musicians, dressmakers, flight attendants – who repeatedly tear tickets in half – sign language interpreters and litter pickers, who repeatedly squeeze the handles on litter collectors. Text messaging has not yet been known to cause the condition, but Virgin Mobile was concerned enough two years ago to advise users to flex their fingers and shake their wrists occasionally.

C Some specialists draw a parallel between the overuse of muscles and joints by RSI sufferers and the stress suffered by marathon runners. An athlete runs to exhaustion, but would never consider doing so every day; the body needs time to recover before the next event. Yet, with computer-related RSI, the fingers are honed to work faster and faster, says Chadwick: 'It is often the hardest and fastest workers, who put in long hours without proper breaks, who develop a disorder.'

D Enoizi's recovery has taken several years' determination and discipline. She missed a lot

IELTS
GENERAL TRAINING TEST A

Exam Essentials

READING MODULE   WRITING MODULE

SECTION 1
SECTION 2
SECTION 3

of work, but her college paid for an amanuensis – a postgraduate student to whom she dictated essays and her exams papers – and for physiotherapy. But even the repeated dictation led to a painful contraction of the neck muscles. 'During finals, I had to lie on the floor to rest my neck,' she says. Enoizi was delighted to graduate with a first, but she then had to take a year off to rest and retrain her body. Her first stop was a residential chronic pain management course. 'I realised that the damage caused by RSI was never going to go away. I had to learn how to control it.' During her year off, Enoizi visited a chiropractor, an osteopath and a kinesiologist. She also tried magnet therapy and herbal supplements. But none of these made a difference. Pilates, with its emphasis on posture and balancing muscles, helped. Physiotherapy also proved crucial. 'It made a big difference when my physiotherapist bandaged my arms and somehow lifted the forearm muscles away from the nerves. There was an instant feeling of liberation – everything felt less tight.'

E Enoizi now uses a curved keyboard. 'This helps me keep my wrists straight, but with my arms slightly curved, so my elbows do not dig into my ribs. Everything is more relaxed. My chair is fully adjustable and I take frequent breaks.' She is now working at Boots as an assistant project manager. 'I do a mixture of computer analysis, meetings and discussions,' she says. 'But, at the end of a long day, I might get a little pain. I walk briskly – jogging can aggravate joints – stretch gently at my desk and keep up the Pilates. I feel optimistic.'

F Enoizi supports the RSI Association's call for prevention. 'I am concerned about schoolchildren,' she says. 'Many use computers for several hours a day, yet are given little advice on posture and injury. Whether they are short, tall, aged 12 or 18, most sit at the same non-adjustable chairs, and at the same height desks. And many send text messages and play games on their computers until late at night.'

Questions 34–39

Complete the summary below using words from the box.

Write your answers in boxes 34–39 on your answer sheet.

What is RSI?

The **34** …. name for RSI is 'work-related upper limb disorder'. The number of people suffering from it is **35** …. , because certain people are not included in the statistics and because for some people the problem is a **36** …. one. RSI is a **37** …. name that includes about thirty unpleasant conditions. Sports people suffer from it, but many other people do as a result of carrying out **38** …. tasks at work. It is not **39** …. whether text messaging can cause it but this is possible.

rising	concerned	general	secret
difficult	false	official	current
likely	complete	constant	characteristic
sure	unknown	clear	routine
simple	flexible	straight	firm

Question 40

*Choose **FOUR** letters A–H.*

Write your answers in box 40 on your answer sheet.

40 Which **FOUR** of the following helped Pia Enoizi?
  A   an amanuensis
  B   an osteopath
  C   magnet therapy
  D   Pilates
  E   physiotherapy
  F   a curved keyboard
  G   brisk walking
  H   jogging

IELTS
GENERAL TRAINING TEST A

Exam Essentials

READING MODULE   WRITING MODULE
TASK 1
TASK 2

You should spend about 20 minutes on this task.

> *An Australian friend is coming to visit you, and it will be his/her birthday during the visit.*
>
> *Write a letter to your friend. In your letter*
> - *say how you feel about the visit*
> - *suggest what you could do on his/her birthday*
> - *try to find out what you friend thinks of your idea.*

Write at least 150 words.

You do **NOT** need to write your address.

Begin your letter as follows:

Dear .... ,

There is a sample answer on page 205.

You should spend about 40 minutes on this task.

You have been asked to write about the following topic.

> *Many young people today are too worried about the way they look and this causes them problems.*
>
> *Do you agree or disagree?*
>
> *What is the situation in your country?*

Give reasons for your answers and include any relevant examples from your experience.

Write at least 250 words.

There is a sample answer on page 205.

IELTS
GENERAL TRAINING TEST B

Exam Essentials

READING MODULE   WRITING MODULE

SECTION 1
SECTION 2
SECTION 3

▶ **Questions 1–14**

Questions 1–7

Read the extract from a leaflet about walking on the following page and answer Questions 1–7.

Do the following statements reflect the claims of the writer of the leaflet?

In boxes 1–7 on your answer sheet write

    YES   *if the statement agrees with the views of the writer*
    NO   *if the statement contradicts the views of the writer*
    NOT GIVEN *if it is impossible to say what the writer thinks about this*

1   The Walk for Life scheme has attracted a lot of publicity.

2   Volunteer Leaders have to put in a lot of effort.

3   Some Volunteer Leaders give up the scheme.

4   Taking up regular walking is a simple decision to make.

5   The Walk for Life rewards are meant to be amusing.

6   It is unlikely that many people will complete 100 walks.

7   Everyone who qualifies for a reward according to the records kept will eventually receive one.

WALK for life

Walk for Life is run by the Health and Sports Development Unit of the council. It is part of a national scheme to encourage one million people to walk regularly for their health. The aim is to achieve this by supporting local co-ordinators to develop Volunteer Led Walks.

Walk for Life relies on the hard work and dedication of the Volunteer Leaders. It's not an easy job to please everyone! Week in, week out, whatever the weather, Leaders can be found welcoming new walkers, greeting regulars, completing essential paperwork and ensuring that everyone has a safe walking experience.

For many new walkers, the decision to walk regularly, and more importantly to continue walking, requires motivation, commitment and often involves a major change in lifestyle.

It is often too easy to start a slippery slope by thinking 'I'll just give it a miss this once' when the weather doesn't look very nice or if you are feeling a bit tired.

But **Walk for Life** would like to recognise the fact that you are dedicated and give you a reward to say 'Well done' and act as an incentive to say 'Keep going'!

Once you hit 20 walks you will receive a certificate. After 50 walks you will be able to pull on a Walk for Life cap and feel proud of yourself – that's about one walk every week for a year.

After 75 walks you can be smug in the knowledge that walking with **Walk for Life** is definitely one of your good habits and be safe in the knowledge that after another 25 walks you can look forward to a Mystery Gift.

There may be a delay between reaching a landmark and receiving your reward as some registers are only examined quarterly. Don't worry – just make sure your name is taken down at the start of every walk you attend. Certificates were recently sent to the first Walkers who reached 20 walks and there are many more of you not too far behind! Who will be the first to reach 50 walks?

IELTS
GENERAL TRAINING TEST B
Exam Essentials

READING MODULE   WRITING MODULE
SECTION 1
SECTION 2
SECTION 3

Questions 8–14

Read the information about a library on the following page and label the diagram below.

Use **NO MORE THAN THREE WORDS** *from the passage for each answer.*

Write your answers in boxes 8–14 on your answer sheet.

---

adult lending area

8 .... and 9 .... sections

children's library

larger space for 10 .... *and* ....
to take place

11 ....

50% more books
teenage section

14 ....

reference section

audio-visual space

place for 13 ....

IT room

toilets

coffee area

12 ....
(can be used for a fee)

LIBRARY PLANS
8 September – 28 November

Have your say on library plans

From 8 September until the end of November, the Council will carry out a consultation exercise giving local people the opportunity to comment on the plans. The options include building a new modern library facility or refurbishing the existing 1938 library building.

The current building is no longer suitable for the delivery of modern library services. In particular, it cannot easily be adapted to meet the needs required by the Disability Discrimination Act or to install a full range of IT learning facilities.

The new building would have almost 60% more floor space and offer the full range of facilities available in other libraries across the borough. A lift service would make sure these facilities were accessible to everyone in the community.

Facilities would include a main adult lending area, a reference section, an audio visual space, separate children's and teenage sections, an IT room with a range of learning software, music listening posts, a coffee area and toilets. There will also be a community hall and a smaller meeting room available for hire.

Adult fiction stock in the new library would increase by about 30% and the emphasis will be on making books easy to find. New fixtures and fittings will enable them to be displayed by genre and there will be different sections for large print and spoken word books.

Teenagers would be given their own seating area and teenage book stock would be increased by around 50%. More children's and teenage videos will be available and the children's library will boast more tables and computers for homework and leisure use and more room for activities and story-telling.

The exhibition at the Library will run for six weeks from 8 September during library opening hours. From 20 October until 28 November the exhibition moves to the Phoenix Cinema, where it will be open for public viewing from 4pm – 9pm each day.

GENERAL TRAINING TEST B

Exam Essentials

READING MODULE   WRITING MODULE

SECTION 1
SECTION 2
SECTION 3

▶ **Questions 15–27**

Questions 15–20

Read the information from a college prospectus on the following page and complete the flow charts below.

Use **NO MORE THAN THREE WORDS** *from the passage for each answer.*

Write your answers in boxes 15–20 on your answer sheet.

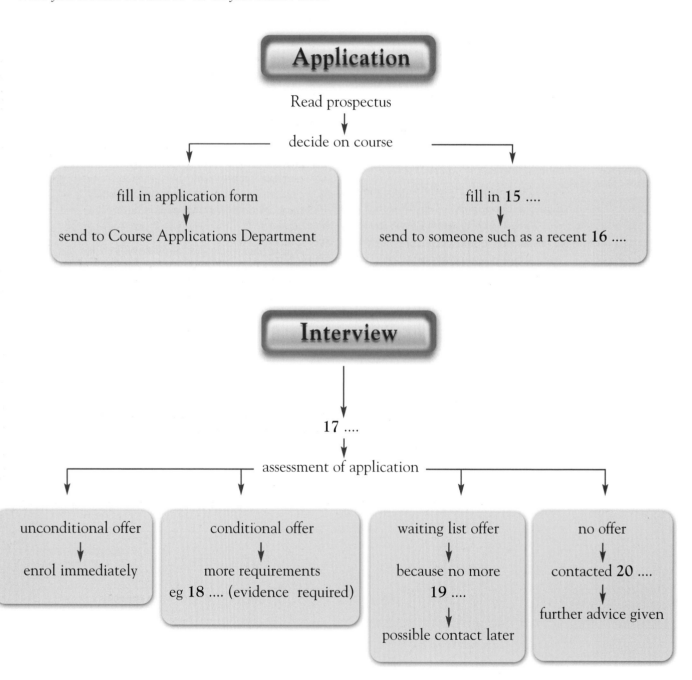

Application

Read prospectus

↓

decide on course

fill in application form

↓

send to Course Applications Department

fill in **15** ....

↓

send to someone such as a recent **16** ....

Interview

↓

17 ....

↓

assessment of application

| unconditional offer | conditional offer | waiting list offer | no offer |

unconditional offer

↓

enrol immediately

conditional offer

↓

more requirements
eg **18** .... (evidence required)

waiting list offer

↓

because no more
19 ....

↓

possible contact later

no offer

↓

contacted **20** ....

↓

further advice given

APPLICATION & INTERVIEW INFORMATION

Application

After you have read through the prospectus and decided which course you want to apply for, please follow the simple procedures detailed below:

1   Detach and complete the centre-fold application form and return it as soon as possible to:
    Course Applications Department, The Admissions Centre, Southgate College, High Street, Southgate, London N14 6BS

2   Complete and forward the reference form to someone who knows of you and your progress. This person would usually be your present or last tutor.

Interview

After we have received your application and reference form, you will be invited in for an interview, during which you will be taken on a tour of the College, and we will assess your application to ensure we offer the right course for you.

After Interview

Unconditional offer

If you have already achieved the entry requirements to join the College, an 'unconditional offer' will be given to you and arrangements will be made for you to enrol as soon as possible.

Conditional offer

You will be given a 'conditional offer' if there are additional criteria to be met; these may include exam results or further practical tests or reports. On receipt of your exam results, you will need to show the College evidence of your grades.

Waiting list offer

If the course of your choice is oversubscribed and there are no longer any places available, you may be included on the 'waiting list', either with a conditional or an unconditional offer. We will then contact you with an offer if a place becomes available.

No offer

If, after the interview, the College considers that you will not benefit from the course of your choice, we will contact you in writing and will offer further advice on your next step.

IELTS
GENERAL TRAINING TEST B
Exam Essentials

READING MODULE   WRITING MODULE

SECTION 1
SECTION 2
SECTION 3

Questions 21–27

Read the information about student services at a college on the following page.

*Complete each sentence with the correct ending **A–J** from the box below.*

*Write the correct letter **A–J** in boxes 21–27 on your answer sheet.*

21   People who are not currently students at the college can find out about courses from

22   Students with problems in their private lives can speak to

23   Students collecting material for a piece of course work can get help from

24   Students having problems with their course may be advised to speak to

25   People trying to decide which course would be best for them should speak to

26   Someone who only wants a brief chat about jobs can go without an appointment to

27   A student may be offered a specially created way of solving their problem by

A a personal tutor.

B the Prospects Careers Service.

C the Inclusive Learning Support Manager.

D the Progression Centre.

E an examinations officer.

F the Library and Learning Resources Centre.

G the College Youth Worker.

H someone in the Admissions Centre.

I someone who is not a member of the college staff.

J a Careers Officer.

STUDENT SERVICES

A wide range of facilities and services is available at the College to assist you with your studies and to help you overcome difficulties. The following is a flavour of what we can offer.

Information

The Admissions Centre provides information about all the College's courses and learning programmes. The staff are here to give you opportunities to discuss your education and training needs and to match them with the right course.

Careers

As well as offering drop-in sessions for quick queries and advice, Prospects Careers Service also provides individual advice and guidance about education, training, career and employment opportunities. You can book an appointment with a Careers Officer in the Progression Centre.

Progression Centre

The Progression Centre aims to help our students and the local community find out more about the opportunities available to them and to help them achieve their next move in education or employment. Students can drop in or book an appointment for advice or opportunities available.

Library & Learning Resources

Our Library & Learning Resources Centre provides a state-of-the-art learning environment offering information and resources to help you succeed. Our specialist team are here to support an appropriate learning environment and to guide you through information-gathering tasks for assignments. A large suite of computers allows access to a wide range of information-based software.

Learning Support

The Inclusive Learning Support Service is available for any student who is having difficulties with their coursework. The Inclusive Learning Manager will see any student for a guidance interview to develop a support programme based on individual need. The support may be on a one-to-one basis with a member of the Inclusive Learning Support team or from outside agencies. The service also applies to examination boards on behalf of students who require concessions due to a disability and/or learning difficulty.

Counselling and Student Services

The Co-ordinator of Student Services, the College Youth Worker and the Nursing Welfare Officers provide information, advice, support and personal counselling on any issues that may cause difficulties or worry.

IELTS
GENERAL TRAINING TEST B
Exam Essentials

READING MODULE   WRITING MODULE
SECTION 1
SECTION 2
SECTION 3

▶ *Questions 28–40*

Read the following passage and answer Questions 28–40.

Natural assets worth saving in the Outback

John Craven meets the conservationist who believes every endangered creature must have its price

A What's the going rate for a hairy-nosed wombat? How much for a yellow-footed rock wallaby? It's hard to believe, but some of Australia's most endangered species are now listed as assets in the annual balance sheet of one of the country's top companies. Earth Sanctuaries Ltd says it is revolutionising conservation by applying the rules of private enterprise to its eight wildlife reserves ... and every animal it protects has a price tag. By the year 2025, the company aims to have turned one per cent of the continent into places where vanishing native species are safeguarded behind high fences.

B For visitors like me, staying in the basic but comfortable sanctuaries and enjoying escorted walks through the bush is a wonderful way of discovering what Australia was like before the Europeans arrived two centuries ago and changed everything. Under the southern stars, beams of powerful torches capture an array of weird and wonderful creatures as they bounce along – most of the inhabitants are nocturnal marsupials. Many I'd never heard of, such as bilbies, potoroos, bandicoots, rufous bettongs and woylies, which – at just a few inches high – are the world's smallest and rarest kangaroos.

C They are also worth a small fortune, according to Earth Sanctuaries, which has, for example, 38 bilbies, 20 more than last year, with a value of £80,000. Those hairy-nosed wombats are worth £525 each and the market price of its 120 rock wallabies is £125,000. They are among 1,189 creatures, worth more than £1.6 million, which have gone on the books of Earth Sanctuaries now that Australian companies can value 'non-human living organisms held for commercial purposes' as assets.

D As I walked through the showpiece sanctuary at Warrawong, in the hills above Adelaide in South Australia, several hundred thousand pounds worth of rare marsupials scattered before me. My guide was managing director John Wamsley, a giant of a man who created Warrawong after making his fortune in the building industry. He spent much of his money and 12 years of his time turning a dairy farm into a landscape which the first European settlers would have recognised – while also teaching maths at the local university.

E 'Then I hit on the idea of making it into a business,' John told me. 'Earth Sanctuaries has to raise nearly half a billion pounds in the next 25 years. As a charity, there's no way we could do that, but it's a trivial amount in the marketplace. We sold shares in the company, using our land and animals as assets. Share values have increased one hundredfold in 14 years, which I think is better than any other company in Australia. And there are 12 species of rare or endangered animals that have grown in numbers because of us. When we listed on the Stock Exchange, we were the first publicly-listed company in the world with conservation as its core business, but I'm sure that in years to come, conservation companies will be everywhere. It's an ideal, incredibly simple way to raise funds.'

F From its beginnings at Warrawong, Earth Sanctuaries is now an £8 million company with a quarter of a million acres of land and eight sanctuaries, each unique. Warrawong, for instance, has at least 20 duck-billed platypuses living in the swamps and ponds that John Wamsley dug out personally. At Yookamurra, 90 minutes' drive from Adelaide, nine miles of 'feral' fencing – keeping out foxes, cats and so on – protects 3,000 acres of mallee trees that are home to near-extinct species such as the numbat. More than a hundred of these delicate, termite-eating marsupials live in the hollows of 1,000-year-old mallees. And John Wamsley says: 'So how can I spend shareholders' money saving the oldest forest in Australia? On the face of it I can't, because the wood is worthless. But now that it has £260,000 worth of numbats living in it, I have to save it because, if I lose those numbats, I'm not looking after my shareholders' assets.'

G And these appealing little animals with extremely long noses are valuable assets – John recently sold half a dozen to the West Australian government for more than £2,000 each. To catch sight of one – something few people have done – I had to keep watch for an hour or so at dawn in absolute silence. Suddenly one appeared, followed quickly by three others – long noses twitching, spikey tails high in the air. For a few minutes they played around the tree before scampering off in search of a termite breakfast. Once, numbats ranged across the whole of southern Australia. Now they are down to a few hundred - and I had just seen four of them. That's what eco-tourism should be all about.

H Before the sanctuary was established, Yookamurra was dying – now it teems with wildlife, some of it quite tame. Wilma the wombat, all muscle and action, trundles between the bush and the tourist huts like a hairy tank. She looks cute but it's best not to get too close because, like her relative the koala, she has quite a bite. Emus and their chicks wander unconcerned past the restaurant terrace, while a small mob – that is their collective noun – of kangaroos hangs around quite shamelessly hoping for titbits.

I The newest and largest sanctuary is Scotia, a £4 million project covering 150,000 acres of the Outback of New South Wales. The world's longest feral fence has just been built to guard creatures such as bridled nail-tailed wallabies, stick nest rats (really appealing animals – honest!) and brush-tailed bettongs.

IELTS
GENERAL TRAINING TEST B
Exam Essentials

READING MODULE | WRITING MODULE

SECTION 1
SECTION 2
SECTION 3

Questions 28–33

*The passage has nine paragraphs labelled **A–I**.*

Which paragraph contains the following information?

*Write the correct letter **A–I** in boxes 28–33 on your answer sheet.*

28   a change in rules concerning companies in Australia
29   a term used for a group of a particular creature
30   a business deal made with another organisation
31   a belief that other organisations like Earth Sanctuaries will be set up
32   a creature that can be dangerous if approached by humans
33   sources of light for seeing creatures

Questions 34–39

Classify the following statements as referring to

       W *Warrawong*
       Y *Yookamurra*
       S *Scotia*

*Write the correct letter, **W**, **Y** or **S** in boxes 34–39 on your answer sheet.*

34   It contains something of no financial value.
35   It contains places for visitors to stay in.
36   It is the most recently created sanctuary.
37   It contains creatures that are said to be more attractive than their name suggests.
38   It was formerly used for a different kind of business.
39   It contains areas of water created by the founder.

Question 40

*Choose the correct letter, **A**, **B**, **C** or **D**.*

Write your answer in box 40 on your answer sheet.

40   Which of the following best summarises the writer's attitude in the passage?
    A   He is doubtful about the approach being taken by Earth Sanctuaries.
    B   He is surprised by how little he knew about endangered species.
    C   He is impressed by what is being achieved by Earth Sanctuaries.
    D   He is amazed that John Wamsley's ideas have not been tried before.

IELTS
GENERAL TRAINING TEST B

Exam Essentials

READING MODULE   WRITING MODULE
TASK 1
TASK 2

You should spend about 20 minutes on this task.

> *You recently visited a tourist attraction and you were very pleased by the help given to you by the staff.*
>
> *Write a letter to the head of staff at the tourist attraction. In your letter*
>
> * *give details of the circumstances of your visit*
> * *describe the help given to you by the staff*
> * *say what you want the head of staff to do.*

Write at least 150 words.

You do **NOT** need to write your address.

Begin your letter as follows:

Dear Sir or Madam .... ,

There is a sample answer on page 206.

IELTS
GENERAL TRAINING TEST B
Exam Essentials

READING MODULE   **WRITING MODULE**

TASK 1

TASK 2

You should spend about 40 minutes on this task.

You have been asked to write about the following topic.

> *Some people think that young people should be ambitious. Others believe that it is fine if young people do not have big aims in life.*
>
> *Discuss both these views and give your own opinion.*

Give reasons for your answer and include any relevant examples from your experience. Write at least 250 words.

There is a sample answer on page 206.

▸ **Test 1**

Task 1 (*page 44*)

The charts show that the number of people who speak a regional language to their children is a great deal lower than the number of people whose parents spoke a regional language to them. For example, over 600,000 people had parents who spoke Alsatian to them habitually and over 200,000 had parents who spoke it occasionally, but only 400,000 speak it to their children now. The fall is even greater in the case of Occitan. Over 600,000 people had parents who spoke this language to them habitually and over 1 million who spoke it to them occasionally, but the number of those people who speak the language to their own children is just over 200,000. In the case of Breton, over 200,000 people had parents who spoke it to them habitually and almost 400,000 had parents who spoke it occasionally, but now under 100,000 people speak it to their own children. There has not been much decrease in the numbers for Creole and Corsican, but these were not as high as the others before. The overall picture presented by the charts is that people are not passing on regional languages to their children as much as they used to.

Task 2 (*page 46*)

These days, stress is a big subject. In all sorts of jobs, people get ill because of it and have time off work. The business world is full of pressure and many people are worried all the time that they might lose their jobs if they don't work harder and harder. Lots of people work very long hours and are given very difficult targets to meet. Their employers expect a lot and sometimes they cannot cope. Young people suffer from stress too – for example, when they have to take exams that will have a big effect on their future. And in general, life is more stressful for a lot of people than it used to be because everything is faster than it used to be. People are always in a hurry to do everything and the pace of life has increased.

But is life really more stressful than it used to be? In the past, people didn't have the comforts that they have now. They had to do a lot more things for themselves. They didn't have all the equipment that people take for granted now, like heating and fridges and microwave ovens and washing machines and telephones and cars. Life was harder for most people. Working conditions for an enormous number of people were much worse than they are today, when a lot of the difficult manual work is done by machines.

The impression I have from talking to older people is that they simply accepted that life was hard and they didn't complain of suffering from stress. They simply got on with their lives. These days there are all sorts of 'experts' talking about how much stress people have – people didn't talk about this in the past.

In my opinion, people today have different pressures from the ones they had in the past, but this does not mean that they have more pressures. In the past, people had harder lives in many ways. It has become fashionable to talk about stress, but it's not a new thing – the difference is that nowadays people complain or become ill because of it, whereas in the past they didn't.

▶ Test 2

Task 1 (page 84)

The table shows that the small companies considered the best to work for have some things in common but also differ greatly in some aspects. In terms of staff numbers, the figures are fairly similar, although the fifth company has a much higher number of staff than the other four.

The best company has a high proportion of female staff, and the fourth best company an even higher proportion of female staff. However, this is not the case for the other companies, and the third company has far more male than female members of staff. As for age of staff, three of the companies have a high proportion of people aged under 35, but the fourth company has a low percentage in that age group. All the companies have no members of staff or only a small percentage aged over 55. The best company has a comparatively low staff turnover figure of 5% and the third company's figure for this is also low at 8%. However, the figure is much higher for the other companies, and the fifth best company has a very high staff turnover of 33%. With regard to salaries, the top company has about a third of staff earning high incomes, the second company has about half and the third company about three-quarters. However, for the other two companies the figure is extremely low.

The overall picture is that, apart from the lack of people in the older age group, there are no consistent features that make a small company popular with its staff. Even salaries do not always seem to be a major factor.

Task 2 (page 86)

People know a lot more about other countries today than they used to. First of all, they can travel there much more easily than they could in the past. You can fly to almost anywhere and air travel is a lot more affordable for many people than it used to be. As a result, more and more people have personal experience of other countries, and they see for themselves how other people live. In some ways, this is a good thing because it helps people of different nationalities and from different cultures to understand each other much better. They have more understanding of each other and this helps people to get on better together.

The media also show people about how others live. People have much more access to international news than they used to, both in newspapers and on television. Satellite television enables people to see programmes from other countries and the internet also gives people access to what is going on all over the world. People are much more informed about other countries. This kind of knowledge is a very useful thing because it can make people change their own attitudes. People in one country can learn a lot about what happens in other countries and use this knowledge to do things differently in their own country.

However, there are disadvantages too. International travel can cause problems when people from richer countries visit poorer countries in large numbers. The people in the poorer countries, though they might make some money, often dislike the attitudes of the visitors. Visitors often make little effort to meet the local people, or treat them as inferiors, and so international travel can cause problems between people rather than increased understanding. A disadvantage of the spread of mass media is that it can make people jealous of how people in richer countries live. If they see rich people living lives of luxury in TV programmes, whereas their own lives are difficult, they may dislike these people. And access to international news may cause problems too because people may decide that they dislike other countries that they knew nothing about before.

In conclusion, I would say that there are both big advantages and disadvantages of these developments. On the whole, I think that the advantages outweigh the disadvantages because the spread of international travel and mass media has led to greater understanding between nations and cultures, and this has been one of the best developments in the world in modern times.

▶ **Test 3**

Task 1 (*page 108*)

The first graph shows that 200,000 drivers were caught speeding in the first year of speed cameras. After that, the number rose steadily until the fifth year, when it began to rise dramatically. Between the fifth and eighth years, it rose from about 450,000 to over 1.5 million. However, the number of road accident fatalities over the same period hardly changed at all. Although it fell slightly during the fourth year, it remained fairly constant at just over 3,000 per year. It would therefore appear that giving people fines for speeding had no effect on the number of serious road accidents. This is the view of the people in the survey. The majority of them felt that speed cameras did not reduce the number of road accidents, and 71% of them felt that the purpose of them was to get money from fines, rather than to improve road safety. Just over half thought that there were too many speed cameras, and the rise in the number of fines indicates that more and more cameras were installed over the eight-year period.

Task 2 (*page 109*)

I don't agree that genuine talent is not valued or appreciated these days. The difference is that people nowadays have access to technology that can enable them to create things they could not have done on their own in the past. As a result, some very talented people whose work nobody would have seen or heard in the past are able to become well-known.

This is particularly true in popular music, where the 'anyone can do it' attitude has always been an important feature. In recent times, computer technology has been invented, which makes it possible for people to create and record their own music at home, with very high quality of sound. They don't have to pay to go to expensive recording studios and because of digital equipment, they can make the sound of a whole group without needing a lot of other musicians. Some very talented people have become rich and famous as a result of making their first recordings at home in this way.

Of course, some people with absolutely no talent do become rich and famous. Some very poorly written books become best sellers, some people with no apparent artistic ability become famous artists and some people who cannot act at all become television stars. The idea that you need special gifts and skills and that you need to train and practise a lot has disappeared in some areas of the arts. There is now a belief that ordinary people who are just like everyone else can succeed, whereas in the past people in the arts were seen as special in some way and admired because they could create things that most people could not. However, in my opinion, genuine talent is still admired. People with no talent do become rich and famous but people still appreciate and value genuine talent.

▶ Test 4

Task 1 (page 128)

To build a water clock, you must first get a stand and attach a bottle at the top of it with some tape. This bottle must have a hole in the bottom of it and a hole at the side, into which you glue a straw. Then you get another bottle, cut the neck off it and place it beneath the first bottle.

You begin the process by turning the tap on and covering the hole at the bottom of the first bottle with your finger. Water drips from the tap into that bottle until it is full and water overflows through the straw. This keeps a constant level of water in the bottle. Then you take your finger away from the hole, so that water drips through it and into the second bottle. As it drips into the second bottle, you mark with a pen on the second bottle what the level of water is after one minute, after two minutes, and so on. When the second bottle is full and you have made marks for each minute, you empty the second bottle. You can then repeat the process to time things, for example because you know how many minutes it takes for all of the water to pass from the top bottle to the bottom bottle.

Task 2 (page 129)

Many older people are forced to end their working lives much earlier than they would like to, and this is a shame because their experience is valuable. Also, it is good for people to work if they want to. If more older people were able to get good jobs, it would be good for business, the economy and society.

One reason why older people find it difficult to get good jobs is that many jobs these days require skills and knowledge that they did not get when they were younger. In particular, computers and information technology play a very big role in many professions, and these are things that only came into existence after older people had finished school or college and after they had begun their working lives.

Another reason is that in many countries these days, there is a view that younger people are preferable for many jobs to older people. Experience is seen as being less important than youth. Many businesses and industries have a majority of workers who are young, and young people are promoted to top jobs much more quickly than they used to be. One way of solving the problem is for older people to be re-trained so that they learn the skills required in the modern world. Training courses should be made widely available and affordable. Older people should be made to feel that they can get good jobs after re-training, and this will encourage them to re-train. Employers should understand that older workers have a lot to offer, and that their experience can be very useful to companies, for example because they can pass their experience of work and life on to younger employees.

▶ *Test 5*

Task 1 (page 148)

The first chart shows that the most popular aspects of living in London were the range of shops, the job opportunities and the mixture of people, followed by museums and art galleries, nightlife, transport and parks. The percentage of people naming these things hardly changed at all over the three years of the survey, although the number of people naming shops and job opportunities fell slightly, and the number of people naming museums and art galleries, nightlife and parks went up slightly.

The second chart shows that the cost of living and traffic congestion were seen as the worst aspects of life in London, followed by crime, the cost of housing and transport. However, the percentage of people choosing these aspects fell over the three years in all cases apart from housing. It is interesting to notice that transport was seen as both one of the best and one of the worst things about living in London.

With regard to major problems, the percentage of people who felt that air quality, noise and litter were major problems fell over the three years, although it rose slightly in the second year for air quality. The overall view given by the charts is that people felt that there were improvements with regard to most things they disliked about living in London over the three years.

Task 2 (page 149)

Most people would say that education is a good thing, and therefore that it is a positive development that more and more people are continuing their education after they leave school. A more educated population must have a positive impact on a country, in both economic and social terms.
From the point of view of the people themselves, they have more choice as to what they can do, and this must also be a positive thing. People can now study subjects that really interest them, rather than subjects they had to do because there was less choice, and they can also study more subjects that are directly related to the kind of work they want to do. There are many more specialised courses on offer that qualify people for specialised jobs.

On the other hand, lots of people these days do courses that may be regarded as a bit silly. You can do courses in all sorts of things that have no connection with jobs and that cannot be taken seriously as academic subjects. I have heard of people doing degrees in subjects like pop music, and it is hard to see how useful such courses and qualifications are. Also, many people now do subjects such as media studies because a lot of young people want to work in the media. However, there are not that many jobs available for these people, and so a lot of them have simply wasted their time doing a degree in a subject that does not help them to get a job.

In general, I think that the increase in people continuing their education after school and the increase in the range of courses available to them is both a positive and a negative development.

▶ *Test 6*

Task 1 *(page 168)*

The first chart shows that, according to teachers, the most common reason why people learn a foreign language is travel, with business and work being another major reason. 19% of teachers said that buying property overseas is the main reason. General interest, social contacts, personal development and having a foreign partner were other, less common reasons.

The second chart indicates recent changes in the reasons why people learn a foreign language. The biggest change is in people learning because of buying property overseas, with 34% of teachers saying that the number of people learning for this reason has increased. The next biggest increase is in the number of people learning for business and work, with a similar increase in the number learning for social reasons. About the same number of teachers report no change in the reasons for learning. According to teachers, the number of people learning for travel has not increased much, and there has also not been much increase in the number of people learning because of general interest, having a foreign partner or personal development.

The charts therefore indicate that more British people are buying property overseas and this is why they are learning a foreign language.

Task 2 *(page 169)*

Some people live for their work. They are obsessed by it and they work and work. Workaholics like this often experience health problems after a while because they do not rest or eat properly and they are in a permanent state of stress. They do not know how to relax and they do not know how to enjoy life. This surely cannot be a good thing. However, some people whose job is the most important thing in their lives are perfectly happy. If you are lucky enough to have a job that you love, doing it all the time is not exhausting or problematic because you enjoy it all the time. People who have careers that make them happy do not need hobbies and leisure pursuits for relaxation - they are happy and satisfied anyway.

Of course it is true that most people have to earn a living and that, unfortunately, this often involves doing a job that you don't enjoy. Lots of people have jobs they hate or that they find very boring or depressing. For such people, hobbies and leisure pursuits are extremely important. They provide something to look forward to at the end of a working day or week, and they provide something that people can give all their enthusiasm and attention to. For example, a big interest in playing or watching sport allows people to forget their jobs and other problems for a while and concentrate fully on something that is simply enjoyable. Hobbies that may seem strange to other people can also give people something they can focus their energies and thoughts on.

In my opinion, hobbies and leisure pursuits are vital. You shouldn't think only about work. You need a balance in your life, you need something that offers simple pleasure and compensates for the unpleasant aspects of work. Some people don't need this because their jobs are also a pleasure for them, but I don't know any people like that!

▸ **General Training Module: Test A**

Task 1 (*page 184*)

> Dear Shane,
>
> I'm really looking forward to your visit here next month, and I hope you'll have a great time meeting my friends and family. There are lots of interesting places I can show you in the area, and there are plenty of places we can go in the evenings to have fun.
>
> I've just realised that it'll be your birthday while you're over here, won't it? I've been thinking about what we could do that day. I think it would be a great idea if we went to the Adventure World theme park, which isn't far from where I live. I haven't been there myself, but friends tell me it's a fantastic place for a day out. It's got some really exciting rides, apparently, including one called The Shake-Up, which everyone talks about when they've been there.
>
> Let me know what you think. I know you like a bit of excitement, and it would be easy for us to get there. Do you fancy it? If so, I can start organising the trip. If it's not the sort of thing that appeals to you, I'll think of something else. If you have a better suggestion, let me know and I'll try to organise that.
>
> Love,
>
> Helena

Task 2 (*page 185*)

> I think it is true that many young people worry too much about the way they look. Certainly, I think this is true where I come from. For example, a lot of girls in my country worry about being too fat and they are always on a diet of some sort. They get the idea that they ought to be thin from magazines and celebrities and this can cause them problems. Even people who aren't really fat think that they are. Sometimes this can make them ill, because they can develop eating disorders. It also makes them depressed because they think there is something wrong with them as a person, and that people won't like them or find them attractive.
>
> Clothes also cause problems for a lot of young people in my country. They are very interested in what make of trainers or jeans they wear, and they all want to buy the clothes that are considered the most fashionable. If you haven't got those clothes, people of your age laugh at you. This is a problem for people who haven't got enough money to buy these 'designer' clothes because these clothes are often very expensive. It's a problem for their parents too because they want their children to be happy, but they can't afford these things.
>
> In my opinion, this is all unnecessary. I think that it's much more important what sort of person you are than what you look like. Young people shouldn't worry so much about their appearance; they should enjoy life more while they are young.

▶ General Training Module: Test B

Task 1 (page 197)

Dear Sir or Madam,

I visited your museum last Saturday with a couple of friends of mine, who do not speak English very well, and who had their small child with them in a pushchair. I would like to tell you how enjoyable our visit was because of the help given to us by your staff.

When we arrived, there was a long queue at the entrance, but a member of staff saw that we had a small child with us and took us immediately to the front of the queue and into the museum. As we went round the museum, we asked members of staff various questions about the exhibits, and they explained everything very patiently and in a way that my friends could easily understand. They are clearly experienced in this sort of situation and very well trained.

Our visit was a great success, and this is mainly because of your staff. I would be grateful if you could thank them on our behalf for treating us so well and helping to give us a memorable day.

Yours faithfully,
J. Dowie

Task 2 (page 198)

Most parents want their children to do well in life and so it is understandable that they expect them to be ambitious. A lot of parents who don't have much money and are not at the higher levels of society want their children to do better in life than they did, to have opportunities that they did not have, to have better jobs than they had and to have money to buy things that they could not buy. It is natural for them to think in this way, and therefore it is hard for them to accept it if their children do not have big things in life that they want to achieve.

However, not everyone can be successful in life. Not everyone is clever enough to get a highly-paid job and not everyone is capable of achieving what their parents would regard as success. Some young people would rather be happy and live a relaxed life than spend all their time trying to achieve ambitions that they might not be able to achieve anyway. And lots of people don't find anything that they desperately want to achieve. They are happy to get ordinary jobs, earn a living and enjoy themselves with their friends and family.

In my opinion, it is understandable that a lot of parents want their children to be ambitious, but it is also natural that not all young people are ambitious. Your youth is a time for enjoying yourself, and there is no reason why everyone should have big goals in life. There are more important things.

 **BRITISH COUNCIL**  **IELTS** idp **AUSTRALIA**  **UNIVERSITY** *of* **CAMBRIDGE** ESOL Examinations

S A M P L E

PENCIL must be used to complete this sheet

Centre number:

Please write your **name** below,

then write your six digit Candidate number in the boxes
and shade the number in the grid on the right in PENCIL.

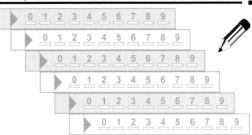

0 1 2 3 4 5 6 7 8 9
0 1 2 3 4 5 6 7 8 9
0 1 2 3 4 5 6 7 8 9
0 1 2 3 4 5 6 7 8 9
0 1 2 3 4 5 6 7 8 9
0 1 2 3 4 5 6 7 8 9

Test date (shade ONE box for the day, ONE box for the month and ONE box for the year):

Day: 01 02 03 04 05 06 07 08 09 10 11 12 13 14 15 16 17 18 19 20 21 22 23 24 25 26 27 28 29 30 31

Month: 01 02 03 04 05 06 07 08 09 10 11 12 Last 2 digits of the **Year:** 00 01 02 03 04 05 06 07 08 09

IELTS Listening Answer Sheet

		✓ x			✓ x
1		1	21		21
2		2	22		22
3		3	23		23
4		4	24		24
5		5	25		25
6		6	26		26
7		7	27		27
8		8	28		28
9		9	29		29
10		10	30		30
11		11	31		31
12		12	32		32
13		13	33		33
14		14	34		34
15		15	35		35
16		16	36		36
17		17	37		37
18		18	38		38
19		19	39		39
20		20	40		40

Checker's Initials		Marker's Initials		Band Score		Listening Total	

IELTS L-R v4.0   DP500/392

S A M P L E

Are you: Female? ▭   Male? ▭

Your first language code:

IELTS Reading Answer Sheet

Module taken (shade one box):   Academic ▭   General Training ▭

	✓ 1 ✗			✓ 21 ✗
1		21		
2	2	22		22
3	3	23		23
4	4	24		24
5	5	25		25
6	6	26		26
7	7	27		27
8	8	28		28
9	9	29		29
10	10	30		30
11	11	31		31
12	12	32		32
13	13	33		33
14	14	34		34
15	15	35		35
16	16	36		36
17	17	37		37
18	18	38		38
19	19	39		39
20	20	40		40

Checker's Initials	Marker's Initials	Band Score	Reading Total

TEST 1

LISTENING Section 1

▶ *Questions 1–4*

Step 1

1 B; **2** C; **3** C; **4** A

Step 2 (Test Questions 1–4)

1 Answer: 90
Note Three figures are mentioned (120, 90 and 200), but the note is about the cheapest, 'the lowest', the price rents 'start at'.

2 Answer: 6 months
Note Two periods are mentioned (9 and 6 months), but the note is about the minimum, the 'standard' which 'can be extended'.

3 Answer: 4 pm
Note Various times (9 am, 5 pm, 10 am, 4 pm and 1 pm) and days (Saturday and Sunday) are mentioned, but the note is about the closing time on Saturday ('open Saturdays until').

4 Answer: (the) internet
Note A list of properties could be sent by post, but the list is available – as the note says – on the internet. This is what interests the woman calling, and what she makes a note of. It would not be grammatically possible to fit a note about the post into the gap. As these are notes, it is not necessary to include words such as 'the' or 'an'. However, the rubric allows up to two words, so you can include 'the' if you want.

Step 3

Man: An important question is how long you're thinking of staying in the property. We don't do short lets.
Woman: I'd want a flat for nine months, perhaps longer.
Man: That would be fine. Our contracts are for a standard six months and that can be extended.
Woman: Fine.

▶ *Questions 5–7*

Step 3 (Test Questions 5–7)

5/6/7 Answers: B/F/G
Note The three correct options are all fully confirmed in the tapescript. The information can come from either speaker, or both together – as in option F here. Option C is ruled out because 'not all' flats include it. Option D is ruled out because the man doesn't 'think any flats have those included'. Option E is ruled out because it's 'up to you to organise'. Option A is ruled out because it is 'extra'.

▶ *Questions 8–10*

Step 4 (Test Questions 8–10)

8 Answer: B
Note You need to follow the order of the instructions carefully. The first 'left' is to turn, then 'right' is also for the road, and the second 'left' is for the position of the block of flats on the road.

9 Answer: H
Note You need to get the correct bridge, and then to recognise which road: the one that 'bends to the right, round the park'. The block of flats is on the 'left side'– you don't turn left.

10 Answer: E
Note You need to choose the correct bridge, pass through the first crossroads and then distinguish between options D and E.

LISTENING Section 2

▶ *Questions 11 and 12*

Step 2

Option D: the whole centre is prepared for blind visitors
Option C: artists that you can watch painting at certain times

Step 4 (Test Questions 11 and 12)

11 Answer: C/A
Note All the activities are mentioned, but only two require booking in advance: 'We need notice of your coming for that' (option C) and 'requiring at least 7 days' notice' (option A).

12 Answer: B/D
Note All the facilities are mentioned, but only two are closed in the winter: 'isn't run in the winter, so the studio is closed then' (option B) and 'during the cold months, so that doesn't operate' (option D).

▶ *Questions 13–17*

Step 1

Suggested answers: It starts on … , It will start on … , It begins on … , It will begin on … , It opens on … , It will open on … , The starting date is/will be … , etc.

Step 2

1 28th August
2 26th August
3 'the chance to have a ride on an old bus'
4 Because 'on' isn't included in the table where the other two dates are given.

Step 3 (Test Questions 13–17)

13 Answer: 28th August
Note The other date mentioned, 26th August, is when the current exhibition ends, not when the next one begins.

14 Answer: *People at Work*
Note The answer is introduced: 'Next, we're running a show called … '. You need to 'translate' this to the table's heading 'Exhibition'. Three words are allowed, so you must write the full title.

15 Answer: careers advice
Note Various things are mentioned (pictures, videos, jobs, coal-mining, flying planes), but these are not a 'service'.

16 Answer: *Land from Air*
Note The answer is introduced: 'Following on from that show, we're putting on an exhibition called … '. You need to write the full title.

17 Answer: balloon trip
Note Photographs are mentioned, but not as a prize for the competition.

▶ *Questions 18–20*

Step 2

1 No; **2** Yes – Question 18; **3** We don't know. See Task guide on page 14.

18 Answer: B
Note You hear about 'a drink from a machine', and you hear that this is 'halfway to the museum entrance'. B must be the answer for Question 18. There is also information about option A, which could help you, although the answer doesn't depend on this.

19 Answer: E
Note You hear that 'for anyone who doesn't have a mobile phone, there are payphones', and you hear that these are 'at the far end of the picnic area'. E must be the answer for Question 19.

20 Answer: C
Note You hear about 'a first aid room', and you hear that this is 'just to the right of the entrance to the main museum'. C must be the answer for Question 20. In this case, the location is described just before the thing is mentioned, so it's important to keep following the directions throughout the recording.

LISTENING Section 3

▸ *Questions 21–25*

Step 3

Option A
1 Yes; **2** No. She says, 'you've got to listen to questions carefully, and be ready to answer quickly'. **3** No

Option B
1 Yes
2 Yes. She says, 'It was my first time using the computerised projector, and I was sure I was going to get the controls wrong, or something. And of course, that's not a good situation … '. This information links to what she said before: 'I was ever so nervous beforehand'. It also explains what she means when she says, 'when you have to get each table of results to come up in the right order, it can make you nervous'.
3 Yes.

Option C
1 Yes; **2** No. She says, 'I must know those statistics inside out'. **3** No

Step 4 (Test Questions 21–25)

21 Answer: B
Note See step 3 above.

22 Answer: C
Note Martin outlines that he has a negative view of the presentations: 'the standard of presentations could be improved'. Option A is not the answer; in fact, the discussion of research is too detailed. Option B is not the answer; Martin appears to sympathise with the lecturers ('although I don't honestly know what they can be expected to do about it'). Option C is the correct answer; students don't make 'any attempt to engage people's interest' by 'looking at your audience's faces'.

23 Answer: C
Note Kate shows that she has a negative view of tutorials: 'they're often a missed opportunity'. Option A is not the answer; 'the reading list … is fair enough'. Option B is not the answer; we are simply told that tutorials happen every week. Option C is the correct answer; if 'the discussion doesn't seem to extract the main issues', then there isn't a clear focus.

24 Answer: A
Note We are told Martin wants to 'make … improvements' next semester. Option B is not the answer; he's already done that. Option C is not the answer; Martin talks about his reading lists, but he doesn't mention prioritising them. Option A is the correct answer: he says he wants 'to learn to navigate my way round them [websites on the internet] more effectively'.

25 Answer: A
Note Martin and Kate both have problems with the library; the question requires you to identify the problem they both describe. Option B is not the answer; Kate raises this point, but Martin says 'I don't know'. Option C is not the answer; Martin mentions the catalogue, but doesn't say it is difficult to use. Option A is the correct answer: the library closes too soon for Martin and opens too late for Kate – they both want it to be open for longer.

▸ *Questions 26–30*

Step 3 (Test Questions 26–30)

26 Answer: C
Note See step 2 in the Step-by-step guide on page 19.

27 Answer: C
Note Both Martin and Kate will select people to interview ('selecting subjects from larger populations'). Although it is clear that Kate knows more about 'the process', this doesn't mean she will do it alone.

28 Answer: B
Note This is only Kate. Martin isn't going to conduct interviews; he is going to type them up after Kate has done the 'face-to-face stage'.

29 Answer: C
Note Martin and Kate will analyse the statistics – 'run (the results) through statistics programmes' – 'as a joint effort'.

30 Answer: A
Note It's important here to distinguish between giving the presentation (which the question does not ask about) and preparing visuals for the presentation (which the question does ask about). Martin and Kate will give the presentation together ('a joint presentation'), but only Martin will make 'the slides and so on'.

LISTENING Section 4

▸ *Questions 31–34*

Step 2

Question 31
1 Greece, Rome, Norway; **2** 'mound' and 'waste disposal'; **3** 'was identified'; **4** Norway

Question 32
1 No. They could form the answer to another question: What type/method of waste disposal was most common? **2** (broken) pottery, metal objects, organic waste; **3** largely; **4** organic

Step 3 (Test Questions 31–34)

31 Answer: Norway
Note See step 2 above.

32 Answer: organic
Note See step 2 above.

33 Answer: disease
Note 'Link' in the question is expressed as 'produced

convincing evidence of the connection between' in the tapescript, and 'waste' in the question is 'rubbish' in the tapescript. 'Health' is not the correct answer, as this refers to part of the tapescript where 'people, such as doctors, claimed' something in relation to the 'natural processes of decay'.

34 Answer: plastic
Note Plastic, we are told, 'has caused the worst headache' – 'is the biggest problem'. 'Modern consumer goods' is not the answer: firstly, they are not a single invention; secondly, you cannot write this answer in 'no more than one word', as the rubric requires.

▸ *Questions 35–37*

Step 2

1 'Industrialised' is an adjective, not a noun. A 'factor' needs to be a noun, or a noun with an adjective.
2 'The advent of manufacturing' is wrong for two reasons. Firstly, it consists of four words, and the question allows a maximum of two. Secondly, the problem of waste is specifically related to mass manufacturing, not just manufacturing.
3 'Damaging' is an adjective, not a noun. It does not make sense, as 'damaging' cannot lead to an increase in waste.
4 'Amount of things' is wrong for two reasons. Firstly, it consists of three words, and the question allows a maximum of two. Secondly, it has been taken from the tapescript without its context, so it doesn't really make sense. In the tapescript, the 'amount of things' is carefully defined as 'on the planet's surface that don't go away by themselves'.

Step 3 (Test Questions 35–37)

35 Answer: mass manufacturing
Note See step 2 above.

36 Answer: packaging
Note 'Transporting things' is not the correct answer. Transporting goods is one of the reasons why packaging is used, but it is the packaging itself which forms waste.

37 Answer: disposable goods
Note Both words are necessary: 'goods' alone would not describe the reason for the increase in waste, which is that more goods are now designed to be thrown away after use.

▸ *Questions 38–40*

Step 3 (Test Questions 38–40)

38 Answer: C
Note See step 2 in Step-by-step guide on page 23.

39 Answer: E
Note Five possible answers are mentioned. E is the correct answer, because it 'is the dominant process used in the UK'. In the other countries, it is used to varying degrees – from 'heavily' in Germany to 'relatively' in Switzerland and Japan – but not as 'the highest proportion', as the question asks.

40 Answer: D
Note Five possible answers are mentioned. Denmark and Germany are 'reasonably impressive', the UK and Japan 'rather poor'. None of these uses 'the highest proportion', as the question asks, but Switzerland 'tops the table in this respect'.

READING Passage 1

▸ *Questions 1–5*

Step 1

1 Section D, first sentence: 'Lomax immediately set to work'.
2 Yes; **3** Section E; **4** Yes

Step 2

Question 1
1 C; **2** 'explore'; **3** 'unpublished'

Question 2
1 B; **2** 'Division'; **3** 'chief'

Test Questions 1–5

1 Answer: song collections
Note Section D: 'He travelled to libraries ... '. The song collections were 'unpublished'; the 'folk song books' mentioned here were published.

2 Answer: Library of Congress
Note Section D: 'During his stay ... '. Engel worked at the Library of Congress. He thought Lomax might run another organisation, the Archive of Folk Song, one day.

3 Answer: portable recording machine
Note Section D: 'Through funds ... '. The recording equipment is said to be 'state-of-the-art' (the latest kind); this is not said about the 'blank records' he was also given.

4 Answer: rural areas
Note Section E: 'This fact ... high percentage of blacks'. He decided that 'black folk music' in these areas would be his 'primary focus' (what he would mainly concentrate on). These areas were in 'sections of the South'.

5 Answer: prisons and penitentiaries
Note Section E: 'But as they went along ... '. They decided before they started the trip to go to 'laboring camps, particularly lumber camps'. But 'as they went along' (while they were on the trip), prisons and penitentiaries also 'emerged' (appeared or became known to them) as a 'focal point for research' (something they should also concentrate on). Therefore, they added these places to the places in which they did their research.

▸ *Questions 6–10*
Question 6

Step 1

1 A; **2** B

Step 2

1 He was asked to deposit the completed records at the Library of Congress.
2 'without hesitation'

Question 7

Step 1

1 C; **2** B

Step 2

1 writing words and melody by hand and asking the singer to perform the song over and over; **2** 'limitations'

Test Questions 6–10

6 Answer: D
Note 'Lomax simply had to … without hesitation.' He had to sign a contract in section C; he had to deal with various people and problems in section G; section D contains the only reference to him responding quickly.

7 Answer: F
Note From 'Most of John Lomax's peers' to the end of the section. Every section contains a reference to Lomax collecting songs or doing research before his trip; section F deals with the normal methods at the time and Lomax's belief that these were not appropriate for the kind of music he was collecting.

8 Answer: D
Note 'Engel felt that Lomax … to direct the Archive of National Song.' The reasons why Engel thought that Lomax was suitable for it were his 'background' and his 'energy'. Jobs Lomax had already had are mentioned in section A. Jobs held by 'various authorities' are mentioned in section G; section D contains the only official job mentioned in connection with Lomax in the future.

9 Answer: B
Note 'Lomax wanted to embark … survey the whole field.' He originally planned to produce 'four volumes' (books) but then 'modified' (changed) his plan and decided to produce 'a single book' (one book). Lomax's plans and intentions concerning collecting songs are mentioned in every section; the only reference to him changing a plan is in section B.

10 Answer: E
Note 'Lomax's library research … '. His theory was that there was 'a dearth of' (a serious lack of) black folk music in printed collections. This theory was 'reinforced' (confirmed, made stronger) when he did his library research. Lomax's theories on collecting methods are the topic of section F; section G refers to his belief that the songs were 'important'; section E contains the only reference to him proving that one of his theories was correct.

▸ *Questions 11–13*

Option A

Step 1

C

Step 2

1 Macmillan Company; **2** H.S. Latham; **3** two days; **4** Yes

Option B

Step 1

Section E

Step 2

1 black folk song material/black folk music; **2** his library research and his early appreciation of African American folk culture; **3** No; **4** No

Test Questions 11–13

11–13 Answer: D/E/F (in any order)
Note Option D, section G: 'As have hundreds … '. Lomax had to 'persuade his singers to perform' and 'explain to them why their songs were important'. This indicates that at first they were reluctant to (they didn't want to) take part in his project.
Option E, section G: 'He faced the moral problem of … '. He

felt that he had to 'safeguard' (protect) the records and the rights of the singers' to make sure that they weren't exploited (that other people didn't take unfair advantage of them to make money).
Option F, section G: 'He had to overcome the technical problems … when recording outside'. The factors were the noise from various things, but his equipment was not able to reduce the noise while recording because it had no 'wind baffles'. He therefore had to 'overcome' these technical problems.

Option A is not the correct answer because in section C we are told that the only publisher we know that he spoke to was impressed and offered him a contract 'two days later'. Option B is not the correct answer because we are told in sections B and E that his aim was always to collect black folk music, and there is no reference to him changing his aim. Option C is not the correct answer because we are told in sections F and G that his method of field recording was unusual and that he had to protect those who took part, but there is no reference to other researchers doubting his methods in section E or to singers thinking his methods were wrong in section G.

READING Passage 2

▸ *Questions 14–20*

Question 14

Step 3

'conventional'

Question 15

Step 3

'also'

Test Questions 14–20

14 Answer: vi
Note The paragraph is mainly about 'the standard answers' people give when asked why children's literature is important.

15 Answer: x
Note The paragraph is mainly about a further reason why children's literature is important, in addition to the reasons given in paragraph A – that it is 'subversive' (opposed to the normal rules of society).

16 Answer: iii
Note The paragraph is mainly about why children's literature appeals to people. It presents an alternative view of life, it makes fun of conventional views of life, it appeals to the imaginative aspects of people, etc.

17 Answer: viii
Note The main topic of the paragraph is the definition of a children's book and deciding whether a book belongs to that category or not; the writer says that children's books have many things in common with adult fiction, but that people find it easy to decide whether a book can be described as children's literature or not.

18 Answer: i
Note The main point of the paragraph is that writers of children's literature base their books on the idea that children are good people or that they can become good people. The paragraph then contains examples of this and of a book that cannot be considered a children's book because the children

in it do not follow this pattern.

19 Answer: iv
Note The paragraph is mainly about the difference between the adults and the children in children's books. The writer says that this difference is something that means a book can be classified as children's literature, and then gives an example of a book that does not have this characteristic and therefore cannot be called children's literature.

20 Answer: ix
Note The paragraph is mainly about how the subjects of sex, money and death are presented in children's books.

▸ *Questions 21–26*
Question 21

| Step 1 |

Sections B and C

| Step 2 |

1 A; **2** C

| Step 3 |

1 Yes; **2** No; **3** No

Question 22

| Step 1 |

1 D; **2** editors, critics and readers; **3** children's books and adult fiction

| Step 2 |

1 'category'; **2** C

| Step 3 |

1 Yes; **2** No; **3** No

Test Questions 21–26

21 Answer: NOT GIVEN
Note In sections B and C the writer says that children's books are subversive and that they make fun of the adult world, but she does not say whether or not adults realise that their children are reading books that contain these features.

22 Answer: NO
Note In section D the writer says that 'editors' and 'critics', as well as readers, 'seem to have little trouble' in classifying books. This means that they continue to classify them in the way they have done previously, and that the distinctions between categories remain clear.

23 Answer: YES
Note In section E the writer says that Mary and Colin have a 'transformation' (major change) in the book, meaning that they become good. They are therefore like the children she talks about in the previous sentence, who she says are typical examples of the children in children's books.

24 Answer: NO
Note In section E the writer says that *A High Wind in Jamaica* isn't a children's book because the children in it do not have the characteristics that children in what she considers to be children's books have. They are 'irretrievably damaged and corrupted' (they are permanently bad and do not change). The characters of the children are the reason why it isn't a children's book, not the language use, which is not more complex than the language in *Treasure Island*, which the writer implies is a children's book.

25 Answer: YES
Note In section F the writer says that one reason why *A Christmas Carol* isn't a children's ('juvenile') book is 'the helpless passivity' of Tiny Tim. This means that Tiny Tim cannot and does not try to change anything, whereas the child in *Little Lord Fauntleroy* is a good example of a child in what the writer considers to be a children's book because he takes action and manages to 'rescue' a bad adult character.

26 Answer: NOT GIVEN
Note In section G the writer says that money in children's books is not presented in 'real-life' situations but has a 'magical' quality that has nothing to do with the 'simple economic survival' that matters in real life. She is therefore saying that the view of money in children's books is unrealistic. However, she does not say that this is a bad thing; she only says that it is a fact.

READING **Passage 3**

▸ *Questions 27–32*
Question 27

| Step 1 |

1 1st sentence, 1st paragraph; **2** 'emergence'; **3** 'marked'

Question 28

| Step 1 |

1 2nd and 3rd paragraph; **2** 'troubled'; **3** 'unsatisfactory'

| Step 2 |

1 'findings'; **2** 'argument'; **3** genetic(s)

Test Questions 27–32

27 Answer: Stone Age technology
Note In the first sentence of the text, the writer says that according to 'the current account' of human evolution, the development of modern man is indicated by a 'creative explosion' 40,000 years ago, not by Stone Age technology.

28 Answer: genetic(s)
Note In the second paragraph, we are told that Lord Renfrew has doubts about 'genetic findings', and that he thinks the 'genetic argument' is 'unsatisfactory' because people had not developed 'culture' at the time when genetic evidence suggests that the modern human mind was fully formed. At the beginning of the third paragraph, we are also told that he thinks that 'genetics does not tell the whole story'.

29 Answer: tools
Note At the end of the third paragraph, we are told that cave art was a much bigger development than the 'detailed changes in tools'.

30 Answer: engravings
Note In the second sentence of the fourth paragraph, there is a reference to the art found in Creswell Crags in Britain. Engravings are an art form involving designs being cut into a hard surface.

31 Answer: permanent villages; agriculture
Note At the end of the fourth paragraph, we are told that Lord Renfrew thinks that major developments in the modern mind 'kicked in' (began to have a real effect) when permanent villages were set up and plants and animals began to be used in agriculture. Agriculture is said to have been 'born' (started, established) then. Plants and animals would not be a correct answer here because they were not 'established' then.

32 Answer: mathematics; written language

Note In the last paragraph, we are told that the 'concept of property' (the idea of owning possessions) began in villages. This, 'in turn' (as a result), produced a need for mathematics so that a 'tally of' (a record of the number of) possessions could be kept, and for written language so that these possessions could be described.

▶ *Questions 33–40*

Step 1

A beginning of 2nd paragraph; second half of 4th paragraph; second half of last paragraph
B 1st paragraph, 3rd paragraph, beginning of 4th paragraph
C second half of 2nd paragraph
D first half of 4th paragraph

Step 2

Question 33

1 the 2nd paragraph; **2** 'fully developed'; **3** 'software (culture)' ('software' here is used to compare the mind with a computer); **4** 'tens of millennia'

Question 34

1 4th paragraph; **2** 'revolution'; **3** 'kicked in'; **4** 'work together in a more settled way'

Test Questions 33–40

33 Answer: C
Note 2nd paragraph: Genetic evidence suggests that the brain was 'fully developed' 60,000 years ago, but Lord Renfrew says humans lacked 'culture' then.

34 Answer: A
Note 4th paragraph: Lord Renfrew thinks that the 'real revolution' happened 10,000 years ago, when people began to 'work together in a more settled way'.

35 Answer: B
Note 1st paragraph: When the 'creative explosion' happened 40,000 years ago, various different art forms began to appear. In this context, an 'explosion' is an enormous increase, and the art forms included art for the body (beads, pendants, tattoos), paintings (of various subjects) and sculptures (stone figures).

36 Answer: B
Note 1st paragraph: the 'cultural Big Bang' is the 'creative explosion' mentioned earlier in the paragraph, which happened 40,000 years ago. This 'coincided with' (happened at the same time as) the time when people 'reached Europe' after a journey that began in Africa. The migration was therefore to Europe.

37 Answer: D
Note 4th paragraph: The art created 70,000 years ago and found in South Africa indicates that people were capable of abstract thought and modern behaviour at a time earlier than had generally been thought to be the case. This art therefore suggests that what is commonly believed is not true – it casts doubts on the conventional view.

38 Answer: A
Note 2nd paragraph: there is a 'dogma' (a firm belief, a fixed idea) that the modern mind developed in Europe 40,000 years ago (as explained in the first paragraph), but Lord Renfrew thinks it developed 10,000 years ago in the Middle East. His view about the location therefore differs from what is generally thought.

39 Answer: B
Note 3rd paragraph: we are told that not much physical change happened 40,000 years ago (there is little difference between *Homo sapiens* and *Homo erectus*), and that the only change then that 'really strikes you' (is really noticeable) is in the art produced.

40 Answer: A
Note Last paragraph: Lord Renfrew says that firm ideas concerning how the modern human developed cannot be gained ('We have not solved anything … ') until people have discovered exactly what happened 10,000 years ago. Research to discover this is taking place in three places that are mentioned.

WRITING Task 1

Step 1

1 B
2 **a** Occitan; **b** 610,000; 1,060,000; **c** 240,000
3 **a** Alsatian; **b** 600,000; 240,000; **c** 400,000
4 Corsican
5 No

Step 2

1 C; **2** C

Step 3

Example sentences
Although in the past over 600,000 people spoke Occitan to their children habitually and over 1 million spoke it occasionally, only about 240,000 people now speak the language to their own children.
The charts show that *not as many* parents speak a regional language to their children as in the past.
It is clear that there has been *a fall in* the number of people speaking regional languages to their children.

See sample answer on page 199.

Notes
Content points
The answer should include an overall view of the data, which is that the number of people speaking regional languages to their children has fallen a lot. It should also contain examples of data from the charts that illustrate this, comparing the number of people who spoke certain languages to their children in the past and the number of people who speak those languages to their children now.

Organisation
The general point comes in the first sentence here. It is followed by comparisons between the numbers in the first two tables and the numbers in the third table. The various languages are discussed in the same order as they appear in the charts. This is a clear way of organising the data, because it begins with the languages spoken the most and progresses to those spoken the least. The last sentence adds a further conclusion. This is optional, but gives a coherent end to the answer and shows a full understanding of the data.

Use of language
Linking: To link information and points, phrases such as *for example*, *in the case of*, etc. are used here. This means that the answer flows well, is easy to follow and presents information and points logically.
Grammatical structures: Structures for comparison are required. Examples here are *a great deal lower than*, *even greater*, *not as high* and *as much as*.

Vocabulary: Words and phrases used for talking about things rising and falling are required. Examples here are *the fall* and *decrease in.*

WRITING Task 2

Step 1

1/2/4/5/7

Steps 2 and 3

See sample answer on page 199.

Notes
Content points
The answer fully addresses each aspect of the task. It discusses the causes of stress today, with examples. It compares stress today with the situation in the past, giving examples of these matters. It presents an opinion on whether amounts of stress today are exaggerated and an opinion on the difference between attitudes to stress today and in the past.

Organisation
The answer follows a logical progression and is easy to follow. Each point is dealt with one by one, with examples. The answer is appropriately divided into paragraphs, each paragraph dealing with a separate aspect: the first paragraph discusses stress today, the second discusses the situation in the past and the final paragraph presents a coherent conclusion, with a clear opinion.

Use of language
Linking: Phrases such as *In my opinion* and *The impression I have* are used to introduce opinions. Phrases such as *These days* and *In the past* are used to introduce periods of time. *Like* is used to link examples with the point they illustrate.
Grammatical structures: *Used to be* is used to talk about something that was true for a long time in the past. *Have to* is used to talk about actions that are necessary for people.
Vocabulary: Words and phrases appropriate for the topic, such as *get ill, meet targets, suffer from stress, have a big effect on, in a hurry, the pace of life, stressful, take for granted* and *get on with* are used throughout.

SPEAKING Part 3

Step 3

1 **c** – Question E
2 **e** – Question A
3 **b** – Question D
4 **a** – Question C
5 **d** – Question B

TEST 2

LISTENING Section 1

▸ *Questions 1–10*

Step 1

1 A; **2** A or C; **3** B; **4** (probably) B or D; **5** A; **6** (probably) A; **7** A; **8** C; **9** A; **10** A

Step 3 (Test Questions 1–10)

1 **Answer: Andrew Sharpe**
   Note 'Surname' (in the tapescript) means 'last name' (on the form). 'Like a knife' refers to 'sharp', and you are told that it

has 'an E on the end'. For the first name, the form asks about who booked the holiday.

2 **Answer: Beaconsfield House**
   Note You need to fill in the middle line of the address, and the word you are not expected to know (Beaconsfield) is spelt out for you.

3 **Answer: 0374 55793**
   Note Two telephone numbers are given. The form asks for a 'daytime' number, which is the woman's work number. She asks, 'Do you mean during the day?' and the man checks that she means 'normal office hours'.

4 **Answer: MH66G4**
   Note You need to listen carefully to avoid writing '7 4'. You also need to listen carefully to take the whole reference from the two parts of what the woman says: 'MH' and then '66G4'. '66' could be expressed as 'six six' or 'sixty-six' or, as here, 'double six'.

5 **Answer: credit card**
   Note The man asks if she booked through her employer, but this was not the company she and her husband used. She says they used a credit card company. When the man fills in the form, he is making notes, so he does not use words like 'a' and 'the'. Be careful: the rubric tells you to write no more than two words, and 'a credit card' would be three words. Notice that there is some support for the answer: she mentions the 'bill', which helps to confirm that she is talking about a credit card company.

6 **Answer: Gold Star**
   Note The man asks if she had insurance which she arranged with the booking, but this is not the answer to the question, as her insurance 'came under' (was covered by) her Gold Star policy. Notice that 'Gold Star' is two words, so you should not write anything else in the gap.

7 **Answer: Mid-winter**
   Note This is the type of holiday – what 'it was called'. You should not try to write anything about the 'brochure'; all the types of holiday will be in the brochure.

8 **Answer: 16 January**
   Note Two dates are mentioned: 21 January and 16 January. The form asks for the date the holiday 'commenced' or 'started', so this is the one which is correct for the form.

9 **Answer: taxi**
   Note The woman explains the first problem in detail. In open situation, several different notes could be made about what she says. However, you must write what will correctly fit the gap and you mustn't change any words. 'Taxi' is the only possible answer; words such as 'meet', 'wait', 'inconvenient', etc. do not fit the gap.

10 **Answer: bicycle**
   Note Although the woman explains the problem in detail, you must write what will fit in the gap on the form. You should not write about 'three' or 'four' bicycles, but simply write in the grammatically fitting 'bicycle'.

LISTENING Section 2

▸ *Questions 11–15*

Step 3 (Test Questions 11–15)

11 **Answer: D**
   Note 'Heavy lifting' is involved in this job. You should not confuse 'a varied job … ' or 'certain times of day' with option B.

12 **Answer: A**
   Note You 'need to have a valid driving licence'. You should

not confuse 'travel by car' with option G. Also, the reference to 'basic computer skills such as word processing' is not the same as option H.

13 Answer: C
Note 'The Hotel will provide you with all your meals' means that they are 'free meals'.

14 Answer: F
Note You need to take this answer in two parts: 'they will also train you … ' and ' … issue you with a certificate'.

15 Answer: E
Note 'The Hotel will require you to work nights' means that you will have to work 'late shifts'. This is on a regular basis, so option B is not correct, although you hear the words 'flexible' and 'work'.

▶ *Questions 16–20*

Step 1

1 Examples could include: *First, you should … , Before anything else, you need to … , The next thing to do is … , After that, you should … , The following task is … ,* etc.
2 Examples could include: *Fill in, fill out, write answers to … ,* etc.

Step 3 (Test Questions 16–20)

16 Answer: personal information
Note The form is clearly described as a 'personal information' form, and it is important to write this with correct spelling. 'Complete' in the flow chart means 'fill in' on the recording.

17 Answer: skills
Note The questionnaire is 'about your skills', so you should write 'skills' in the gap.

18 Answer: general
Note The word order in the flow chart is different from that on the recording, and you should extract 'general' as the correct word to describe the course. 'Go on' in the flow chart means 'attend' on the recording.

19 Answer: role-play
Note Various answers might appear possible here – 'helpful', 'realistic', 'fun' – but only 'role-play' actually describes the activities within the course.

20 Answer: video
Note 'About themselves and the work involved' on the recording means 'about the hotel' in the flow chart. In the flow chart, the passive 'will be sent' (from a job candidate's point of view) means 'they'll post you' on the recording.

LISTENING Section 3

▶ *Questions 21–26*

Step 2

1 following the plan; **2** experience of collaborating; **3** we've fallen behind our schedule; **4** The rubric tells you to write no more than three words; 'actually' is not an essential piece of information for the gap in the sentence.

Step 3 (Test Questions 21–26)

21 Answer: following the plan
Note This is the only answer that you can take from what David says to fit the gap in the sentence grammatically. He refers to 'problems of various kinds', a lack of 'experience of collaborating on projects' and 'co-ordination', but these will

not fit the gap. 'Progress on the project has been slow' in the sentence means 'we've fallen behind our schedule' on the recording.

22 Answer: individual responsibilities
Note Both words are needed for the sentence to reflect the recording accurately. 'Targets' are mentioned, but as something that had been established adequately.

23 Answer: advice service
Note 'Suggests' in the sentence relates to 'I think you'd find … useful' on the recording. 'Group meetings' is not the correct answer, as these are what they have had.

24 Answer: reference section
Note David is worried about the fact that there may be too many people to interview, but not enough in the reference section. Not being 'adequate' in the question means not being 'solid enough' on the recording.

25 Answer: methodology
Note Dr Wilson refers to being 'pragmatic', but this adjective would not fit the gap grammatically. 'Results' are also mentioned, but not the thing to focus on by the project group members. 'Focus on' in the question means 'ensure … is really strong' on the recording.

26 Answer: websites
Note 'Could make more use of' in the question means 'haven't exploited as fully as we might' on the recording. 'Some' before the gap in the sentence would not fit with 'the internet', but does with 'websites'. 'Journals' is not the answer, because these are things that she has made full use of already.

▶ *Questions 27–30*

Step 2

1 A, E, H; **2** A; **3** H; **4** C, F, H; **5** H
Option H is the correct answer.

Step 3 (Test Questions 27–30)

27 Answer: H
Note This is introduced with 'get down to work after lunch'. Dr Wilson talks about 'an exhibition at the library in the university'. Although 'photographs' and 'newspapers' are heard on the recording, they are both the contents of the exhibition, so option A is not correct.

28 Answer: B
Note This is introduced with 'the following morning'. 'Interview' is 'talk to' on the recording, which is supported by mention of 'tape recorder', 'questions' and 'tells you'. 'Local historian' is 'expert on the area's history' on the recording. Option C is not correct; although Jarvis Gregson works at the City Library, the activity is not to listen to tapes there, but to make them of the interview.

29 Answer: G
Note This is introduced with 'back to work on Wednesday morning'. 'Tour city centre' is 'walk round (the central area) methodically' on the recording. 'Old maps' are 'plans … from different periods' on the recording. Option D is not correct; although shops are mentioned, the task is not to study shop ownership as such, but to follow a wider task, which includes shops' development.

30 Answer: E
Note This is introduced with 'in the afternoon'. 'Take photographs' is 'use a camera to get some pictures' on the recording. The castle 'area' is 'the buildings and spaces around it' in the recording. Option F is not the answer, although you hear a reference to the City Library's archives.

▶ *Questions 31–35*

Step 3 (Test Questions 31–35)

31 **Answer: competition**
Note 'For a' introduces 'competition' on the recording – the reason for or function of their drawing it. 'Kitchen table' would need 'on a' before the gap; 'millennium landmarks' would need something like 'as one of a number of' before the gap.

32 **Answer: British Airways**
Note 'Formed a partnership with' means 'became a partner' on the recording. The press are mentioned, but not as partners.

33 **Answer: invented**
Note 'Components had to be' means 'parts … needed to be' on the recording. Notice that although the recording provides detail about the reason for this ('simply because they had never existed before'), the task presents a summary text, which does not reproduce everything that is heard on the recording.

34 **Answer: tides**
Note 'Co-ordinated with' means 'timed to coincide with' on the recording. 'Bridges' is not the correct answer you can only co-ordinate things which you can manipulate, and you cannot manipulate a bridge in this sense.

35 **Answer: distilled water**
Note 'Only … is used to clean the glass' means 'demands such as washing all its glass with nothing but … having to be met' on the recording. Water alone would not be an adequate answer, as there is nothing unusually demanding about using water to clean glass.

▶ *Questions 36–40*

Step 3 (Test Questions 36–40)

36 **Answer: tension**
Note This is introduced with a reference to the ground, and then we are told that 'tension piles' were being driven into the ground. We are also told that 'this was the first step'.

37 **Answer: base cap**
Note We are told that the 'base cap was installed over them as a kind of lock', and then that the plinths – the next step, and listed element of the diagram – were on that, 'pointing up'.

38 **Answer: A-frame**
Note We are told about this between the mention of the plinths and the spindle. We are told that the A-frame 'was attached' to the plinths. Although A-frame is perhaps a rather technical term, the visual similarity of it to the alphabetical letter 'A' is made clear: 'like a giant letter'.

39 **Answer: rings**
Note We are told about these between the passenger capsule and the final element. The difficult word 'mounting' is given, and their function is explained ('linked by mounting rings that would support eager viewers … ').

40 **Answer: boarding platform**
Note We are told that this is 'underneath', so it can be located easily on the diagram. Information about its purpose is suggested ('the first thing the visitor encounters').

▶ *Question 1*

Step 2

Option A
1 Yes; **2** No
Option B
1 Yes; **2** No
Option C
1 Yes; **2** smaller
Option D
1 Yes; **2** No

Test Question 1

1 **Answer: C**
Note The answer is located in the sentence beginning 'Historians may come to discern … '. The writer is saying that emigration from Africa, Asia and South America in the 20th and later centuries may be seen to be far greater than emigration from Europe to the US in the period in the past he is describing (the 19th century). Option A is incorrect because he is saying that emigration may be greater in later periods. Option B is incorrect because he does not say that he doubts the figure of 35 million. Option D is incorrect because, although he mentions that the French differed from other nationalities because they didn't emigrate as much as the others, he doesn't talk about what happened to different nationalities after they emigrated in the 1st paragraph.

▶ *Questions 2–9*

Step 1

1 the 2nd paragraph; **2** No. It deals with particular reasons.

Step 2

Question 2
1 'maintained'; **2** 'huge'

Question 3
'heavier'

Question 4
'avoid'

Test Questions 2–9

2 **Answer: armies; navies**
Note The writer says that every great European power 'maintained' (kept) 'huge armies and navies', and that these became more expensive because of the 'increasing cost' that resulted from the need to have 'up-to-date equipment'.

3 **Answer: taxes**
Note Big armies and navies 'implied' (meant, resulted in) bigger and bigger ('heavier') taxes to finance them and many people couldn't pay.

4 **Answer: mass conscription**
Note Big armies and navies required lots of people to be forced by law to join them, and many people didn't want to do that.

5 **Answer: peasants**
Note Agricultural developments in other countries and improvements in the transport of agricultural goods meant that it became too expensive to pay peasants in Europe for agricultural work. Peasants could not 'compete effectively in the world market' (they were too expensive to employ in comparison with workers from other countries).

6 **Answer: free trade**
Note Restrictions on trade were removed and free trade was introduced instead. In this context 'arrival' means 'introduction' or 'establishment'.

7 **Answer: literacy**
Note One reason why newspapers became much more widely read was that a lot more people could read. Literacy was 'rapidly spreading' – there was a much greater amount of it and it was quickly becoming more widespread.

8 **Answer: New states**
Note A number of major events in Europe resulted in the formation of new states and the disappearance of old ones. In this context, 'came into being' means 'had been formed'.

9 **Answer: new industries**
Note There were many changes connected with trade and one was that new industries created ('stimulated') 'new wants' – people began to want the new goods produced by the new industries.

▶ *Questions 10–13*
Question 10

Step 1

1 the 3rd paragraph; **2** 'was over'

Step 2

B

Question 11

Step 1

1 the 3rd paragraph; **2** 'adventurers'

Step 2

B

Test Questions 10–13

10 **Answer: E**
Note 3rd paragraph: The writer says that after the Great Famine, the situation was 'not much better' because other famines followed and the Irish economy was weak. These problems clearly affected the people living in Ireland.

11 **Answer: C**
Note 3rd paragraph: The writer says that people who had emigrated sent letters and money back to people in Ireland, and that these things 'encouraged' the people receiving them to emigrate, too.

12 **Answer: G**
Note 4th paragraph: the writer says that there was a 'drift' (movement) of American people away from agriculture at the time, but that it was not big enough to supply enough American workers for factories. Because 'times were good on the family farm', the 'supply of Americans' moving off the land and going to work in factories was 'too small to meet the demand', and so employers needed to employ immigrants.

13 **Answer: B**
Note 4th paragraph: the writer says that the 'transcontinental' railroad companies 'badly needed settlers' on their land because they couldn't make profits if people were not producing crops on the land near the railroads which would then be transported on the railroads. The 'settlers' were therefore agricultural workers.

READING Passage 2

▶ *Questions 14–20*

Step 1

A 1; 5; last; **B** 2; **C** 4; **D** 5; 6; 7; 8; **E** 8

Step 2

Question 14
1 the 2nd paragraph; **2** 'hitch-hiked a ride'

Question 15
1 B; **2** the 2nd paragraph; **3** Streptococcus; **4** Captain Conrad

Test Questions 14–20

14 **Answer: B**
Note 2nd paragraph: The 'colony of bacteria' found on the Moon had arrived on board the Surveyor probes.

15 **Answer: A**
Note 1st and 2nd paragraph: It was amazing that the Streptococcus bacteria had survived after their journey to the moon and because of the environment on the Moon. They arrived in the Surveyor probes, but they were discovered by the Apollo craft that Captain Conrad took to the Moon.

16 **Answer: D**
Note 8th paragraph: Beagle's heat shield was also its 'biological shield'. It was intended that it became so hot that no bacteria could survive on it. Therefore, bacteria on the 'casing' (outer structure) were not a problem.

17 **Answer: E**
Note 8th paragraph: Mars Express was designed so that its 'trajectory' (the direction of its flight) could be changed during its journey ('corrected en route') if something went wrong.

18 **Answer: A**
Note Last paragraph: At first, moon rocks found on Apollo missions were brought back in vacuum glove boxes, and in later missions they were kept in nitrogen.

19 **Answer: C**
Note 4th paragraph: The Galileo probe was destroyed because there was a fear that it might have bacteria on it that would be harmful to Europa, which was its destination. This action was carried out by 'smashing it' into Jupiter (causing it to crash into Jupiter and be broken into small pieces).

20 **Answer: A**
Note 1st paragraph: The writer says that some people believe that Apollo's most important discovery was rocks, but others think its most important discovery related to 'technological spin-offs' – advances in technology that resulted from what was discovered.

▶ *Questions 21–26*

Step 1

1 6th paragraph, 1st sentence; **2** 7th paragraph, last sentence

Step 2

Question 21
'specially put together'

Question 22
mikes, monitors, a piece of paper

Test Questions 21–26

21 **Answer: clean room**
Note 6th paragraph: This was built in a building that used to be a garage where vehicles used by the BBC (British Broadcasting Corporation) for broadcasting from outside studios were stored.

22 **Answer: glass wall**
Note 7th paragraph: The people assembling Beagle were given information from outside the part where it was being assembled through the wall by use of microphones (mikes) and monitors (screens), or pieces of paper stuck onto the wall, and the people giving the information did not go in and out of the part where it was being assembled.

23 **Answer: electronic equipment**
Note 7th paragraph: Bacteria on electronic equipment were killed at low temperatures by something created in a microwave because the high temperatures used on other things would have damaged the electronic equipment (it 'can't cope with those sorts of temperatures').

24 **Answer: gamma radiation**
Note 7th paragraph: Bacteria on parachutes and gas bags were destroyed by gamma radiation. They were 'zapped with' (treated with great force, hit hard by) gamma radiation.

25 **Answer: beards/facial hair**
Note 6th and 7th paragraph: Beards and facial hair in general were not allowed (there was 'a ban on' beards and facial hair was 'banned'), presumably because they could carry bacteria. This applied to the people going into the part where Beagle was actually being assembled.

26 **Answer: fans**
Note 6th paragraph: In the part where Beagle was assembled, 'an enormous set of' (a very large number of, a lot of) fans 'circulated and filtered' the air (distributed it round the room and kept it pure).

READING Passage 3

▶ *Questions 27–34*

Step 1

1st sentence, 1st paragraph

Step 2

Question 27
1 'element'; **2** 'genres'; **3** 'lacks'; **4** 'narrative'

Question 28
They 'often cannot understand it'.

Test Questions 27–34

27 **Answer: story-telling**
Note This has the same meaning as 'narrative' in the text.

28 **Answer: confusing**
Note People 'cannot understand' television news, which means they find it confusing.

29 **Answer: crucial**
Note The text states that 'the main point (the headline) comes right at the beginning'. This means that the most important (crucial) information comes first.

30 **Answer: secondary**
Note The text states that 'less and less important things' come next. 'Secondary' means 'of less importance'.

31 **Answer: step-by-step**
Note The text refers to fiction having something that is

'gradually solved'. This means that it is solved in stages, not all at once; 'step-by-step progress' is progress involving various stages towards a final result.

32 **Answer: mysterious**
Note The text says that 'there is no enigma' in television news. An enigma is something that people do not understand or find strange but are fascinated by or very interested in; 'mysterious' means strange and interesting.

33 **Answer: creative**
Note The text refers to people trying to 'design' a television programme, which means have the ideas for and create one. The 'creative' process therefore refers to designing a programme.

34 **Answer: contrary**
Note The text is saying that if people actually tried to create a programme that had all the features a programme should not have, they would design the television news; in other words, television news has all the features a programme should not have. It is therefore completely different from what an interesting programme is like. 'Contrary to' means 'completely different from' or 'opposite to'.

▶ *Question 35–40*

Step 1

1 the 1st and 2nd paragraph; **2** the 2nd and 3rd paragraph
3 the 4th paragraph; **4** B

Step 2

Question 35
1 'Moreover': 2nd paragraph
2 'overstress the importance of'
3 'content'

Question 36
1 the 3rd paragraph; **2** Yes; **3** No; **4** No

Test Questions 35–40

35 **Answer: TRUE**
Note 2nd paragraph: The writer of the text says that there are problems with Lewis's theories; there are 'counter-examples of his arguments' (examples which suggest that his theories are not correct), and he concentrates too much on the 'formal features' of programmes rather than on the important matter of their content.

36 **Answer: NOT GIVEN**
Note 3rd paragraph: Lewis says that people prefer soap operas to television news because their own lives have more in common with what happens in soap operas than with what they see on television news. They can 'identify with' people in soap operas, but television news presents them with a world that is 'remote' and 'distant' and they feel 'disconnected' from what happens in it. However, we are not told that he thinks it is a pity that this is the case; we are not told whether or not he gives a view on whether this is a good or bad thing.

37 **Answer: FALSE**
Note 3rd and last paragraph: According to Lewis, the television news could come 'from another planet' as far as many viewers are concerned. It shows them a 'distant world' that is 'disconnected from' their own experience of life. They feel 'alienated' from it but have no 'alternative perspective' to use in order to evaluate what they see. This means that they have no personal knowledge or experience that is useful to them when watching the news. The problem is not that the

news differs completely from (contradicts) what they have experienced, it is that it has no relationship with what they know or have experienced.

38 **Answer: TRUE**
Note Last paragraph: 'This is not to suggest …'. Lewis says that people talk about 'not believing what you see on television' and have a generally 'cynical' attitude to it, but that they also 'fall back on what it said on TV' (use or rely on because they have nothing else to use or rely on). In other words, they have an inconsistent attitude (one that changes at different times) – they say they don't believe what they see on television news, but in fact they do believe it because they have no knowledge or experience that would enable them to know it is wrong.

39 **Answer: TRUE**
Note Last paragraph: 'Parkin had argued …'. Parkin says that working-class people 'accept propositions from the dominant ideology at an abstract level' (in theory, they accept the beliefs that are most commonly held in their culture), but in practice, they find ways in which these beliefs do not have to apply to them in their own lives (in the 'particular circumstances of their own situation'). They therefore regard themselves as exceptions to these general rules.

40 **Answer: NOT GIVEN**
Note Last paragraph: In the last sentence, the writer says that people tend to disbelieve the media in general, but that on every individual matter that arises they are 'pushed back into reliance on' (forced to rely on) what the media are saying, because they have no way of proving that it is untrue. He is therefore saying that they are forced to be passive consumers of the media, but he does not say that they are wrong in this or that there is anything they can do about it.

WRITING Task 1

Step 1

1 B
2 **a** 190, 5ᵗʰ company; **b** 56, 1ˢᵗ company
3 **a** two; **b** 4ᵗʰ company
4 **a** 93%, 5ᵗʰ company; **b** 8%, 4ᵗʰ company
5 three
6 two

Step 2

1 B; 2 A

Step 3

Example sentences
Apart from the company that came fifth, all of the companies have fewer than 100 members of staff.
The company that came fifth has a *far* higher staff turnover than the company that came first.
The five companies *differ from* each other in many ways.

See sample answer on page 200.

Notes
Content points
The answer should include the fact that there is no consistent pattern in what makes these companies popular with their staff. It should mention each category and point out examples of where companies have things in common and where there are exceptions and differences.

Organisation
The general point comes first here, and the rest of the answer

illustrates ways in which this general point is true. Each category is discussed in the same order as they appear in the table – this is a logical and clear way to present the information. The last section of the answer presents further general conclusions. This is optional, but it demonstrates a full understanding of the data and an ability to bring together the data as a whole.

Use of language
Linking: To link information and points, phrases such as *In terms of, As for* and *With regard to* are used to introduce the different categories. *Apart from* is used to talk about an exception. *Although* and *However* are also used to introduce contrasts in the data.
Grammatical structures: Structures for comparison are required. Examples here are *fairly similar, even higher, far more, comparatively low* and *extremely low*. Note that the present simple verb tense is used throughout, but that the past simple could also have been used; the important thing is that the present or the past is used consistently throughout. It would be wrong to use a mixture of present and past.
Vocabulary: Words and phrases used for talking about differences and similarities are required. Examples here are *have some things in common, differ greatly* and *no consistent features*.

WRITING Task 2

Step 1

1/3/5/6/9

See sample answer on page 200.

Notes
Content points
The answer deals with everything mentioned in the task. It discusses the increase in international travel and the spread of mass media, and the advantages of each of these. It then discusses disadvantages of each of these. It ends with a firm conclusion that answers the question asked.

Organisation
The answer flows well, with a clear progression. Each aspect of the task is dealt with in a logical order. Ideas and views follow each other logically and are linked well. The answer is appropriately divided into paragraphs.

Use of language
Linking: Phrases such as *First of all* and *In conclusion* are used to introduce parts of an argument. *On the whole* is used to introduce a general conclusion. *As a result* is used to introduce a result. *Although, though* and *whereas* are used for linking contrasting facts and ideas.
Grammatical structures: Comparatives such as *more ... than* are required. Phrases beginning with *what* and *how* are used (*how others live, what is going on, what happens,* etc.) as objects of verbs. Reflexives are also used appropriately (*see for themselves, understanding of each other*).
Vocabulary: Words and phrases connected with things being available are used (*affordable, give people access to*). Words connected with feelings (*envious, understanding*) are required. Words and phrases linking causes with results are also required (*cause, lead to*).

SPEAKING Part 1

Step 1

Generally, it is quite easy to understand what this person says. They provide adequate answers to the examiner's questions. The information they give is more than the minimum, with useful detail. However, there are a number of grammar mistakes, and several of these are basic mistakes.

Step 2

1 to; **2** on; **3** the; **4** read; **5** —; **6** are; **7** delayed; **8** at; **9** —; **10** being

SPEAKING Part 2

Step 1

This is a clear and informative performance. The requirements of the task are addressed, and the information is presented in a logical fashion. The listener would know what had happened and understand the effect of the conversation on the speaker's life. There are one or two minor mistakes. In places, greater use of linking devices could be made to make the talk more coherent.

Step 2

1 b; **2** g; **3** f; **4** a; **5** d; **6** h; **7** e; **8** c

SPEAKING Part 3

Step 1

This person engages fully and effectively with the examiner's questions. The answers provided use a wide range of language and present clear and thoughtful responses. Linking devices and vocabulary are employed to help fluency and the result is a very good performance.

Step 2

A 1 rely **2** consider **3** clarify; **B 1** calculate **2** considerable **3** imitate; **C 1** claim **2** suspect **3** significant; **D 1** develop **2** immediate **3** remote; **E 1** beneficial **2** increasingly **3** hunched

TEST 3

LISTENING Section 1

1 **Answer: 76**
   Note You have to pick out the number which answers the question of how many members are in the club at the present time. 70 is wrong (last year's figure); 60 is wrong (regular attendance); 85 is wrong (next year's predicted figure).

2 **Answer: £30 per year**
   Note It is important to write all the elements of the answer. '£' is important, as '30' on its own does not tell you how much you need to pay. 'Per year' is important too, as £30 is a very different expense if it is a one-off payment or monthly or yearly. You also need to rule out £40 (Standard membership) and £25 (Family membership).

3 **Answer: teacher or parent**
   Note You need to put both types of person here to answer the question properly. 'And' would not be correct, as it would suggest that you need to get two signatures. Notice that 'get a signature' in the question matches 'to sign your form' on the recording.

4 **Answer: 3 weeks**
   Note Here you need to match the question ('process a membership application') with the recording ('deal with it and get a confirmation of acceptance with a membership card out to you'). You should not write 'a year' or 'one month' as these refer to other aspects of membership.

5 **Answer: every month**
   Note Write what you hear on the recording ('every month'). Don't try to change it. 'Two weeks' is not correct: that is how often the rides might take place in future.

6 **Answer: 60 km**
   Note 'Usually' in the question matches 'is about average' on the recording. '100 km' is how far they do not go. It is important to include 'km'. The rides would be very different if they were 60 meters or miles.

7 **Answer: (a) safety certificate**
   Note You need to read the question carefully and see that 'What' requires an answer that includes a noun. 'Roadworthy' and 'checked' are not nouns. 'Shops' is a noun, but would not make sense as an answer to the question. The rubric allows three words for the answer, so you can include 'a' if you want, but it is not a mistake to leave it out.

8 **Answer: (on) July 14**
   Note The question asks 'when' (not 'how often') and 'next', so you must not write 'twice a year' or 'August 17th'. It is not necessary to write 'on', but it is not a mistake.

9 **Answer: (a) picnic**
   Note You hear the man say 'May 5th' on the recording. You should not try to write anything about the membership being 'through', as this is not an event that will take place on May 5th. It is not necessary to write 'a', but it is not a mistake if you do.

10 **Answer: 15%**
    Note You can hear the information for this question being prepared on the recording The man says 'discount with Wheels' and the woman confirms that this is 'the shop'. 'Discount' in the question matches 'a … reduction' on the recording. You do not need to write anything else because the '15%' answers the question completely.

LISTENING Section 2

11 **Answer: 2.30/7.30 pm**
    Note The information is clearly introduced on the recording with 'Times for the event'. You need to put both times: this is clear in the timetable (' … and … ') as well as on the recording ('twice each day').

12 **Answer: CD**
    Note You hear 'the foyer shop will be selling a' in the recording, and this matches the timetable's 'Can get a … in shop'. All you need to write is 'CD'.

13 **Answer: separate programme**
    Note 'See the' in the timetable matches 'look in the' on the recording. It is important to include the word 'separate' because this is different from the normal one. Information such as 'details of performers' or 'ticket prices' would not be relevant here: the heading in the timetable is 'Times'.

14 **Answer: dance festival**
    Note 'Annual' in the timetable matches with 'this year … again … last year' on the recording. 'Performances' would not be correct: it does not represent enough information. Both 'dance' and 'festival' must be included to provide complete information for the timetable.

15 **Answer: 4 continents**
    Note The word 'from' in the timetable is important to notice. It helps you to match the timetable with 'groups representing as many as 4 continents' on the recording. It is not relevant to try to include 'as many as', and you are told to use no more than three words and/or a number. 'Styles' would not be a correct answer because it could not follow 'from'.

16 Answer: 14–20 March
Note You know that this part of the timetable is for dates, so you need to be ready to hear and write a date or dates. You should follow the pattern of this part of the timetable to write your answer.

17 Answer: *Love and Hope*
Note The recording says 'cinema', so you should be ready for a reference to a film. The : and the '...' round the answer space tell you that you need to write a name or title. All three words are important because this is the actual title of the film.

18 Answer: producer
Note 'Talk' in the timetable matches 'short lecture' on the recording. 'By' in the timetable tells you that you need to write who talks, not who they talk to (the 'audience').

19 Answer: singing competition
Note 'To be confirmed' in the timetable matches 'the times aren't fixed yet' on the recording, so you know that the next information should be what the event is. You need to write both 'singing' and 'competition' to present the complete information. It is not necessary to include 'a', because 'a' or 'the' are not used in the timetable for the other events. However, because you can use up to three words, it is not a mistake if you do write 'a'.

20 Answer: shown on TV
Note 'It will be' in the timetable tells you that the answer here is not only a noun. These words in the timetable match 'is going to be' on the recording. It would not be enough to write only 'TV'. It would not make sense as a note within the timetable.

21 Answer: B
Note 'Illustrations' in B matches 'pictures, the diagrams and photos' on the recording, and we are told that these 'were quite strange' – 'unusual' in option B. Although 'detail' is mentioned, this is not the same point as in option C. 'Arguments' are also mentioned, but not 'clear' ones, as in option D.

22 Answer: I
Note 'Not suitable for new students' in option I matches 'high level ... first year' on the recording. Although we are told that 'it was rather dense' on the recording, this is not fully the same as option C. The index is 'excellent', not 'inadequate', as in option A.

23 Answer: D
Note 'Presents clear arguments' in option D matches 'easy to follow ... step-by-step' on the recording. 'Index' is mentioned, but not as in option A. 'Photos' are mentioned, but not as in option B. 'Translated' is mentioned, but not as in option G.

24 Answer: F
Note 'Omits important historical facts' in option F matches Ben and Tom's exchange on the recording. This is the opposite of options C and H.

25 Answer: A
Note 'Inadequate index' in option A matches what Tom says about this dissertation. What he says is the opposite of options C and D; other options are not referred to.

26 Answer: large private houses
Note Ben mentions 'plans' and 'layout', so you should be prepared for a reference to 'drawings'. Jane says that 'small houses' will not be useful enough. This means that it is important to include all three words of the answer here in order to make the distinction.

27 Answer: window designs
Note 'Internet' in the flow chart matches 'web' on the recording. 'Get images' matches 'do a search', 'find' and 'illustrations'. You must write what you hear on the recording ('window designs'). Do not try to change this to 'windows' or 'designs of windows'.

28 Answer: typical furniture
Note We are led to 'books' from 'libraries'. 'Find' in the flow chart matches 'get hold of' on the recording. You should write both words of the answer: all furniture is not typical furniture.

29 Answer: outline plan
Note Ben first suggests showing his 'section headings' to Dr Forbes, but then agrees to 'give' his 'outline plan' to him 'to look at' – 'show' in the flow chart.

30 Answer: references
Note 'Ask Dr Gray for more' in the flow chart matches 'go and see Dr Gray ... he'd be happy to provide you with further' on the recording.

31 Answer: shake
Note We are told that 'cameras such as the American Biograph' were part of the 'competition' ('rival cameras'), and that it was 'asserted' ('claimed') that these 'did not shake as much as' ('shake less').

32 Answer: bomb
Note 'Russia' is matched in the sentence and on the recording. We are told that the camera's ticking noise led people to believe it was ('suspected it of being') a bomb. 'Ticking noise' would not make sense within the sentence.

33 Answer: journalism
Note We are told that the filming 'marked the beginning of a new concept of' ('led to the creation of a new approach to') journalism. It would not be correct to write 'filming' (already in the sentence) or 'technology' (not the result of filming) in the sentence.

34 Answer: functioned
Note We are told that 'historians of cinema face difficulties' (have a 'problem') 'establishing if' ('knowing whether') 'an apparatus' ('equipment') 'functioned in the way its makers asserted' ('as it was claimed'). Although you hear 'was the best', this is three words, not one or two, and would not make good sense within the sentence.

35 Answer: regular movement
Note It is important to listen carefully for Marey's 'difficulties', as his successes are also described on the recording. We are told that 'he found it impossible initially to ensure' ('encountered difficulties achieving') 'regular movement'.

36 Answer: structure
Note 'Comic strips' are clearly introduced on the recording. Their 'structure was applied to' ('influenced' in this context) 'the planning of films' ('the way films were planned').

37 Answer: travelling
Note We are told that documentaries 'led the way ... in the use of travelling shots' ('used travelling shots before fiction films did').

38 Answer: chase
Note We are told that 'greater numbers of shots' ('increased numbers of shots') came when chase films 'became popular' ('the popularity of').

39 Answer: telephone conversations
Note We hear about 'splitting the screen image into two parts' ('the screen might be divided') 'to show' ('when filming') telephone conversations. It would not be enough to write 'the telephone' in the sentence, because the point is that two people are shown talking to each other.

40 Answer: editing
Note We are told that 'as the filming developed into multiple shots' ('as films became more complex'), editing 'emerged as an essential ingredient of the process' ('became an important part of film-making'). It would not make sense to write 'audience' as an answer.

READING Passage 1

▶ *Questions 1–5*

Task location: 3rd and 5th paragraph

1 Answer: timing
Note 3rd paragraph, 2nd sentence: 'Synchronising the subtitles to the dialogue and pictures' means 'matching the subtitles to what is said and seen'.

2 Answer: insert; delete
Note 3rd paragraph: 'You insert … disappear.' You press the insert key to record the time on the tape when you want the subtitle to appear on the screen, and the delete key to record the time on the tape when you want it to disappear from the screen.

3 Answer: (a) manual review
Note 3rd paragraph: 'This process is then … '. After setting the places where each subtitle appears and disappears, you then check each one by pressing the necessary keys.

4 Answer: synchronisation
Note 3rd paragraph: 'This process is then … '. While checking all the subtitles, some may be 'adjusted' (changed a bit) to 'improve synchronisation' – to make sure that the subtitles match the dialogue and the pictures better.

5 Answer: spotting list
Note 5th paragraph: This is all the subtitles in English, all timed to fit in at the correct places in the film; these subtitles are then translated into the required language by a translator, who does not have to fit them into the correct places because this has already been done.

▶ *Questions 6–9*

Task location: Spread throughout the text

6 Answer: TRUE
Note 1st paragraph: 'As translating goes … DVD'. The writer says that if you work as a translator, there is nothing more 'entertaining or glamorous' than subtitling films. The best work is on new blockbuster films before they come out, but you are also lucky if you work on films being translated for video or DVD. All translators therefore want to do any work that involves subtitling films.

7 Answer: TRUE
Note 3rd paragraph: 'You have to be more concise', you have to say things in fewer words than in traditional translation work.

8 Answer: FALSE
Note 4th paragraph: Two different methods are described. The second is said to be 'just a different method', which means that it is neither better nor worse than the first. It is simply a different approach. The two methods are therefore equally effective.

9 Answer: NOT GIVEN
Note Last paragraph: Comedies are said to be particularly difficult to translate and provide subtitles for, but we are not

told whether or not only a few people manage to do it successfully.

▶ *Questions 10–13*

Task location: 6th and 7th paragraph

10 Answer: the source language
Note 6th paragraph: 'Mistakes usually occur … '. If the translator 'does not master' (is not excellent at) the source language, they will make mistakes when subtitling.

11 Answer: reformat the timing
Note 6th paragraph: 'If subtitles were done … '. The timing of the subtitles has to be changed when a video version of the film is made because the subtitles for the film version may not match those required for the video version for technical reasons.

12 Answer: thin black border
Note 7th paragraph: 'Characters usually appear … '. A border is something that surrounds something. Most subtitles have white letters with a thin black border round them, we are told.

13 Answer: the hearing impaired
Note 7th paragraph: 'We can also use … '. The words spoken by different characters can be put into different colours for each character, so that people who are deaf or cannot hear well will know which character is speaking while they are reading the subtitles.

READING Passage 2

▶ *Questions 14–19*

Task location: Spread throughout the text

14 Answer: C
Note 10th paragraph: Dr Nurrish says that complementary medicine gives people the chance to 'talk to someone and be listened to sympathetically', and that this opportunity is 'lacking' (is not available) in medicine in general.

15 Answer: A
Note 7th paragraph: Dr Bron says that in the field of alternative medicine, 'the general public has a hard time to distinguish between scientific myth and fact'. Some things they are told are not true, but they may not know that.

16 Answer: D
Note 11th paragraph: The neuroscientist has a 'withering' (very critical) opinion of alternative medicine. He says that the only difference between aromatherapy ('the latter') and the other kinds of therapy he mentions is that aromatherapy has a 'cadre of professional practitioners' – there are a number of people who earn a living from aromatherapy – whereas this is not the case with the other kinds of therapy. He suggests that the other kinds of therapy are not taken seriously and that aromatherapy should not be taken seriously either.

17 Answer: E
Note Last paragraph: Professor Moore says 'there should be no such thing as complementary or alternative medicine' – it should not exist. He thinks that every form of treatment that has been scientifically proved to work should be considered medicine and that any form of treatment that has not been scientifically tested cannot be considered medicine of any kind.

18 Answer: B
Note 8th paragraph: The molecular biologist says that there is enough 'anecdotal evidence'(evidence from what people have said about their own experiences) that some alternative therapies 'are effective'(do work) and that therefore research should be done into them.

19 Answer: A
Note 5th paragraph: Dr Bron says that homoeopathy is a 'scam' (a clever and illegal way of cheating people out of money), and that claims made about the content of homoeopathic treatments cannot be trusted.

▶ *Questions 20–22*

Task location: 1st, 2nd and 3rd paragraph
20 Answer: C
Note 1st paragraph: 'This' at the beginning of the last sentence refers to the question of whether complementary or alternative medicine can be considered to 'warrant' (deserve) 'scientific investigation' and whether scientists should 'conduct research' into it.

21 Answer: E
Note 2nd paragraph: The Mintel survey found that one in five British people (20%) used complementary medicine, so, clearly, the number of people using it was one of the subjects of that survey.

22 Answer: B
Note 3rd paragraph: The writer says that 'our sample' – the scientists asked in the survey the writer was involved in – used complementary medicine more than the general public. It therefore tried to find out how many scientists used it.

▶ *Questions 23–26*

Task location: Spread throughout the text
23 Answer: D
Note 6th paragraph: Scientists felt that homoeopathy has not been definitely proved to work and are 'baffled by how' – they cannot understand how – it could be effective, but they think it has 'no side effects' – no unpleasant and unintended results.

24 Answer: C
Note 9th paragraph: The scientists felt that acupuncture, chiropractic and osteopathy should all receive money for research, 'as should herbalism' – and herbalism should receive money for research too.

25 Answer: A
Note 4th paragraph: Acupuncture is said to be one of the 'more established areas' that scientists 'place more trust in' because they have 'professional bodies' (organisations to run them) and 'recognised training'.

26 Answer: D
Note 5th paragraph: 'Some of the comments ... scathing'. The writer says that 10% of the scientists they asked in their survey had used homoeopathy, but that comments made about it were 'scathing' (extremely critical).

READING Passage 3

▶ *Questions 27–32*

27 Answer: v
Note A 'momentous occasion' is an important event that has important results. The paragraph describes the event – Luke Howard's talk at the laboratory – and its effect on the audience, who realised that what they were hearing was of great importance.

28 Answer: viii
Note The paragraph refers to theories about cloud formation that people were still 'in thrall to' (still strongly believed in), such as the vesicular or bubble theory. Howard's ideas showed these theories to be incorrect. In addition, the popular theories at the time had replaced the 'earlier

speculations' – theories that had appeared before them but were now forgotten or considered strange.

29 Answer: iii
Note It is stated in the paragraph that Howard's theory that clouds should be regarded as having things in common with the rest of the natural world was not a new one, and that 'many of the more scientifically minded' people held the same view.

30 Answer: ix
Note We are told that people may have thought that classifying clouds would involve hundreds or thousands of different types of cloud, but that Howard showed that there were 'just three basic families of cloud'. Therefore, he showed that classifying clouds was a less complex matter than people might have expected.

31 Answer: i
Note At the beginning of the paragraph, we are told that Howard's system for classifying clouds involved giving them names that were connected with what they looked like and using Latin names because people of many nationalities would understand them. The rest of the paragraph gives examples of his names.

32 Answer: x
Note We are told that Howard's system was 'clear and self-evident' to the audience and that, because it was so clearly the right way to describe clouds, they wondered why nobody had done it before.

▶ *Questions 33–36*

Task location: Paragraph B (but not in sequence there)
33 Answer: dizzy heights
Note Paragraph B, last sentence. This is what the situation shown in the diagram was called by balloonists, we are told.

34 Answer: major cumulus cloud
Note The situation described is when a balloon has gone up so high in the sky that it is now in the middle of this type of cloud.

35 Answer: oxygen
Note At this point, the 'oxygen concentration' in the air begins to 'thin quite dangerously' – there begins to be so little oxygen that breathing becomes difficult.

36 Answer: 6.5°C; thousand/1000 metres
Note As the balloon goes up into the air, the air temperature goes down at the rate described.

▶ *Questions 37–40*

Task location: Spread throughout the text (but not in sequence there)
37 Answer: E
Note Paragraph E, last sentence: The cloud type that Howard called Nimbus was later given a different name – nimbostratus – by meteorologists.

38 Answer: F
Note Paragraph F, last sentence: Howard's system for naming clouds is said to have been similar in a way to the system of words used by Eskimos for different types of snow.

39 Answer: A
Note The paragraph lists all the kinds of information that Howard gave. In the last sentence, we are told that there was 'much that needed to be taken on board', which means that there was a lot of information for the audience to understand and think about.

40 Answer: F
Note 'Some must have wondered ...'. The writer is saying

that he is certain that people in the audience asked themselves why nobody had come up with a system for naming and grading clouds before Howard.

WRITING Task 1

See sample answer on page 201.

Notes
Content points
The answer should compare the number of fines with the number of accident fatalities and point out that the number of fines greatly increased over the period, but the number of fatalities remained much the same. The answer must also refer to the survey and point out what the majority opinions were. The answer should also link the results of the survey with the information in the two graphs.

Organisation
In this answer, the information in the two graphs is compared first. Individual figures for each year are not required and would make the answer too long. Instead, the only actual figures presented in the answer are those that relate to the key points. The results of the survey are then discussed, with reference made only to the majority views, and with the only actual percentage being the most relevant one. At the end, the survey and the graphs are linked.

Use of language
Linking: *After that* and *when* are used for linking information in terms of time. *However* and *Although* are used for contrasting information and *therefore* is used to introduce the result of something.
Grammatical structures: Passive verbs are used appropriately, for example *were caught* and *were installed*. Pronouns are used for reference to things and people previously mentioned, for example, *This, them* and *it*.
Vocabulary: Words and phrases connected with things increasing and decreasing are used, for example, *rose steadily, rise dramatically, hardly changed at all, fell slightly* and *remained fairly constant*.

WRITING Task 2

See sample answer on page 201.

Notes
Content points
The answer discusses the attitude that 'anyone can do it' in the arts and gives the example of developments in popular music involving technology. It then addresses the question of whether such developments have resulted in genuine talent being undervalued and people with no talent becoming highly successful. It ends with a conclusion involving both agreeing and disagreeing with the statement. It is not necessary to completely agree or completely disagree.

Organisation
The answer is divided into clear paragraphs, making it flow well. The first deals with the general topic of the 'anyone can do it' attitude. The second presents an example and how this relates to the idea. The third deals with the question of talent or lack of talent with regard to people who become rich and famous in the arts, and ends with a clear conclusion.

Use of language
Linking: *As a result* and *as a result of -ing* are used for linking causes and results. *However* (at the beginning of a new sentence) and *whereas* are used for contrasting facts and ideas. *Of course* is used to introduce an idea considered obviously true.
Grammatical structures: Relative clauses are used throughout, introduced with the relative pronouns *that, which, who, whose* and *where*. The auxiliary *do is* used for emphasis, to say that

something really is true or really happens, in the phrase *do become rich and famous* (first sentence, last paragraph).
Vocabulary: Words and phrases appropriate to the topic, such as *enable, talented, high quality, poorly written, apparent* and *gifts* are used.

TEST 4

1 **Answer: James Bowen**
   Note The form asks for 'full name', meaning both first and last name. The man gives his first name, James, and does not spell it out because it is a common name in English. He does spell his other name. It would be acceptable in this case to put the two names in either order.

2 **Answer: 4 Lion Road**
   Note Although James mentions the Youth Hostel, the woman asks for the address of the flat he is going to move to. James does not spell 'Lion', but he does say that it is 'like the animal'.

3 **Answer: 09954 721 822**
   Note The woman writes James' mobile number down because it is the only one he has at the moment. You need to be prepared for numbers such as this in various ways.

4 **Answer: history diploma**
   Note Both words are necessary here – either one on its own would not be enough information. The form asks for qualifications, so 'college', etc. would not be a proper answer.

5 **Answer: computer skills certificate**
   Note 'IT course' would not be correct because the form asks for 'qualifications'. All three words are necessary to correctly complete the form.

6 **Answer: hospital**
   Note This is introduced on the recording as 'worked, just as a general assistant, in a … '. Because of the 'in a … ', you should not try to write anything about 'assistant'.

7 **Answer: tour guide**
   Note James checks that part-time work is included ('if you include part-time work … ') before saying that he worked as a tour guide.

8 **Answer: swimming club**
   Note James talks about 'various sports', but he only mentions being a member of ('I'm in … ') the swimming club.

9 **Answer: playing piano**
   Note 'Enjoys' on the form is matched by 'love' on the recording, and the woman also writes '10 years' on the form. 'Music' would not be a correct answer, because the reference to 10 years would not fit with it.

10 **Answer: June 28**
   Note Two dates are heard, June 20th and 28th. The form asks for when James is available (for work). James says he will be 'back and ready to start on June 28th'.

LISTENING Section 2

11 **Answer: breakfast**
   Note Various kinds of food or meal are mentioned (dinner, a drink or a snack), but only breakfast must be booked in advance: 'if you do want it, you should tell the Hotel that you do the night before'.

12 **Answer: paintings**
   Note 'Some interesting' in the sentence matches 'a collection of fascinating' on the recording.

13 Answer: castle
Note 'Has been cancelled' in the sentence matches 'we won't be going to the castle after all' on the recording. We can understand that they were going to go there. The recording gives the reason for this, but this is not required by the sentence.

14 Answer: famous people
Note 'A talk about' in the sentence matches 'a lecture on' on the recording. The sentence is about the content of the talk (about/on), not the person who gives the talk (by).

15 Answer: antiques show
Note 'The visit to' in the sentence matches 'the trip to' on the recording. The arrangement has been changed to Sunday.

16 Answer: old postcards
Note Both words are necessary here. If you wrote only 'postcards', it would suggest (new) ones that you could buy, but these old ones are on show in the art gallery.

17 Answer: E
Note The recording clearly provides the starting point for the instructions – the bus station. You are directed to the railway bridge and beyond. You need to listen carefully to avoid confusing E and I: for E you go left and it is on the right, but for I you would go right and then it would be on the left.

18 Answer: F
Note The recording gives you the starting point – the bus station – and says it is 'near' there. You are told the names of the two streets where F is.

19 Answer: A
Note The recording tells you that the Tourist Information Office is 'up around the train station area'. You are also told the names of three streets that go towards it from the bus station. You have to be careful to decide which of A, B or C it is.

20 Answer: D
Note The recording tells you how to get to the restaurant from the bus station. G is not correct – Cromwell Road is one you should go past. Choosing between D and H correctly depends on understanding that the restaurant's entrance is on the left corner.

LISTENING Section 3

21 Answer: A
Note 'Student support services' are the 'services to support students' on the recording. Dr Smith is 'not absolutely sure about the situation at Haines' but says that 'certainly Forth has a good reputation in that regard'.

22 Answer: C
Note 'Residential accommodation' is 'room or flat' on the recording. Dr Smith says that 'all colleges ... have decent rooms or flats ... and Forth and Haines are no exception'.

23 Answer: A
Note 'On-line resources' matches 'on-line provision' on the recording. This is 'limited' at David's present college, and Dr Smith says that Haines is 'developed' to the same level, but that Forth 'has developed some pretty impressive stuff'.

24 Answer: B
Note Forth's 'splendid' library is for law, which is not 'particularly relevant' for David, but Haines' 'collections' are 'better suited' to David.

25 Answer: B
Note 'Teaching staff' are 'lecturing staff', and these are 'adequate' at Forth, but 'inspirational' and 'very cutting edge' at Haines.

26 Answer: B
Note 'Record' matches 'reputation for results'. Although Haines 'has consistently scored very well', Forth has 'a little bit of an issue with non-completing doctorate students'.

27 Answer: B
Note David is 'concerned': he is 'anxious' and 'daunted' on the recording. He himself does not feel competitive, and he says he will have to use the fact that he is motivated to help him when he feels isolated ('out on my own ... compared to the sense of community here').

28 Answer: B
Note Dr Smith mentions all three possibilities, but only publishing articles matches 'should aim to' in the question: 'it would be sensible to think in terms of ... that'll stand you in good stead ... '.

29 Answer: B
Note Dr Smith refers to all three possibilities, but the question asks for which one he thinks has improved in recent years. The only one which has changed for the better is B: 'what I've found impressive is the way courses have developed to be more adaptable ... '.

30 Answer: C
Note David mentions all three things, but time management is the only one he wants to improve from now on; he has already improved the other two.

LISTENING Section 4

31 Answer: crisis
Note 'Start with a' matches 'begin with a' on the recording. It would not be logical (or possible in two words) to write 'slow build up of interest'.

32 Answer: specialist knowledge
Note 'Tell publishers about your' matches 'give them details of ... you have' on the recording. 'Topic' and 'idea' are not directly things you should tell the publisher on the recording.

33 Answer: definite market
Note 'Write for a' matches 'produce your article for a' on the recording. 'Focus' would not fit logically.

34 Answer: obvious
Note 'Meaning shouldn't be too' matches 'the message of a poem oughtn't to be overly' on the recording. 'Subtle' is a good thing in this context, so it would not be logical as an answer.

35 Answer: director
Note 'Movements usually decided by the' matches 'things such as "moves towards the sofa" and so on are for the director to come up with' on the recording. Neither the playwright nor the actors decide these things.

36 Answer: regional stations
Note 'To begin with' on the recording introduces 'first' here. 'National radio' is what you should probably avoid to start with.

37 Answer: age group
Note 'Decide on an' matches 'fix on one' on the recording. This is what you should 'aim at'. The illustrator and the pictures do not fit logically.

38 Answer: C
Note The question is about a disadvantage, so you must ignore things which are advantages. Option C is the answer because it refers to the idea of it being 'restricting' if you can only 'put' certain 'things' into a story on the recording.

39 Answer: B
Note The question requires you to identify a mistake when writing novels. The recording alerts you to this with 'pitfalls', but you have to wait until you hear 'inexperienced' and 'all

too often' introducing a negative aspect. The mistake is represented by 'spoil' and this relates to 'spelling out what they mean by it' – that is, 'trying to explain'. This confirms option B as the correct answer.

40 Answer: C
Note This question requires you to identify the advice relating to something you should do in order to make dialogue 'seem natural'. Option C is represented by 'insert minor descriptions and actions to vary the pace ...' on the recording.

READING Passage 1

▶ *Questions 1–4*

Task location: 1st, 2nd and last paragraph
1 Answer: NOT GIVEN
Note 1st paragraph: We are told that Groucho was 'as proud' of his work as a writer as he was of his work in other media, and that not enough attention is paid to his writing because he was so good at his other work, but we are not told whether or not some of his writing was better than some of his other work.

2 Answer: YES
Note 2nd paragraph: We are told at the end of the paragraph that, because they sometimes pretended that Sheekman's work had been written by Groucho, some critics suspected that Groucho had not written any of the things that had his name on them. Critics were caused to believe that he wasn't a good enough writer to have written these things.

3 Answer: NO
Note Last paragraph: We are told that Groucho gave the money for articles Sheekman had worked on to Sheekman, and that this money was useful to Sheekman because he was 'periodically unemployed'. It is therefore clear that they did not disagree about money. Groucho was happy to give it and Sheekman needed it.

4 Answer: NOT GIVEN
Note Last paragraph: At the end of the paragraph, we are told it is strange that Groucho did not include Sheekman's name on some of the things they had produced together, because he usually put collaborators' names on things they had worked on with him. However, we do not know why he left Sheekman's name out or whether or not this was because he sometimes regretted the arrangement – it is a mystery.

▶ *Questions 5–8*

Task location: 3rd, 4th and 5th paragraph
5 Answer: no input
Note 3rd paragraph: 'The letters indicate ... at all'. In the first category, the essays were written by Groucho alone.

6 Answer: editorial assistance
Note 4th paragraph, 1st sentence: In the second category, Groucho wrote the essays and sent them to Sheekman for him to make comments and suggest changes.

7 Answer: Sheekman compositions
Note 5th paragraph, 1st sentence: In the third category, Sheekman wrote most of each essay and Groucho made contributions to them of various kinds.

8 Answer: his own style
Note 5th paragraph, 2nd sentence: For some pieces in the third category, Groucho rewrote some parts so that they had his style of writing rather than Sheekman's.

▶ *Questions 9–13*

Task location: Spread throughout the text
9 Answer: E
Note 4th paragraph: 'By the time Groucho ... polishing job.' In this letter, Groucho referred to his own 'glaring illiteracies' – obvious poor uses of language.

10 Answer: G
Note 5th paragraph: 'The letter continued ... like me'. Groucho explained that he had changed a piece not to make it better, but so that it would have his style.

11 Answer: D
Note 4th paragraph: 'Shortly thereafter ... again'. 'Shortly thereafter' means 'a short time after that' and refers back to the letter previously mentioned, on July 20, 1940, so this letter must also have been in 1940. In this letter, Groucho says that Sheekman's comments about the beginning of the piece are right, and that therefore he will write that part again.

12 Answer: B
Note 3rd paragraph: Groucho refers to a piece he calls 'my drool' – by this he means 'my rubbish' – that is to going to be published the following week. In the letter mentioned previously in the paragraph, he refers to a piece that has already been published.

13 Answer: F
Note 5th paragraph: In this letter, Groucho suggests that Sheekman should write about a political campaign, and that in the piece Sheekman should 'complain about' various things.

READING Passage 2

▶ *Questions 14–17*

Task location: 2nd, 3rd and 4th paragraph
14 Answer: D
Note 2nd paragraph: In this paragraph, the writer says that their work has not only been important in connection with the movement of continents, it has also had a variety of other results in connection with looking for oil and minerals, learning about volcanoes and earthquakes, and understanding climate changes.

15 Answer: E
Note 3rd paragraph: People had observed that South America and Africa appeared to fit together very well if they were put together, and Wegener explained that they had once been joined together, using fossil evidence he had found to demonstrate this.

16 Answer: B
Note 3rd paragraph: We are told that he was 'ridiculed' (laughed at) because of his theories because he was an 'outsider' and because he couldn't prove that continents actually moved. His theories were therefore not considered believable.

17 Answer: F
Note 4th paragraph: Their theory is described as 'just a hunch' (a feeling that something is true, but without any evidence to prove that it is true). They felt that their theory must be correct, but they couldn't show that it was.

▶ *Questions 18–22*

Task location: 5th and 6th paragraph (but not in sequence)
18 Answer: mid(-)ocean ridge(s) / ridge crest(s)
Note 5th paragraph: 'He found what ... each side of the ridge.' All the activity described here happened on both sides of the mid-ocean ridge (a raised part in the middle of the ocean

floor), particularly on each side of the ridge crests (the very top of the ridges) where the stripes appeared.

19 Answer: molten rock rose
Note 5th paragraph, last sentence: They decided that molten (hot and in liquid form) rock rose, with the result that new ocean floor was formed, which created the stripes.

20 Answer: (Earth's) magnetic field
Note 6th paragraph: When the rock became solid again, the magnetic field changed around, so that north became south and south became north. 'Flips' are changes from one side to the other.

21 Answer: parallel/symmetrical/magnetic (zebra) stripes
Note 5th paragraph: The stripes formed are described firstly as 'parallel zebra stripes' and they are then described as being 'symmetrical' and 'magnetic'.

22 Answer: pushed aside/(further) apart
Note 6th paragraph: 'As the new sea floor ...'. The creation of new sea floor meant that the continents on either side of the ocean moved further away from each other.

▶ *Questions 23–26*

Task location: Last two paragraphs
23 Answer: plate tectonics
Note 7th paragraph, 1st sentence: This term is given to the theory that resulted from proof that the sea floor spreads.

24 Answer: climates
Note Last paragraph: 'The distribution of ...'. Vine says that the movement of continents has had 'a profound effect' (an enormous influence) on climates and has caused some huge climate changes.

25 Answer: Earth Systems Science
Note Last paragraph: 'The recognition that ...'. Their work led to an understanding that there was a link between the movement of continents and the other things listed, and this 'spawned' (led to the birth of) this new branch of science.

26 Answer: integrated
Note Last paragraph: He thinks there should be an 'integrated approach' and is quoted as saying that 'the whole of environmental science should be integrated'. He says that he really disliked (it was 'anathema' to him) the idea that science was separated into completely separate areas (the 'polarisation').

READING Passage 3

▶ *Questions 27–30*

Task location: Paragraph B, C and D
27 Answer: science of wellbeing
Note Paragraph B, first sentence: The use of inverted commas means that the writer is quoting the term used for the subject of the conference.

28 Answer: scientifically rigorous methods
Note Paragraph C, second sentence: They want to 'deploy' (use) such methods to find out why some people are happy all the time and others are often miserable.

29 Answer: positive psychology
Note Paragraph D, first sentence: He is a lecturer in this subject. Again, the inverted commas mean that this is the actual term used for his subject when he is teaching it.

30 Answer: self-help gurus
Note Paragraph D, first sentence: He accepts that this area of research may sound 'woolly' (imprecise) and 'is at pains to distance himself from' (is very keen not to be included

among) the groups of people who consider themselves experts on how people can help themselves, but who have no academic background for this.

▶ *Questions 31–36*

Task location: Paragraph F
31 Answer: entertainment
Note One of the things that causes his first type of happiness is 'watching a good film', which is a form of entertainment.

32 Answer: illusion
Note He thinks that people are given the false belief that these things lead to 'lasting happiness'. If you are 'under the illusion' that something is true, you have a false belief that something, usually something good, is true.

33 Answer: ability
Note His second type of happiness comes from being 'good or talented at' something, which means that it is connected with your ability at something.

34 Answer: participation
Note He believes that this type of happiness comes from identifying what you are good at and 'taking part in' things that use your abilities. 'Participation' means 'taking part'.

35 Answer: conviction
Note His third type of happiness involves finding something you 'believe in' and then taking action to help others in connection with this belief. A conviction is a strong belief, especially a moral one.

36 Answer: permanence
Note Involvement in things you strongly believe in can lead to 'long-lasting happiness', according to Seligman. If something is long-lasting, it has permanence, rather than being only temporary.

▶ *Questions 37–40*

Task location: Spread throughout the text
37 Answer: H
Note Lewis Wolpert says that he would not trust someone who was 'totally happy', and he would regard them as being incapable of doing anything. He thinks that people need some 'discomfort' in order for them to do anything.

38 Answer: C
Note Baylis and his colleagues want to find out what makes people happy and then use this information to make people happier. They think this may affect people's social lives, their health, how long they live and how good they are at work.

39 Answer: B
Note The fact that the conference is being held at such an important place as the Royal Society indicates that the subject 'is being taken very seriously indeed'.

40 Answer: E
Note Seligman asked why science investigated unhappiness but not happiness. This shocked people who heard him and, if he had not been so well-known, it 'could have spelt the end of his career'. People would have found his words unacceptable, and he would have been unable to find work as a result.

WRITING Task 1

Task guide – A process or sequence of events
• As with all Task 1 tasks, you must select the key information and summarise it.
• Start by studying the diagram(s) carefully until you are sure that

you fully understand the process or sequence of events shown. Make sure that you are clear about what happens at the beginning, in the middle and at the end.

- In this task, the stages are labelled and information is given on them. In other tasks, the stages of a process or the order of a sequence of events may be indicated with arrows pointing from one stage or event to the next.

- You must use any information given in words with the diagram to build parts of your answer, but you will not be able to simply copy whole phrases.

- Make sure that your answer is clear and that it clearly describes each stage in the process or each event in the sequence. Do not try to use highly complex language – instead, concentrate on a clear and straightforward description.

- Make sure that you include all relevant information. Do not leave out any important stages or events.

- As you create your answer, imagine that you are explaining the diagram to someone you are talking to. Concentrate on making it absolutely clear to another person.

See sample answer on page 202.

Notes
Content points
The answer should contain a description of the equipment required, and how it is set up. It should then describe each stage, one after the other, using the information in words below the diagram, and the information given for each stage in the diagram.

Organisation
The answer should be organised in the only logical way, with a brief description of the equipment and how it is set up, followed by a brief description of each stage in the correct order.

Use of language
Linking: Words like *then*, *as*, *after* and *until* are used for linking things in terms of time. *So that* is used for linking an action with its purpose.

Grammatical structures: The grammar is fairly simple to ensure clarity. Modals such as *must* and *can* are required, and so are the present simple and present perfect verb forms. Imperative forms could also be used because instructions are given. The phrase *begin by -ing* is a good way of describing the beginning of a process.

Vocabulary: Words and phrases such as *attach*, *beneath*, *turn a tap on*, *drip*, *mark* and *pass from* are required to explain this process clearly.

WRITING Task 2

See sample answer on page 202.

Notes
Content points
The answer describes the situation mentioned in the statement in the task, gives reasons for it and suggests possible solutions. It therefore covers everything in the task.

Organisation
The answer is appropriately divided into paragraphs, and it has a clear progression. The first paragraph describes the situation and makes clear that it is a problem by saying that it is *a shame* and pointing out the benefits of solving it. The second and third paragraphs discuss causes of the problem. The last paragraph suggests solutions and discusses the benefits of these solutions.

Use of language
Linking: *Also* is used for introducing an additional point. The phrases *One reason why* and *Another reason is that* are used for introducing reasons.

Grammatical structures: A second conditional sentence is used for describing a hypothetical situation and its result in the first paragraph. Passive verb forms are used throughout for generalising. The structure *verb + as* is used for describing a general point of view in the third paragraph (*is seen as being less important*).

Vocabulary: Words and phrases appropriate to the topic, such as *be forced to do*, *play a big role*, *come into existence*, *preferable*, *widely available*, *have a lot to offer* and *pass something on to someone else* are used.

TEST 5

LISTENING Section 1

1 **Answer: 2 km**
   Note The question is clearly reflected in the woman's question to the man. Two distances are mentioned, but only one of them answers the question ('from the very centre of town').

2 **Answer: www.cheapstay.com**
   Note The website address is clearly spelt out, and is supported by 'go to … ' and the fact that you can 'email them directly from it'.

3 **Answer: street festival**
   Note The woman refers to March, and the man mentions the 22nd within this context. You need to include the word 'street' – there are many different kinds of festival.

4 **Answer: local musicians**
   Note The concert is clearly mentioned on the recording. The 'point' that the man is making is that the music (which is of various kinds) is played by 'local musicians', so this is the answer. Different types of music ('classical' and 'rock') or 'mixture', etc. would not be correct answers to the question 'who'.

5 **Answer: natural history**
   Note March 24th is clearly mentioned on the recording, and the paintings are exhibited before this date. We are told that the 'exhibition' changes to 'natural history'.

6 **Answer: sports centre/center**
   Note Do not write 'swimming pool' or 'park', which are open in March.

7 **Answer: C**
   Note All three times are mentioned, but only option C answers the question: 'depart' matches 'sets off' on the recording.

8 **Answer: A**
   Note All three possibilities exist, but only option A answers the question because it is the only one that the man 'recommends' – he says this way is 'more convenient'.

9 **Answer: B**
   Note All three figures are heard on the recording, but the question is about the group discount, and only option B answers this – 'if there are more than 10 of you travelling together'.

10 **Answer: C**
   Note The question asks about the 'excursion' – that is, the whole trip. The total length of the trip is four hours, consisting of three hours when the train travels and two half-hour breaks in which you do what you want. You are told that four hours is the answer; you do not need to do any mathematical calculating to get the answer.

11 Answer: A
Note The director says that in year 1 (that is, 5 years ago), 'sales climbed': this is true of all three graphs. Then he says they went 'flat' for 3 years: this is true of graphs A and C (but not graph B). Then he says he is 'delighted' (a positive reaction) that in the 'last year' (year 5) they 'rose again': this is only true of graph A.

12 Answer: B
Note All three types of the business are mentioned. Read the question carefully: it is about 'this year', not other years. Graph B is correct because it shows the three departments as the same: 'equally balanced on all fronts at the present time'.

13 Answer: B
Note You need to understand that the numbers for this year are more than last year and the numbers for next year will be more than this year: the numbers are going up every year.

14 Answer: creating value
Note The word 'phrased' on the recording tells you that the exact words for the '......' of the question begin at this point.

15 Answer: line manager
Note 'Help' in the notes matches 'assistance' on the recording. 'Colleagues' are who you should not ask.

16 Answer: positive
Note 'Customers to have a' matches 'everyone who shops here feels they have had a' on the recording. 'Routine' is the kind of experience for customers not to have.

17 Answer: special offer
Note 'Tell' matches 'informed' and 'let them know' on the recording. 'Goods' matches 'products'.

18 Answer: newsletter
Note 'Read the' must be followed by something you read – the newsletter. You could not write 'about these', for example, in the space.

19 Answer: progress meetings
Note This is a certain kind of meeting, so you need to write both words. You cannot write 'section leader', as this would not follow 'attend' correctly.

20 Answer: E/B
Note All five things are mentioned on the recording, but only options E and B must be done today – 'this evening' for option E, and 'by the end of the day' for option B.

21 Answer: A
Note We are told that Gentoo penguins 'look carefully down ... ' before jumping. This should not be confused with options B or F.

22 Answer: E
Note 'Climbing' in option E matches 'get up somewhere' on the recording. Other references to movement such as those in options A, B or C should not be chosen.

23 Answer: F
Note There are references to looking twice here on the recording – 'first to one side then the other', 'each eye in turn', 'double-checked'. This is different from option A – 'always hesitate'.

24 Answer: G
Note Options G and C refer to positions penguins use with their bodies. However, here it is the flippers that are discussed. You should not be confused by the idea of jumping in option A.

25 Answer: standing
Note Emily introduces the reference to 'sleeping'. Brian talks about the penguins lying 'flat' sometimes, but the question is about 'usually', which is what Emily goes on to say – 'normally'.

26 Answer: stick out
Note Two kinds of feather on the Rockhopper are mentioned, the black and the yellow; the question asks about the yellow ones.

27 Answer: white patches
Note 'Recognise' matches 'spot' on the recording.

28 Answer: find food
Note You need to find an answer that fits the space in the summary grammatically, and in one or two words only. Reference to 'a bigger catch' helps to explain what is meant by 'best way to find food' ('makes it easier'), but is not the correct answer in itself.

29 Answer: calm
Note 'Appear' matches 'seemed' on the recording. Emily had thought the penguins might have been 'frightened', but in fact this is what they were not apparently feeling.

30 Answer: social nature
Note 'All the types have a social nature': this is what characterises them and what Emily responds to. 'Security' is mentioned but not as a characteristic.

31 Answer: demolish
Note 'Have been mistaken' matches 'proved disastrous' on the recording. 'Demolish', as a basic verb, is the only possible answer that fits into the space here.

32 Answer: real consultation
Note 'Often' matches 'frequently'. It is important to write both words of the answer, as 'real' consultation is distinguished from 'token gestures'.

33 Answer: self-help
Note 'Housing policies' matches 'strategies for providing accommodation'. 'Based on principles of' matches 'an approach rooted in'. 'Independent' is part of the idea, but this adjective would not fit the space grammatically.

34 Answer: services
Note 'Some' matches 'a number of'. 'Be provided' matches 'have to be laid on' on the recording.

35 Answer: invest money
Note 'Feel secure' matches 'have a sense of security, of long-term commitment' on the recording. Both words of the answer are necessary in this case. Answers involving other words such as 'time' would not fit logically or grammatically.

36 Answer: community values
Note 'Governments often underestimate the importance of ... ' matches 'too many governments fail to appreciate that ... are a crucial component of that' on the recording. You should not try to write an answer to do with 'belong'. It would not fit grammatically, and it is the community values that create the sense of belonging, not the other way round.

37 Answer: employment
Note The point made on the recording is that the question of 'how much employment is going to be available' should be considered before housing is built.

38 Answer: freedom
Note There is a reference to the 'economy', but this could not fit into the space – ' ... of individuals'. 'Effect' here matches 'impact' on the recording.

39 Answer: **specialist activities**

Note 'The population size of cities' matches 'the sheer volume of people' on the recording, but you need to wait a little while for the link in the sentence to 'range' ('variety'). 'Work' would not be an adequate answer the point is the kinds of work – 'activities' are 'specialised', unlike in villages.

40 Answer: **understanding**

Note 'Raise the level of' matches 'increases our degree of' on the recording. This is what city living does in relation to understanding – the result of 'thinking or going about things' in many different ways.

READING Passage 1

▶ *Questions 1–4*

Task location: 1ˢᵗ, 2ⁿᵈ and last paragraph

1 Answer: **rockdoves**

Note 1ˢᵗ paragraph: 'It has been suggested … sea-girt cliffs'. The pigeons today are descended from birds from the medieval period, and they were descended from rockdoves. The pigeons lived on buildings, while the rockdoves lived on cliffs.

2 Answer: **stale bread**

Note 1ˢᵗ paragraph, last sentence: People first started to be kind to them in the 19ᵗʰ century, when they gave them oats. Before that, it was common to give them stale (old and not good to eat) bread.

3 Answer: **fly(-)lines**

Note 2ⁿᵈ paragraph: 'Those who look up … history of use'. The use of inverted commas indicates that this is the special term used. You can see these lines all over London if you look up, we are told, and examples of places in London that birds fly to and from are given.

4 Answer: **building work; tree(-)felling**

Note Last paragraph: 'The rooks of London … tree-felling'. The places where rooks live (rookeries) have been destroyed by these two activities, and this is why they have disappeared.

▶ *Questions 5–9*

Task location: 3ʳᵈ paragraph

5 Answer: **friend**

Note Cockneys (people born and brought up in London) pronounced the word as 'sparrer'; they had a word, 'cocksparrer', which meant 'friend'. They used the bird's name in this word because they felt the bird was like a friend, 'sweet and yet watchful' (pleasant but also taking care of others).

6 Answer: **lose body heat**

Note London is called a 'heat island' (a place where heat is concentrated), and the bird is 'perfectly adapted' to such a place because it loses its body heat very quickly, so it can stay warm in London.

7 Answer: **(an) occupied building**

Note It was said that it 'never breeds at any distance from an occupied building'. It always breeds close to buildings with people in them.

8 Answer: **sociability**

Note This means that it likes people and being with people. This characteristic is 'bred upon the fondness of the Londoner' – caused and encouraged by the fact that people in London like the bird.

9 Answer: **interrogation**

Note The birds seem to be 'uttering a little plaintive note' – making a sad sound that suggests they are asking for something.

▶ *Questions 10–13*

Task location: Spread throughout the text

10 Answer: **D**

Note 4ᵗʰ paragraph, 1ˢᵗ sentence: Chaffinches are 'less approachable and trustful in the city than in the country'. They are happier to have people near them when they are in the countryside than when they are in the city.

11 Answer: **B**

Note 2ⁿᵈ paragraph, 1ˢᵗ sentence: Woodpigeons 'were quickly urbanised' (rapidly became used to living in a city) and they increased in numbers and 'tameness' (they became less wild and more used to living with people).

12 Answer: **F**

Note Last paragraph: 'They were venerable … preferring to cluster around ancient churches and the like'. They used to gather in groups at very old churches and at similar very old buildings.

13 Answer: **A**

Note 1ˢᵗ paragraph: 'A man fell … the Bishop … complained of malignant' (very nasty, very unpleasant) people who 'threw stones at the pigeons'.

READING Passage 2

▶ *Questions 14–20*

14 Answer: **vi**

Note The first sentence states that we assess other people's personalities frequently during our 'daily lives', and the rest of the paragraph gives examples of everyday situations in which this happens.

15 Answer: **ix**

Note The paragraph lists situations in which it is important that correct assessments of people's personalities are made.

16 Answer: **iii**

Note The paragraph begins by stating that it becomes very clear when inaccurate assessments of people's personalities have been made, and then examples are given of the results when this has happened. (Paragraph B is about needing to make accurate assessments, while Paragraph C is about what happens if inaccurate assessments are made.)

17 Answer: **vii**

Note The paragraph begins by stating that little attention has been paid to the question of how personality can be assessed or how accurately personalities are assessed. It then states that people have been attracted by a number of 'unscientific systems' for assessing personality because they realise there are 'weaknesses in their judgments', and they are 'desirous of' (they want) better methods for assessing personality. This means that people know they are not very good at it and want to get better at it.

18 Answer: **ii**

Note The main point of the paragraph is that a lot of psychologists consider that their main role is to deal with 'general laws and principles' concerning human behaviour and thought. They think it is not their role to find 'practical uses' for their knowledge, and they do not think they have great skill at judging other people themselves. As a result, they do not want to give 'definite predictions or decisions about other people'. Some psychologists are moving into work that involves doing this, we are told at the end of the paragraph, but the main point is that psychologists think they should deal with general theories and not try to give practical guidance.

19 Answer: viii

Note The main point of this paragraph is that 'unscientific methods of assessment' are still used because, although psychologists have done research on personality assessment, they have not produced techniques for doing this that 'are sufficiently reliable and accurate to win general acceptance'. They have therefore not made much progress towards coming up with methods that are of practical use in society in general.

20 Answer: v

Note In the first half of the paragraph, we are told about unsuccessful approaches to personality assessment by a variety of people who 'inaccurately ... diagnose personality' and make 'bad appointments' because of poor personality assessment methods. In the last part of the paragraph, we are told about attempts to find 'better methods' (more successful ones) that have been used by certain organisations.

▶ *Question 21*

Task location: Paragraphs E and F

21 Answer: C/D/E (in any order)

Note C: Paragraph E, last sentence. They are 'under constant fire' (constantly criticised severely) by 'other psychologists' (ones not working in the area of personality assessment)
D: Paragraph F, first sentence. Psychologists involved in personality assessment have shown people who have to make important decisions in society how difficult it is to assess personality.
E: Paragraph F, second sentence. The writer is saying that psychologists have shown people that their judgments of personality are poor, but they have not managed to 'provide something better' (suggest a better method).
Option A (paragraph E, third sentence) is not a possible answer because depth psychologists have been studying personality assessment for longer than other psychologists, but the writer does not say they are better at this than other psychologists. Despite the work of depth psychologists, a widely accepted approach has not developed.
Option B (paragraph E, last two sentences) is not a possible answer because their methods are criticised, and it is not easy for them to 'prove their worth' (to prove that their methods are right), but we are not told that they themselves agree that their methods don't work.
Option F (paragraph F) is not a possible answer because we are told about the existence of different methods used by different people and in different organisations, but we are not told that the same psychologists keep using different methods or changing from one method to another.

▶ *Questions 22–26*

Task location: Spread throughout the text

22 Answer: YES

Note Paragraph B, last sentence: We know that 'misinterpretations easily arise' (it is easy for people to make inaccurate personality assessments), and we feel that this happens particularly when other people judge us (rather than when we judge others).

23 Answer: NOT GIVEN

Note Paragraph C: Various 'unscientific systems' are mentioned in the middle of the paragraph. The writer says that these have become popular because people want to get better at assessing personality, but he does not say whether or not any of them have actually been useful in a practical way.

24 Answer: YES

Note Paragraph D, last sentence and paragraph E, first sentence: The writer says that it is 'natural' (understandable) that people think that psychologists are experts on personality, but that this belief is 'hardly justified' (not really correct at all) because they are not experts on this.

25 Answer: YES

Note Paragraph F: The writer refers to 'university psychologists' and says that when they appoint a new member of staff, they 'probably make at least as many bad appointments as other employers do'. They assess personality using the same 'traditional methods' that other people use, and they judge personality as inaccurately as other people do.

26 Answer: NO

Note Paragraph F, last sentence: The research since 1940 that the writer mentions has involved 'the experimental development of better methods', which means it has tried new methods and has not been based on the theories that led to the previous methods.

READING Passage 3

▶ *Questions 27–29*

Task location: 1st, 2nd and 3rd paragraph

27 Answer: C

Note 2nd paragraph: He had the most important role in Research & Development (coming up with new products) and was not as 'extrovert' (lively, confident and enjoying talking to people) as his partner, whose role was to represent the company in public.
Option A (1st paragraph) is incorrect because he still has the same personality and is happier exchanging ideas with 'techies' (experts on technical matters) than being involved in selling products or talking to shareholders in the company.
Option B (1st paragraph) is incorrect because he was considered not to be someone who could ever be a manager, but the psychologist did not say he was in the wrong kind of business. Option D (1st paragraph, 1st sentence) is incorrect because the opposite is probably true. Although he is funny and 'self-deprecating' (he talks as if his achievements and abilities are not big or important), he is actually 'shrewd' (he is clever and makes good judgments).

28 Answer: B

Note 2nd paragraph: The company was 'laid-back' (had a calm and relaxed approach and atmosphere), but this never 'implied lack of ambition' (meant that the company wasn't ambitious). Option A (2nd paragraph) is incorrect because the company was 'distinctively Californian' (it was clearly very typical of companies in California at the time). Option C (2nd paragraph) is incorrect because it may have been unconventional – people wore casual clothes and Moore did not have special treatment even though it was his company – but there is no suggestion that these aspects attracted attention. Option D (2nd paragraph) is incorrect because the emphasis was equally on 'intellectual pizazz' (having clever and exciting ideas) and the 'ability to deliver a product' (they saw having clever ideas and producing products as equally important).

29 Answer: D

Note 3rd paragraph, 1st sentence: They got paid well, but they were frustrated because the company did not provide funding for research and development, and so they left and set up their own company.
Option A is incorrect because money was available for setting

up companies at that time, but this is not why they set one up, it is what helped them set it up after they had decided to do so. Option B is incorrect because their business plan 'said essentially nothing' (this means that it had very little detail in it, not that it left out secret information). The competition was seven years behind Intel in terms of research and development because of what they did after they set the company up, not because they kept things secret at the time when they set it up. Option C is incorrect because their first microprocessor came out three years after they set up the firm, but it did not exist when they set it up. They set up the firm to develop products themselves, not because they had a particular product in mind.

▶ *Questions 30–35*

Task location: Spread throughout the text

30 Answer: FALSE
Note 3rd paragraph: Intel was seven years ahead of the competition in terms of research and development, and we are told that it did not 'relinquish' this lead (it never lost this advantage). The competition therefore did not catch up with Intel.

31 Answer: NOT GIVEN
Note 4th paragraph: It seems clear that it was successful, but we are not told anything about Moore's expectations concerning how successful it would be.

32 Answer: NOT GIVEN
Note 6th paragraph: His estimation in 1975 of how much growth there would be was 'pessimistic' (it was too low), so it was inaccurate, but we are not told how much evidence he based the prediction on.

33 Answer: TRUE
Note 7th paragraph: Moore says that every time the cost of producing more computer power falls, an enormous number of new products using microprocessors appear, because they can now be produced more cheaply. Flashing trainers are an example of such a product.

34 Answer: FALSE
Note 7th paragraph: 'I suspect I shared …'. Moore says that he agreed in the past that there would be a point where no more development was possible, but he had been proved wrong about this because the 'barriers' (problems connected with making components even smaller) had 'melted away' (disappeared because people had found ways of solving these problems).

▶ *Questions 35–40*

Task location: 5th paragraph

35 Answer: sophistication
Note He referred to the fact that the 'complexity' of integrated circuits had 'doubled' (they had become twice as complex'). In this context, 'sophistication' means 'complexity'.

36 Answer: accuracy
Note His prediction proved to be more 'spot-on' than he had expected. If something is 'spot-on', it is completely accurate or correct.

37 Answer: cost
Note Before then, integrated circuits had been 'expensive', so cost was an issue.

38 Answer: use
Note Before then, integrated circuits had had 'principally military applications' – they had been used mainly in military equipment.

39 Answer: influence
Note The cost of producing them and the main way in which they were used had obviously affected the development of

integrated circuits. Moore felt that this was going to change, and that these factors would no longer be such an influence.

40 Answer: cost-effectiveness
Note He predicted that there was going to be a dramatic change in the cost of producing integrated circuits – it was going to come down a lot. They were going to become 'the cheapest way to make electronics'. If a product can be made cheaply in comparison with how much it can be sold for, it is cost-effective.

WRITING Task 1

See sample answer on page 203.

Notes
Content points
The answer should present only the most noticeable information from the first two bar charts. This should include any significant changes over the three-year period and any information that stands out. The answer should not list details of all the figures in all the categories. The information in the bar charts should be summarised and the general trend in the figures should be explained. The conclusion here links the bar charts and the line graph. This is optional, but shows a full understanding of what all the data as a whole indicates.

Organisation
The answer should begin by discussing the first bar chart, move to the second bar chart and then discuss the graph. Changes and contrasts should be included for each one.

Use of language
Linking: *Although* and *However* are used for contrasting data. *With regard to* is used for introducing an analysis of a different element of the information given. *Followed by* is used for linking things in a list. *Apart from* is used for introducing an exception.
Grammatical structures: Passive verb forms are used, for example, *were seen as*. Relative clauses involving a past participle but no relative pronoun or form of *be* are used, for example, *the percentage of people choosing* (the percentage of people who chose) and *the overall view given* (the overall view that was given).
Vocabulary: Words and phrases for describing changes, such *as fell slightly* and *went up slightly*, are used appropriately. The verb *felt* is used to describe people's opinions. The phrase *the percentage of* is required here, and so is the word *aspects*.

WRITING Task 2

See sample answer on page 203.

Notes
Content points
The answer discusses the situation mentioned in the statement in the task in general terms and in terms of the people involved. It discusses both elements of the statement – people continuing their education and the range of courses now available. Both positive and negative opinions are given on these developments. A clear conclusion is presented.

Organisation

The answer begins with a general point about people continuing in education and a positive view. In the second paragraph, the range of courses is discussed, with a positive view. The third paragraph moves to negative views and gives examples to support them. The final paragraph provides a general conclusion.

Use of language

Linking: *From the point of view of* is used for introducing someone's attitude or situation. *Therefore* is used to link a cause and result. *Rather than* is used for linking alternatives. *On the other hand* is used for introducing an opposite view. *However* is used at the beginning of a new sentence for linking contrasting ideas or facts. *In general* is used for introducing a general point.

Grammatical structures: The modal *must* is used for saying that something is obviously true (1st and 2nd paragraph). The structure *waste time + -ing* is used.

Vocabulary: The following phrases relevant to the topic are used: *have an impact, directly related, on offer, a bit silly* and *taken seriously.*

TEST 6

LISTENING Section 1

1 **Answer: Grieves/Anna**
   Note The form requires last and first names. The woman gives both, and in this case in that order. She spells out her last name and confirms the double 'N' in 'Anna'.

2 **Answer: Holiday World**
   Note The man asks Anna 'where you heard about' Go-Travel, which matches 'source of enquiry' on the form. Anna's reply ('it was your advertisement') matches 'saw ad'. 'Magazine' is written on the form, so you should not repeat it, particularly since you are told to write no more than two words.

3 **Answer: FT4551**
   Note 'Reference' matches 'code' on the recording. You need to be prepared for the various ways of saying such combinations of letters and numbers.

4 **Answer: 3**
   Note Anna and two friends makes a total of three. Mathematics is not necessary, as you are told the actual number.

5 **Answer: August 16**
   Note Anna also refers to the 'end of August', but this is when she needs to return by, not when she needs to depart ('going on').

6 **Answer: 11**
   Note Darren mentions three possible numbers of nights, out of which Anna chooses 'the middle one'.

7 **Answer: Super**
   Note Darren lists three available types ('levels') of insurance. Anna rules out the first, Standard, and selects ('let's say') Super.

8 **Answer: G**
   Note Having said no to option E, picnic lunches ('we'd leave that'), Anna agrees to option G ('is a must').

9 **Answer: A**
   Note Anna says no to option D ('we'll pass on the night bus one') and option C ('museums aren't really my sort of thing'). But she says yes to option A ('the demonstration of local arts could be fun').

10 **Answer: F**
   Note Anna says yes to option F ('sounds delightful ...'), but says no to option H ('well, sitting in a coach on those winding roads ... '), which Darren confirms with 'I understand'.

LISTENING Section 2

11 **Answer: 1992**
   Note It is important to read the page of notes you are required to complete carefully. Question 11 is about when the charity was 'set up'. The recording mentions 1987 (when the founder took up running) and 1997 (when the runs were being filmed). It is in 1992 that the charity was 'set up' ('established').

12 **Answer: hospital**
   Note 'Aim' matches 'with the idea that' on the recording. The money goes to the hospital; people who are unwell will then (presumably) benefit.

13 **Answer: numbers**
   Note This is the correct answer, which fits the space both grammatically and logically. Neither 'ideas' nor 'standard' would fit. Here, 'supply' matches 'reproduce' on the recording.

14 **Answer: train**
   Note The space requires a verb, and one that can go before 'together'. We are told that teams do not 'compete side by side' but that they 'should' ('we do recommend') 'train as a group'.

15 **Answer: food and drink**
   Note The space requires a noun or nouns. You should not try to make 'eat and drink' fit, but you must write 'food and drink'. 'Enough' matches 'sufficient' on the recording.

16 **Answer: main square**
   Note You need to pay attention to prepositions here. 'In' goes only before 'main square' on the recording. The 'race' ('course') goes 'through' the town and park. 'Finish' matches 'concluding' on the recording.

17 **Answer: minister for health**
   Note The note here is about who gives the prizes. One prize (only) has been donated by Zoom Fashions. The Mayor will make a speech, but does not give the prizes to the runners – only the Minister for Health does that.

18 **Answer: C**
   Note Option C is recommended: 'A sponsored swimming event ... did very well'. Options B and F are not recommended, although they are mentioned on the recording: 'Selling home-made cakes and bread' and 'a large picnic' 'failed to justify the efforts put into them'.

19 **Answer: A**
   Note Option A is recommended: 'It is possible to raise useful funds by selling ... badges'. Option G is neither recommended nor advised against (and so does not answer the question correctly): 'We're currently checking to see'. Option I is not recommended: 'The returns have not been very high on this'.

20 **Answer: H**
   Note Option H is recommended: It 'went very well, and it would be good to see more such activities'. Option D is neither recommended nor advised against (and so does not answer the question): 'We'll have to see how plans for that progress'.

LISTENING Section 3

21 **Answer: A**
   Note The question matches 'people's names in terms of culture' on the recording. The conclusion to include this is reached across things that all three speakers say.

22 Answer: B
Note The question matches 'ways in which naming practices are similar across different languages' on the recording. Joe expresses reservations about this ('not sure ... ') which Angela supports ('maybe you need ... '), so its inclusion is neither sure nor ruled out.

23 Answer: A
Note The question matches 'what first names mean' on the recording. All three speakers express enthusiasm about the idea, and Joe confirms its inclusion by saying he will enjoy creating the projection slides for it.

24 Answer: C
Note The question matches 'place names' and 'sea ... ' on the recording. Martin is critical of the suggestion, and Joe concedes ('perhaps you're right'), so the conclusion is that it will not be included.

25 Answer: B
Note The question matches 'the way migrants often used to name places after somewhere in their country of origin' on the recording. Martin is critical or doubtful about its inclusion, and Angela and Martin agree that he should wait until he decides whether to include it or not – in other words, he might include it.

26 Answer: A
Note The question matches 'country names, the origins of those' on the recording. All three speakers find this interesting, and Joe's idea of projecting a map of the world during the presentation is supported ('that seems a foregone conclusion'), so that it is clear this topic will definitely be included.

27 Answer: meaningless words
Note 'Many' words in the summary matches '108 words' and 'the list' on the recording. Once you have identified 'common' in the summary as matching 'ordinary' on the recording, the sequence of types of words is clear.

28 Answer: capital letters
Note 'Shown' in the summary matches 'displayed' on the recording; 'easier' matches 'more readily'; 'identify' matches 'recognise'.

29 Answer: colour/color
Note 'Visual features' on the recording introduces the thing you need to focus on. 'Helping to store ... ' on the recording matches with this sentence in the summary. Because you only write two words, you should not try to include 'for example' from the recording.

30 Answer: associations
Note 'Create' in the summary matches 'conjure up' on the recording; 'within' matches 'inside'; 'a number of' matches 'a range of'.

LISTENING Section 4

31 Answer: spies
Note After the introduction, 'US civil war' in the notes is repeated on the recording. The idea of 'replacing' on the recording matches 'instead of' in the notes. It would be wrong to think that something like 'enemy lines' was being replaced.

32 Answer: maps
Note You must find a word or two words that fit grammatically as well as logically into the space. The verb 'to make' in the notes matches 'were employed in the creation of' on the recording.

33 Answer: collect data

Note This is what fits the space in the notes in terms of grammar and meaning. There are references to 'knowledge and understanding' on the recording, but they are not precise enough for the space you must fill.

34 Answer: climate
Note Something that is 'part of studies of' matches the idea of 'ongoing investigations into' on the recording. 'Instruments' are used to carry out this research, but are not, in this sense, part of 'the studies'.

35 Answer: lift
Note There are various comparisons going on or implied here – 'cheaper and safer', but 'create' in the notes matches 'generate' on the recording. You need to process the transfer from 'less' to (not) 'as much as'.

36 Answer: weather protection
Note 'The first airships' matches 'early examples' on the recording. 'Had no' matches 'didn't provide any'.

37 Answer: framework
Note 'Be efficient' matches 'work effectively' on the recording; 'needed' matches 'have to have'. 'A' before the gap in the notes shows you that you need to write a noun here, not a verb or adjective.

38 Answer: airliners
Note You need to find the first of two causes here. 'Success of' in the notes matches 'speed and popularity of' on the recording. The fact that airships 'appeared superseded' matches 'stopped because of' in the notes.

39 Answer: crashes
Note You need to find the second of two causes here. 'Series of' in the notes matches 'number of alarming' on the recording. This is in the context of 'the decline of' the airship and the fact that this 'put people off'.

40 Answer: cargo
Note 'Recent interest' in the notes matches the idea that 'their popularity seems set for a slight revival and in the past few years there has been renewed attention paid to the possibility of' on the recording. 'Transport' can be a verb or a noun; on the recording it is a verb and would not be a correct answer for the space in the notes. The note is about the specific 'cargo', not passenger(s), that may be carried.

READING Passage 1

▶ *Questions 1–2*

Task location: Paragraphs A and B
1 Answer: B
Note Paragraph A: The fact that you would need 'plenty of room for expansion' in your library of management books means that the increase will continue and many more books will be produced. Also, 'the trend continues' – the increase is still happening.
Option A (paragraph B) is incorrect. The number of management books has grown so much that it has created its own 'mini-industry', but the writer does not say that the growth surprised people in the industry. Option C (paragraph B) is incorrect. The writer says how much money is made from management books, but does not say that this figure is higher than the amount made from other kinds of book. Option D (paragraph A) is incorrect. The writer talks about the period during which the growth has happened, but does not say that it was possible in the past to predict that this growth would happen.

2 Answer: C
Note Paragraph B: The writer lists all kinds of people who have produced management books. These people felt a 'need

to get into print' or were 'aspiring authors', which means they wanted to write the books, rather than that someone else asked them to do so.

Option A (paragraph B) is incorrect. The writer says that all sorts of books have been written and that 'the quality is uneven' (some are better than others), but does not say that the content of any of them is completely irrelevant. Option B (paragraph B) is incorrect. It's likely that the books by business leaders are more practical and the books by academics more theoretical, but the writer does not say that there are more of one kind than another. Option D (paragraph B) is incorrect. The writer says that some books are better than others, but does not say which ones are better than others.

▶ *Questions 3–7*

Task location: Spread throughout the text

3 Answer: H
Note Drucker's and Handy's books are said to deserve their success because they are well-written, clear and relevant to a wide range of people.

4 Answer: E
Note 'Add to that ... '. The writer lists here reasons why managers are 'in a permanent state of confusion' and need advice on management.

5 Answer: D
Note We are told that Caulkin 'is philosophical about the inevitability of finding so much dross'. He is not surprised that it is certain that most management books are rubbish.

6 Answer: C
Note Last sentence: Some books 'never make it to the review pages' (are not considered worth reviewing) because they are 'unreadable'.

7 Answer: G
Note Kennedy says that consultants 'are among the worst offenders'. They are a group of people who are particularly guilty of writing books full of jargon that cannot be understood.

▶ *Questions 8–13*

Task location: Spread throughout the text

8 Answer: C
Note Paragraph E, last sentence and paragraph F, 1st sentence: This book is about publishers' desire to find 'the next big management idea', which will result in very high book sales. It 'tracks' (examines the progress of) 'blockbusters' (books that have sold in enormous quantities) in the management genre over the past 20 years, making big profits for publishers and authors. The *Next Big Idea* therefore looks at management books that have been very successful.

9 Answer: D
Note Paragraph F: This book made claims that 'started to look less than solid' (began to appear not to be based on fact) because some of the companies used in it as examples of good companies suffered a rapid 'reversal of fortune' (quickly changed from being successful to being unsuccessful) and became 'basket cases' (in a hopeless situation).

10 Answer: B
Note Paragraph C: This book is said to 'over-promise' and 'under-deliver', which means that the writer of it makes claims about how good it is, but the book itself does not fulfil the promises made, and does not contain what it is said to contain.

11 Answer: E
Note Paragraph F, last sentence: This book suggested a certain way of improving a company's position, but people who followed this advice realised that it 'caused more problems than it solved'.

12 Answer: A
Note Paragraph C, 1st sentence: This book provides an 'overview' (a general look) at people whose ideas and books have been the most influential.

13 Answer: B
Note Paragraph C: There is a reference to the 'banality' (stating of things that are obvious and therefore not worth saying) of this book, and the fact that the writing is 'leaden' (very dull), with the result that Kennedy had completely lost interest in it after 31 pages.

READING Passage 2

▶ *Questions 14–18*

14 Answer: viii
Note The whole paragraph consists of the writer's argument that the architecture of a stadium is important. Throughout the first paragraph, he gives reasons in support of his strongly held belief that the architecture of stadiums is just as important as the architecture of other buildings because sport itself is important in people's lives.

15 Answer: iv
Note In most of this paragraph, the writer contrasts stadiums that are popular with stadiums that are considered attractive. The most popular stadiums are not, in his view, attractive ones, and the ones that are considered attractive are also said not to be very good from a practical point of view.

16 Answer: vi
Note In this paragraph, the writer says that Sydney 'set about' (started) its programme of urban regeneration 'in a wholly impressive way' when it was preparing to stage the Olympics. His main point in the paragraph is that, although he does not normally like the buildings produced for Olympic Games, staging the games can be good for 'urban regeneration', – in Sydney the work that was carried out at the beginning of the process of getting ready for the Games (listed in the 2nd half of the paragraph) was very good and suggested that the outcome would be a good one.

17 Answer: v
Note This paragraph describes the special arrangement for the funding and ownership of Stadium Australia. That it was a special arrangement is indicated by the fact that it had a special name ('BOOT').

18 Answer: ii
Note This paragraph mainly describes the ways in which various aspects of the stadium met the general requirement of being environmentally friendly.

▶ *Questions 19–22*

Task location: Paragraphs A, B and C

19 Answer: NOT GIVEN
Note Paragraph A: 'What better way ...'. The writer is saying that the public would be more aware of and appreciate 'quality design' if sports stadiums were examples of good design. His point throughout paragraph A is that people expect buildings in which cultural events take place to be 'grand' and 'inspirational' (magnificent and exciting), and that stadiums should also be like that. However, he does not say whether or not the public complain about the quality of the design of stadiums.

20 Answer: TRUE
Note Paragraph A, last sentence: The writer says that it's possible that 'better stadiums might make for' (help to create) 'better citizens'. By this he means that they might encourage people to behave better as members of society.

21 Answer: NOT GIVEN
Note Paragraph B: The writer talks about different opinions of various stadiums, saying that what people think of some stadiums is connected more with the events that happen there than with the building itself, and also saying that some stadiums are 'rather poorly designed'. However, he does not compare any stadiums in terms of the amount of criticism they have received.

22 Answer: FALSE
Note Paragraph C: 'Nor, as a spectator ...'. The writer says that 'the bloated Games programme' places certain demands on stadium designers. He means that designers are forced to produce certain designs because of the large number of events that have to be staged in the Olympics. They are therefore not free to choose what they might consider to be good designs, and so it is not their fault that the designs have not been better.

▶ *Questions 23–26*

Task location: Paragraph E
23 Answer: natural lighting
Note 'In order to reduce ... '. The design made it possible to use this 'in as many public areas as possible'.

24 Answer: mechanical air-conditioning
Note 'Wherever possible ... '.

25 Answer: storm water
Note This ran off the roof and into storage tanks and was then used in toilets.

26 Answer: pitch irrigation
Note This was collected separately from storm water, ran off the roof and into storage tanks, and was then used on the playing area.

READING Passage 3

▶ *Questions 27–29*

Task location: 1st, 2nd and 3rd paragraph
27, 28, 29 Answer: C/D/E (in any order)
Note Option C: 1st paragraph.'I say "attempted" ... '. The writer refers to the 'absence of community', which means that the people could not be considered a single group with much in common. They were all different from each other and lived separate lives.
Option D: 1st paragraph, same sentence. The writer refers to the 'intensely private nature of London households', which means that people did not want to give private information on their personal lives.
Option E: 3rd paragraph, 1st sentence. The writer says that he has had to 'gloss over' the fact that (avoid drawing attention to the unfortunate fact that) the amount of his involvement differed greatly with different households. Some he only talked to about their shopping, and some he visited at home and accompanied when they went shopping. He would clearly have preferred to have the maximum involvement with all the households, but he was not able to do so.
Option A is not a possible answer. 1st and 2nd paragraphs: He says that he aimed to carry out an ethnography (a kind of study) of shopping in a certain place and that his part would focus on 'shopping itself'. He does not say that he was ever not sure what the study should be about.

Option B is not a possible answer. 1st paragraph: He found 76 households, but he does not say what number he tried to find. He was not able to get very involved with some of them, but he does not say he found it hard to get enough people willing to take part in his study.
Option F is not a possible answer. 3rd paragraph: He was more involved with some people than with others, but he does not say that some people agreed to take part and then changed their minds.

▶ *Questions 30–37*

Task location: 4th, 5th and last paragraph
30 Answer: NOT GIVEN
Note 4th paragraph: The writer describes both traditions and says that he intends to 'emphasize the latter' (anthropological generalisation), but he does not say whether one is more generally used than the other.

31 Answer: YES
Note 4th paragraph, last part: The writer says that he intends to use anthropological generalisation because almost all of the acts of shopping in his study 'exhibit a normative form'. This is clearly something which he feels makes anthropological generalisation appropriate.

32 Answer: YES
Note 4th paragraph, last sentence: He says that he believes that the 'heterogenous' (consisting of many different kinds of people) group he studied carried out 'homogenous cultural practices' (ones that are all of the same type). He is therefore saying that he can generalise about shopping because the people he studied all did the same things.

33 Answer: NO
Note 5th paragraph, 1st sentence: The writer says that his ideas are 'at odds with' (opposed to) 'most of the literature on this topic'. His conclusions will therefore not agree with those of other research.

34 Answer: YES
Note 5th paragraph: 'My premise ... shopper'. The writer is saying that the basis of his theory is that people usually don't do shopping for their own benefit but for other reasons.

35 Answer: NOT GIVEN
Note 5th paragraph, second half: The writer gives two purposes he believes shopping to have and analyses in both cases the motives of people when they are shopping. However, he does not say whether or not he thinks people analyse their own motives when they are shopping – the analysis is his.

36 Answer: NO
Note 5th paragraph, last sentence: The writer says that shopping 'transcends any immediate utility' (its aim is higher than simply the practical use of the things that are bought). He is saying that shopping is concerned with general values in life more than with the actual things people buy.

37 Answer: NO
Note Last paragraph, 1st sentence: The writer says that he never thought while he was carrying out his study that the subject of sacrifice would come into it. However, that subject did come into it later. His study was not an attempt to test the theories he now has; the theories, which include the area of 'sacrifice', developed after he had done the study. He therefore did not know before he started the study what theories would result from it.

▶ *Questions 38–40*

Task location: Last paragraph
38 Answer: thrift
Note 'The literature ... chapter 3'. He says that he first

thought that the research most closely connected with his own research in London was research on thrift (being careful with money).

39 Answer: Hubert and Mauss
Note 'The crucial element ... my interpretation'. He says that work done by Bataille led him to the area of sacrifice, but that the work done by Hubert and Mauss is 'the primary grounds for my interpretation'. His interpretation is mainly based on their work.

40 Answer: colloquial/metaphorical
Note He says that he uses the colloquial sense of the word 'only rarely', and that the metaphorical sense may be useful at some point, but it is 'secondary' (of less importance) in comparison with the sense of the word in connection with 'structure' (here he means in connection with 'ancient' or 'traditional' sacrifice').

WRITING Task 1

See sample answer on page 204.

NOTES
Content points
The answer should focus on the most important points shown in the two charts – the main reasons in the first chart and the main reasons in the second chart. It should link the two charts by comparing the percentages in each of them and commenting on any important differences. The general conclusion at the end here is the most important change shown in the two charts.

Organisation
The answer should begin by discussing the first chart, move on to the second chart, comparing it with the first, and then end with a conclusion drawn from the two charts.

Use of language
Linking: The phrase *according to* is required for referring to what the teachers report. *Therefore* is used for talking about the result of something. In this case, it is used for what can be concluded as a result of the information. *With* is used for linking parts of a sentence, to introduce an additional piece of information or the result of something.
Grammatical structures: Superlative structures such as the *most common*, *the biggest change* and *the next biggest increase* are required. Present participles are used instead of relative clauses, for example *people learning* (people who are learning), *the number learning* (the number who are learning). The *-ing* form of verbs is used as the subject of clauses, for example, *having a foreign partner*.
Vocabulary: The verb *indicate* is used for talking about what the information shows or means. Words and phrases describing changes, such as *increase in* are also required.

WRITING Task 2

See sample answer on page 204.

Notes
Content points
The answer discusses both kinds of people referred to in the statement in the task – those for whom work is the most important thing in life and those for whom hobbies and leisure pursuits are more important than work. General points and details are given for both attitudes. Opinions are given on the causes and results of both attitudes, and an opinion is given as a conclusion on the subject as a whole.

Organisation
The answer deals with the two attitudes in the same order as they appear in the statement in the task. In the first paragraph, the disadvantages of the first attitude are discussed, and in the second paragraph positive views of that attitude are discussed. In the third paragraph, the second attitude is discussed, and reasons for it and opinions on it are given. The final paragraph presents general opinions on the subject as a whole, referring to both attitudes.

Use of language
Linking: *Because* is used throughout to link causes and results. *However* is used at the beginning of a new sentence to contrast ideas. *Of course* is used to introduce something considered obvious and *unfortunately* is used to link a fact with an undesirable result.
Grammatical structures: A conditional structure with *if* and two present simple verbs is used to talk about a general fact in the second paragraph. The structure *make someone* + adjective to talk about the cause of a feeling is used in the last sentence of the second paragraph. The structure *involve + -ing* is used at the beginning of the third paragraph to talk about a feature of something.
Vocabulary: Words and phrases appropriate for the topic used here include: *live for something, be obsessed by, workaholic, in a state of, earn a living, balance* and *compensate for*.

GENERAL TRAINING

 TEST A

READING Section 1

▶ *Questions 1–7*

1 Answer: over 300
Note First section, second box: 91 is the number of routes (places buses go to and from) with new buses that have been added, not the number of new buses.

2/3 Answer: 3/three doors; low floor (in either order)
Note Second section, second and third sentences: Both features make it easy and quick for people to get on and off.

4 Answer: before boarding
Note Second section, last sentence: People do not get on the bus and then buy a ticket; they already have one.

5 Answer: monthly; annual
Note Last section, second sentence: Together with annual Bus Passes, these can be bought online and by phone.

6 Answer: (a) Saver
Note With this, you pay a maximum of 35p less than the normal price per journey.

7 Answer: Travel Information centres
Note We are told that 'like all other tickets', Saver tickets can be bought here. This means that all tickets can be bought in Travel Information centres.

▶ *Questions 8–14*

8 Answer: NOT GIVEN
Note The text is about how the scheme works. In the first section, it gives the background to the scheme and why it has been set up, but there is no information on how popular it is.

9 Answer: TRUE
Note 1st section: The text says that people in the area may have to wait 'several years' until a suitable property is available for them, which means that there are not enough properties in the area for everyone.

10 Answer: TRUE
Note 2nd section: The text says that 'you can still contact' an officer and apply to councils 'outside the area' if your situation does not match any of those listed.

11 Answer: FALSE
Note 2nd section: It is 'unlikely' that someone with 'rent arrears' (money owed for rent) will be offered a home through the scheme; this means it probably won't happen, but it is not completely impossible.

12 Answer: NOT GIVEN
Note 2nd section: The text refers to other areas outside the one covered by this council, and it also states that you can ask to move to 'more than one area', but it does not say that you have a better chance of finding a home in some areas than in others.

13 Answer: FALSE
Note 3rd section: An officer will 'send you a form' and 'arrange' the trip. The officer will 'arrange for you to go'. This means that the officer does not go with you.

14 Answer: FALSE
Note You will receive 'reasonable expenses' for the trip to visit a property, but you do not have to agree to live in that property 'if you do not like it'. This means that you receive the expenses for the trip even if you don't decide to live in the property.

READING Section 2

▶ *Questions 15–21*

15 Answer: B
Note This is said to be 'the perfect setting' (location) 'for international students'.

16 Answer: C
Note 'Health & Social Care' courses take place here. Various kinds of nursing come into the category of 'Health Care'.

17 Answer: D
Note This place is 'a short step' (a very small distance) from 'busy shopping streets' (ones with a lot of people in them).

18 Answer: A
Note Here, 'the latest addition' (the newest thing) is a 'professional media make-up studio' (a place for people to learn how to do make-up for performers in the media).

19 Answer: B
Note This centre is in a 'leafy, residential area' – a place with a lot of trees and houses, rather than shops, main roads, offices and factories, etc. This indicates that the area is a pleasant one.

20 Answer: E
Note The 'Tudor Hall' here was built and used as a school in the 16th century.

21 Answer: E
Note The Belling Suite is a 'purpose built' (built for a specific use) 'unit', which contains PCs. This means it was specially created as an IT facility.

▶ *Questions 22–27*

22 Answer: Learning centres
Note 2nd section, last sentence: Here, we are told that the staff 'are always on hand to help'.

23 Answer: Youth Work team
Note 3rd section: We are told that you should 'contact' (get in touch with) the Youth Work Team leaders 'for more information' (to find out about the Student Union).

24 Answer: debates
Note 4th section: In the list of activities, debates (formal discussions of a topic involving speeches in favour of and against something, followed by a vote from the audience) are included.

25 Answer: student common rooms
Note 4th section: Details of events can be found on notice boards, and you can also find out about them if you 'drop into' (visit without arranging to do so beforehand or making an appointment) the student common rooms.

26 Answer: Poppins shops
Note These places sell 'stationery' (paper, pens and other equipment needed by students or used in offices).

27 Answer: an induction course
Note You have to 'complete an induction course' (a course introducing you to how to do something) if you want to use the equipment there.

READING Section 3

▶ *Questions 28–33*

28 Answer: v
Note The second and biggest part of the paragraph is about the problem starting with difficulty lifting a pan, the problem continuing and then the problem getting very bad, with 'intense' pain and cramp and 'horrific pins and needles' (these are all words used for different kinds of pain).

29 Answer: viii
Note This paragraph deals with the number of British people who have the problem. We are told that the figure is probably higher than the one officially given. Having talked about the number of sufferers, the paragraph then mentions some of the groups of people included in this number.

30 Answer: iii
Note In this paragraph, we are told that specialists 'draw a parallel between' RSI sufferers and marathon runners; this means, they say, that the two groups are similar or the same in some way. We are then told about how the two groups differ. This means it is wrong to compare the two because they are not the same or similar.

31 Answer: x
Note This paragraph describes the many things that Pia Enoizi did, and the different people she went to for treatment, in order to deal with the problem. It is therefore about the different things she tried in order to solve the problem.

32 Answer: vi
Note This paragraph is about the fact that she now suffers less from the problem because of using a curved keyboard and because of the nature of her job, but she still suffers 'a little pain', so the problem is not completely solved.

33 Answer: ii
Note The main topic of this paragraph is her belief that schoolchildren could start to suffer from the problem and her belief that something should be done to prevent this from happening.

▶ *Questions 34–39*

Task location: Section B
34 Answer: official
Note 'Work-related upper limb disorder' is the 'official' name because it is the one used by 'specialists' (doctors who specialise in a particular area of medicine). This name is contrasted with the term 'RSI', which is not an official name used by medical experts, but used commonly by the public and people who are not doctors.

35 Answer: unknown
Note Various kinds of people who suffer from the problem are not included in the figure of half a million, which means that the real number of sufferers is not known.

36 Answer: secret
Note Some sufferers are not included in the figure because they are people who suffer from the condition 'in silence'. They hide the fact that they have the problem because they don't want to 'lose their jobs'.

37 Answer: general
Note RSI is said to be 'an umbrella term' – a general name used for something that has a variety of different forms or categories.

38 Answer: routine
Note Some of the people mentioned are people who do things 'repeatedly' as part of their jobs. Something that is done repeatedly as part of a job is a routine task.

39 Answer: clear
Note We are told that there is no evidence that text messaging can cause the problem, but that advice has been given to help people avoid the problem when text messaging. It is therefore not clear whether or not it can cause the problem, but one company thinks it is a possibility, so they have given advice about it.

▶ *Question 40*

Task location: Sections D and E
40 Answer: D/E/F/G (in any order)
Note D: We are told that Pilates, because it emphasises 'posture and balancing muscles', helped her.
E: We are told that physiotherapy 'proved crucial' (was extremely important) and 'made a big difference', giving her 'a feeling of liberation'.
F: The keyboard helps because it means that she uses her wrists, arms and elbows in a 'more relaxed' way.
G: She does this rather than jogging, which she says can 'aggravate joints' (damage them and make them painful). This means that brisk walking must be good for the condition.
Option A is incorrect: This involved telling another student what to write down, but doing this caused 'a painful contraction of the neck muscles'.
Option B is incorrect: The sentence 'But none of these made a difference' refers back to the treatments previously mentioned that she tried, and going to an osteopath is one of those.
Option C is incorrect: This is another of the treatments that didn't work, referred to by 'none of these'.
Option H is incorrect: See note on option G.

WRITING Task 1

Note: General Training Writing answers are marked according to the same criteria as Academic Training Writing answers.

See sample answer on page 205.
Notes
Content points
The three bullet points required are all covered. The answer refers to the writer looking forward to the visit, contains a suggestion as to a place to go on the birthday and asks the friend for their opinion on this.

Organisation
The answer follows the order of the bullet points, with each one in a separate paragraph. It is common in these tasks for one bullet point to produce more of the answer than the other bullet points.

In this case, the part about the proposed trip is the longest. The letter has an appropriate opening line and an appropriate ending. It begins with a reference to the forthcoming visit and ends with a reference to further contact.

Use of language
Linking: Several sentences are linked by *and* so that the letter does not contain a lot of short, simple sentences and flows well. Other good uses of linking words and phrases include *while, including,* and *If so.*
Grammatical structures: Tag questions (in this letter *won't it?* in the second paragraph) are often appropriate in this kind of informal letter. The third sentence of the second paragraph includes a conditional structure and a relative clause with *which.* The question form *do you fancy?* and the request form *let me know* are very useful in informal letters of this kind.
Vocabulary: Good and appropriate vocabulary in this answer includes: *look forward to, have a great time, have fun, apparently, appeals to.*

WRITING Task 2

See sample answer on page 205.

Notes
Content points
The answer fully addresses the issues in the task. Two different aspects (weight and clothes) are discussed, and examples are given of the problems they cause and the reasons why they cause these problems. Both questions asked in the task are answered. The answer states clear agreement with the statement and discusses the situation in the writer's own country.

Organisation
The answer flows logically from one point to the next and is appropriately divided into paragraphs. It begins by agreeing with the statement in general. In the first paragraph, the issue of weight is discussed, with causes and results of worrying about this and reference to the writer's own country. In the second paragraph, clothes are discussed in the same way. The third paragraph presents a clear opinion as a conclusion.

Use of language
Linking: In several sentences, *because* is used to link causes and results so that there are not a lot of sentences that are short and too simple. Other words and phrases used for linking are *Certainly, For example, Even* and *In my opinion.*
Grammatical structures: The modal structures *ought to, shouldn't* and *should* are used for expressing opinions on what is right and wrong. The structure *make someone + adjective* is used for describing the cause of a feeling. The structure *cause someone something* is used for describing the result of something.
Vocabulary: Words and phrases appropriate for the topic used here include: *on a diet, of some sort, disorders, something wrong with* and *laugh at.*

TEST **B**

READING Section 1

▶ *Questions 1–7*

1 Answer: NOT GIVEN
Note 1st paragraph: We are told that it is a national scheme, and that the aim is to get a million people to walk regularly, but we are not told how much publicity has been given to the scheme.

2 Answer: YES
Note 2nd paragraph: The Volunteer Leaders are said to do

'hard work' and to have 'dedication' (willingness to work hard and make a lot of effort for something you consider important).

3 Answer: NOT GIVEN
Note 2nd paragraph: We are told about many things leaders have to do, even in bad weather, and this might cause some of them to give up, but we are not told that this happens.

4 Answer: NO
Note 3rd and 4th paragraph: We are told that people who do it need to have 'motivation' and 'commitment', and that they need to change their lifestyles very much. This means they need to have a strong desire to do it, they need to keep doing it even if it proves difficult, and they need to change the way they live in a big way. None of these things are simple things, and it is easy for people to decide not to walk one day, for example because of the weather or because they are tired.

5 Answer: NO
Note 5th and 6th paragraph: Although they have informal names, they have a serious purpose. They show that people are 'dedicated' and people who get them can feel 'proud'.

6 Answer: NOT GIVEN
Note 7th paragraph: When you've done 75 walks, you can be satisfied with yourself that you have a 'good habit', and when you do another 25 and reach 100, you will get a gift. The writer does not say whether or not many people are expected to do 100 walks.

7 Answer: YES
Note Last paragraph: There may be a 'delay' before you get a reward because the registers are only looked at 'quarterly' (every three months). But if your name is on the register for each walk because it was 'taken down' (written down) when you went on the walk, you will definitely get the reward at some point.

▶ *Questions 8–14*

8, 9 Answer: large print; spoken word (in either order)
Note 5th paragraph: This paragraph is about 'adult fiction'. Books in this category will be displayed 'by genre' (according to what category of fiction they belong to), and there will be separate sections for large print books (for people with poor eyesight) and spoken word books (books on audio tape).

10 Answer: activities; story(-)telling
Note 6th paragraph: If there is 'room for' something, there is space for it. There will be more of various items, but these are the two things that we are told there will be a bigger area for.

11 Answer: community hall
Note 4th paragraph: The two rooms not labelled in the diagram are the community hall and the meeting room. As the meeting room is described as the 'smaller' of the two, this room must be the community hall.

12 Answer: meeting room
Note 4th paragraph: This is said to be 'available for hire' (a charge is made for using it).

13 Answer: music listening
Note 4th paragraph: In this context, 'posts' are fixed places with equipment attached to them.

14 Answer: seating area
Note 6th paragraph: This is a seating area specially for teenagers in their own section of the library.

▶ *Questions 15–20*

15 Answer: reference form
Note This is the second step described. You 'complete' the reference form.

16 Answer: tutor
Note You send the reference form to someone, 'usually' (but not always, it could be someone else) your 'present or last' tutor, so that they can write about you.

17 Answer: tour of college
Note The first thing mentioned for the day of the interview is the tour of the college.

18 Answer: exam results
Note A conditional offer may require certain exam results, practical tests or reports. Evidence is required for the exam results (proof of the grades that you got).

19 Answer: places available
Note This offer may be made because too many people have applied for a course (it is 'oversubscribed') and so all the places have already been filled.

20 Answer: in writing
Note In this situation, the college will write to you and suggest what you might do next (instead of going to the college).

▶ *Questions 21–27*

21 Answer: D
Note The Progression Centre gives information and advice not only to students of the college but also to 'the local community' (people who live in the area but are not students at the college).

22 Answer: G
Note 'Counselling and Student Services' section: The College Youth Worker is one of a number of people listed who provide 'personal counselling'. This means advice on things causing 'difficulties or worry' in students' personal lives, rather than problems connected with the college or course.

23 Answer: F
Note The staff here are said to 'guide' students when they are doing 'information-gathering tasks for assignments'.

24 Answer: I
Note 'Learning Support' section: In the first sentence, we are told that this concerns problems connected with coursework. In such cases, the support given may involve 'outside agencies'.

25 Answer: H
Note The staff here will help you to 'match' your education and training needs with 'the right course'.

26 Answer: B
Note 'Careers' sectio: This place has 'drop-in sessions' (when people can go without making an appointment beforehand) for people who have 'quick queries' (questions that can be answered quickly).

27 Answer: C
Note 'Learning Support' section: This person will speak to students and then 'develop a support programme based on individual need'.

▸ *Questions 28–33*

28 Answer: C
Note Last sentence: The phrase 'now that' refers to the current situation in contrast with the situation in the past. Companies are now allowed to do something connected with accountancy that they couldn't do before.

29 Answer: H
Note Last sentence: We are told that a 'mob' is the 'collective noun' for a group of kangaroos.

30 Answer: G
Note 1st sentence: John has made an agreement to sell half a dozen numbats (the 'appealing little animals' named at the end of section F) to the West Australian government.

31 Answer: E
Note Last sentence: John believes that in the future, conservation companies 'will be everywhere' (lots of companies like his will be started).

32 Answer: H
Note Wilma the wombat looks 'cute' (sweet and nice) but has 'quite a bite' (will bite and hurt you).

33 Answer: B
Note 2nd sentence: Both the stars and the 'powerful torches' are said to 'capture an array' of creatures as they move along (make it possible for a variety of creatures to be seen).

▸ *Questions 34–39*

34 Answer: Y
Note Section F: John is still talking about Yookamurra (second sentence) when he says that 'the wood is worthless' later in the section.

35 Answer: Y
Note Section H: The 'tourist huts' referred to in the second sentence are in Yookamurra, which is the sanctuary described in this section (see first sentence).

36 Answer: S
Note Section I: This is the 'newest' sanctuary, as well as the largest.

37 Answer: S
Note Section I: The writer comments 'really appealing animals – honestly' about stick nest rats, suggesting that he thinks that people would not expect creatures with such a name to be nice.

38 Answer: W
Note Section D: This section is about Warrawong (first sentence), and we are told that John 'turned a dairy farm into' a sanctuary there. It used to be a dairy farm, but he changed it.

39 Answer: W
Note Section F, second sentence: We are told that John 'dug out personally' the 'swamps and ponds' there.

▸ *Question 40*

40 Answer: C
Note Throughout the text, the writer approves of or is excited by what he sees and learns, and he makes no criticisms.
Option A is incorrect: He describes John's attitude to the business and the fact that animals are given a financial value; this surprises him, but he does not say that he thinks it may be a bad thing.
Option B is incorrect: Various endangered species are mentioned, but the writer does not refer to his previous knowledge of the subject.

Option D is incorrect: The ideas have not been tried before, but the writer does not say that he thinks this is very surprising.

WRITING Task 1

See sample answer on page 206.

Notes
Content points
The answer deals with everything contained in the question. A description of the visit is required, including the writer's situation. A description of what the staff did and why it was helpful is given. A request for the head of staff to give the writer's thanks is included.

Organisation
The answer follows the order of the bullet points, with a paragraph for each. It begins with a description of the background – when the writer visited the museum, who the writer was with – and it also contains the reason why the writer is writing the letter. The second paragraph deals with what happened with regard to the help given by staff, and the last paragraph concludes with a request for the head of staff to thank the staff.

Use of language
Linking: Several sentences are linked by *and*, so that sentences that are not too simple and too short are created. *When* and *As* are used in the second paragraph to link parts of sentences in terms of time.
Grammatical structures: A relative clause with *who* is used in the first sentence. The structure *I would like + infinitive* is used appropriately in the first paragraph. The structure *I would be grateful if you could* is used in the last paragraph.
Vocabulary: Good and appropriate vocabulary includes: *enjoyable, a long queue, patiently, a great success, treating* and *memorable*.

WRITING Task 2

See sample answer on page 206.

Notes
Content points
The answer deals with both views, discussing why parents think that their children should be ambitious and also discussing the opposite view – why ambition may not always be a good thing and why some young people are not ambitious. The writer's opinions are given throughout, and the answer ends with a general opinion and conclusion.

Organisation
The first paragraph deals with the first view, describing the attitude of parents and giving reasons for it. The second paragraph deals with the second view, giving reasons for it. The last paragraph presents the writer's opinion on the issue in general.

Use of language
Linking: The second sentence of the first paragraph presents a list, with each desire on the part of parents in the infinitive form. *Therefore* links a cause and a result at the end of the first paragraph, and *However* (at the beginning of a new sentence) links contrasting ideas.
Grammatical structures: The following good structures are used appropriately: *hard for someone + infinitive, not everyone + positive verb, capable of + -ing, would rather + infinitive without 'to', spend time + -ing* and *there is no reason why*.
Vocabulary: Good and appropriate vocabulary includes: *understandable, at the higher levels, natural, accept, achieve, desperately, youth* and *goals*.

Section 1

Man: Easylet. Good morning. How can I help you?

Woman: Hello. I saw your advertisement in the paper and I'm calling to ask about renting a flat.

Man: Certainly. What kind of flat had you in mind?

Woman: Well, er, I don't know exactly … I mean, it depends on price, to some extent.

Man: OK, now we have properties across the whole range. The average is probably £120 a week.

Woman: Oh, I was hoping for something a little cheaper.

Man: They start at £90, that's the lowest we have usually. And they go up to £200.

Woman: I could manage the lowest figure.

Man: An important question is how long you're thinking of staying in the property. We don't do short lets.

Woman: I'd want a flat for nine months, perhaps longer.

Man: That would be fine. Our contracts are for a standard six months, and that can be extended.

Woman: Fine. I'd need to come in and see you?

Man: Yes, our office is open from 9 am to 5 pm.

Woman: I'd need to come in on Saturday.

Man: OK, then we're here between 10 am and 4 pm. We also open on Sunday mornings, until 1 pm.

Woman: Saturday is fine. If possible, I'd like to see details of some properties first.

Man: We can post you a list. Or you may find it easier to look on the internet.

Woman: Oh, yes, I have the address here, thank you.

Man: What else would you like to know?

Woman: I wonder what I might need to buy for a flat. What's included in the rent?

Man: That depends on the flat, to a certain extent, although some things are standard in all flats. For example, every flat has kitchen equipment provided for your use.

Woman: Good. Does that also mean tableware, cups, glasses, plates?

Man: In some flats, but not all.

Woman: OK. And bathroom towels, sheets, and so on?

Man: I don't think any flats have those included.

Woman: I can easily buy some. I don't suppose flats come with a TV?

Man: In fact they all do – although they may not be the most modern models.

Woman: Oh, that's fine.

Man: But it's different with the telephone. That's up to you to organise. These days, most people seem just to use their mobile phone.

Woman: I can imagine. What extra charges would I get? Is heating extra?

Man: Yes, it is, but the water bill is part of the rent, so you don't have to pay for that.

Woman: Right, I've noted all that.

Man: Are you looking to move into a flat soon?

Woman: I hope so, yes.

Man: The thing is, we have a few flats at the moment that we'd like to get rented out by the end of the month.

Woman: I see.

Man: They're all good flats, and at the price you want. There's one in Eastern Towers, one in Granby Mansions and another in Busby Garden. All three are nice blocks of flats.

Woman: Could you tell me where they are? I'm at the train station at the moment.

Man: Eastern Towers, if you're coming from the station, isn't very far. Cross over City Bridge. Then go left, and where the road divides, you want the right-hand fork. You'll see Eastern Towers on the left side of the road. It's a lovely building, with trees around it.

Woman: That sounds nice. What about Granby Mansions?

Man: The best way to get there from the station is probably to go down River Road and then cross over Old Bridge. The road bends to the right, round the park, and if you follow along, you'll find it there, on the left side. That's a great location, with lovely views of the park.

Woman: Very nice. And you said there was one more?

Man: Busby Garden, yes. OK, from the station, cross over City Bridge, keep going through the first crossroads until you come to the second crossroads. Busby Garden will be facing you, over to the right side. It's very convenient for the shops.

Woman: Fine. Thank you. Well, I'll see you on Saturday.

Section 2

Guide: It's nice to see so many of you here. I'm going to tell you something about Hollylands – our facilities and activities, and the exhibitions we have coming up. I hope you'll find it interesting and bring your pupils along. For most of what we have to offer here, you can just turn up with your party. I'm pleased to say that recent work has meant that the whole centre is prepared for blind visitors. There are a couple of activities where we ask you to book a week in advance. We only have artists that you can watch painting at certain times, so we need notice of your coming for that. The other activity requiring at least 7 days' notice is the drama workshop – again, it's a question of organising the staff at this end. But the video you work yourself, and so that's available any time. Another activity where you need to think ahead is the garden sculpture experience, but that's a question of the weather, which of course we can't control! Speaking of weather, we run a reduced range of facilities in the winter months. While the café and the shop provide welcome shelter from the cold and rain, I'm afraid our artist in residence scheme isn't run in the winter, so the studio is closed then. And the animals in the mini zoo are kept indoors for warmth during the cold months, so that doesn't operate either. The adventure playground does – though make sure the children are wrapped up well!

OK, now we run a programme of exhibitions through the year, so I'll tell you about the next few. Our current exhibition, *Local Lives*, ends on 26th August, and then one called *History in Pictures* starts on 28th August. This includes all sorts of objects and experiences from the past, such as farm machinery and some cars. We're sure children will love the chance to have a ride on an old bus. Next, we're running a show called *People at Work*, and this will open on 19th September. There will be pictures and videos depicting all sorts of jobs, from coal mining to flying planes. And there's a careers advice service available for everyone to consult. Following on from that show, we're putting on an exhibition called *Land from Air*. This starts on 11th November and includes hundreds of aerial photographs. A competition accompanies the show, with the exciting prize of a balloon trip for two. So, we hope to see you at at least one of the exhibitions.

Now, the area occupied by Hollylands is rather large, and we don't want people to get lost, so I'll just give you a few pointers to help you orientate yourselves. So, whether you come by car or bicycle, you'll come in from the road. Cars then park to the left, through the gates into the car park, and bikes to the right, through the gates opposite. Cyclists in particular might be feeling thirsty at this point, and you can get a drink from the machine at the end of the bike park, halfway to the museum entrance. You can enjoy your drink in the picnic area, which is opposite the car park. For anyone who doesn't have a mobile phone, there are payphones at the far end of the picnic area. Over at the opposite end of the picnic area, across the path, are the toilets. Next to them, and just to the right of the entrance to the main museum, is the first aid room, which we hope you won't need, but it's there in case you do. If you have any queries, please go to the manager's office, which is behind the picnic area. And, last but not least, you'll need to buy your tickets or show your group pass to the ticket office on the left of the museum entrance. OK, I'll pause there – are there any questions at this point?

Section 3

Kate: Hi, Martin.

Martin: Hi, Kate. How are you?

Kate: Fine. I'm relieved to have done my presentation!

Martin: I'm sure! How did it go?

Kate: Oh, OK in the end, but I was ever so nervous beforehand. It's silly, because I do know my stuff quite well. I must know those statistics inside out, but when you have to get each table of results to come up in the right order, it can make you nervous. It was my first time using the computerised projector, and I was sure I was going to get the controls wrong, or something. And of course, that's not a good situation, if you know you've got to listen to questions carefully, and be ready to answer quickly.

Martin: But it was fine once you got going?

Kate: Yes.

Martin: I do feel that the standard of presentations could be improved in general. I think a lot of the lecturers agree with me, although I don't honestly know what they can be expected to do about it. Students need to appreciate the difference between style and content. Too many presentations are just a mass of detailed content – all very worthy – without any attempt to engage people's interest. Basic things, like looking at your audience's faces, seem to get forgotten. And that makes it harder to concentrate on the points made about the research itself.

Kate: Yes, there are quite a few improvements I'd like to see. Take tutorials, for example. I feel they're often a missed opportunity. I come out not feeling sure about what I've learnt. Week in week out, I faithfully plough through the reading list, which is fair enough, but then the discussion doesn't seem to extract the main issues. It's frustrating.

Martin: Hmm, I know what you mean. Mind you, we have to take some responsibility ourselves. I actually got quite a lot from that skills workshop I went to on taking notes, and I'd like to make similar improvements in the next semester. The reading list we get has several websites each time, and I want to learn to navigate my way round them more effectively.

Kate: That's sounds a good idea. Mind you, it means spending more time in the library ...

Martin: If you can get in ...

Kate: You mean because it's too crowded? It isn't big enough, is it?

Martin: Well, I don't know. I mean, I like to work late in the evening, and it shuts before I want to finish. But I know you can access the catalogue from a laptop.

Kate: Which personally I haven't got. Actually, the problem for me is that I like to get up early and start work straight away, and they don't start until 9. I wish they'd change that.

Martin: Look, we ought to start working out what to do next for our project.

Kate: Yes, enough moaning!

Martin: OK, the main thing is to allocate the various tasks between us, isn't it?

Kate: Yes. Well, we're going to need the questionnaire before we can do much else, aren't we? Do you want to handle that?

Martin: I'd assumed we'd do it together?

Kate: You have more experience than me. Maybe you could think up the main questions, you know, a first version of the whole thing, and then I could read it through.

Martin: And make suggestions? Well, OK. My experience on projects has all been with closed groups. I don't really know how you go about selecting subjects from larger populations.

Kate: Actually, it's quite straightforward. You use tables of randomised numbers.

Martin: Could you show me?

Kate: Yeah, I'll take you through the process. That way, you'll learn, and I'll feel surer for having someone else there. Now, that brings us to the interviews themselves.

Martin: Right. Would you like to do them? Or are there too many?

Kate: Well, your typing's pretty fast, isn't it? So, if you agree to handle the transcribing afterwards, I'm prepared to do the face-to-face stage. Does that sound fair?

Martin: It does to me. But tell me if you find it takes longer than you thought.

Kate: And vice versa! And when we get the results altogether, they'll need to be run through statistics programmes, won't they? That's where I always feel a bit unsure about which tests are the correct ones to choose.

Martin: Same here. But we can get advice from the lecturers about that. Shall we do all that as a joint effort?

Kate: I think it'd make us feel more secure about what we were doing.

Martin: Yes, it would be terrible to get that wrong after all the hard work leading up to it.

Kate: And then we've got to present the whole thing to the group. Will you feel up to doing that?

Martin: I think we should do a joint presentation. It's all both our work, after all.

Kate: I guess you're right. But would you mind getting the slides and so on ready? I find that takes me ages, and still doesn't look any good.

Martin: Whereas I quite enjoy that kind of thing. OK. Now, we need to think about ...

Section 4

Lecturer: Good afternoon, everybody. Today I'll be talking about the issue of waste, which has become an immense problem in today's society. We face huge challenges in terms of reducing its creation in the first place and then in dealing with it when it has been created. Now, the model of nature would be our ideal – a completely cyclical system in which no excess waste is generated that can't be processed by itself. However, we humans have proved, despite our apparent intelligence and ingenuity, quite incapable of achieving this. Where did it all go wrong? We have evidence that in ancient Greece and Rome governments operated municipal waste collection, and a huge Stone Age mound was identified some years ago in Norway as waste disposal, so we can see that people have been generating waste for a very long time indeed. However, during the Dark Ages, sophisticated municipal waste processing disappeared. The medieval answer to waste was to throw it out of the window. But this waste, apart from broken pottery and a few metal objects, was largely organic. This meant, of course, that it was quickly absorbed into the environment by the natural processes of decay. However, many concerned people, such as doctors, claimed that this created health problems, although it wasn't until science produced convincing evidence of the connection between rubbish and <u>disease</u> that governments began to see the importance of dealing with the problem effectively. Unfortunately, their response has remained slower than the generation of waste. It is very hard to deal with waste that won't melt into the environment, as so many of our modern consumer goods won't, and that's why the invention of <u>plastic</u> has caused the worst headache for the environment – it's more than nature can deal with.

In order to address the root of the problem of waste, we need to think about what has made the quantity of waste accelerate in growth. I'd identify three main reasons. As many countries became industrialised, we saw the advent of <u>mass manufacturing</u>. This has been enormously damaging, as it has greatly increased the amount of things on the planet's surface which don't go away by themselves. Closely related to this is <u>packaging</u> – necessary for transporting things around the world, but then extremely difficult to get rid of properly. And a third aspect to the problem has been <u>disposable goods</u>. We have become accustomed to so many things being to use and then discard that we find it hard to imagine life without them. And yet we spare little thought for where they go when we do discard them.

Right now, let's move on from where all this waste comes from to what is done with it all now it's here. Different countries deal with waste differently. Of course, each country also changes what it does, so the figures for waste treatment I've got here are likely to change in the future. Let's look at Municipal Solid Waste, or MSW. MSW is important to consider because it's effectively a measurement of consumerism – how much waste people produce that goes beyond the absolute basic requirements in life to eat and drink. One of the main ways of dealing with MSW is <u>incineration – burning</u> it. This is adopted variously around the world. The UK burns relatively little waste, as does the US, while Denmark burns about half of all waste, and <u>Japan uses this method for as much as three quarters</u>. These are broad brush strokes, of course, because an important issue is how efficient and clean the burning process is. Another major form of waste treatment is using <u>landfill</u> sites – basically, burying the waste in the earth. Currently, this method is the <u>dominant process used in the UK at over 80%</u>, and is also heavily used in Germany and in the US, while densely populated and mountainous countries such as Switzerland and Japan dispose of relatively little this way. A third – and much better way of dealing with waste is to <u>recycle</u> it, turning it back into more things we need. It must be said that much depends here on whether further waste is generated by the recycling processes themselves. The UK and Japan have rather poor records in recycling, while <u>Switzerland tops the table in this respect</u>, and reasonably impressive levels are achieved by Denmark and Germany. I really hope that if we all gathered here again ten years from now, these figures would be much higher. Time – and a lot of effort – will tell.

IELTS TEST 2

Section 1

Man: Good Times Holidays. John speaking. How may I help you?

Woman: Oh hello. I'm calling to complain about a holiday we've just had.

Man: Oh dear. I'm sorry to hear about that.

Woman: Yes, we're very disappointed.

Man: What I need to do is to take some information from you, so that I can look up the relevant files, and then we can

discuss the specific problems. Would that be alright with you?

Woman: Yes – I hope it doesn't take too long.

Man: Oh no – let me just get a form ready ... First, the name, please. Of the person who booked the holiday.

Woman: Well, our surname's <u>Sharpe. S-H</u> ...

Man: <u>Like a knife?</u>

Woman: <u>Yes, but with an E on the end.</u>

Man: And a first name?

Woman: I'm Alice, but I think it was my husband who actually booked the trip – his name's <u>Andrew</u>.

Man: Fine. And then the address, please.

Woman: It's Flat 4, <u>Beaconsfield – that's B-E-A-C-O-N-S-F-I-E-L-D – House</u>. That's Winchester, and it's S-O-2, er, 4-E-R.

Man: Thank you. And could I take a telephone number?

Woman: We're on 0374 56561 at home, or – do you mean during the day? – then my work number's <u>0374 double-5 793</u>.

Man: I'll put the work one down, assuming that's normal office hours?

Woman: Oh yes.

Man: The next thing is, do you have a note of your booking reference?

Woman: I think so ... would it start 7–4?

Man: Er, no, usually with two or three letters ...

Woman: Uh-huh ... is this it – <u>MH</u> ... ?

Man: That sounds like it.

Woman: And then <u>double-6-G-4</u>.

Man: Thank you. Right, what's next ... uh-huh, now, did you book in conjunction with any kind of special offer?

Woman: Er ...

Man: Or did you book directly with us? Or maybe through a scheme your employer's part of?

Woman: Oh, OK, no, I think – yes, we were using an offer from a <u>credit card</u> company. They always seem to have offers on – you get something with every bill, don't you?

Man: Yes, so many. Fine, and ... now, insurance. Did you have an insurance policy that came with your booking?

Woman: Well, no, I mean it came under our <u>Gold Star</u> Policy ... so we didn't need extra –

Man: No, that's fine, it's just to check. Alright, nearly there. Now, what type of holiday was it?

Woman: Well, not very ... no, OK, it was called a <u>Mid-winter</u> Break in the brochure.

Man: Thank you. And when was the holiday?

Woman: We just got back – on <u>January</u> the twenty-first. And we started on <u>the sixteenth</u>.

Man: Fine. Right, I'm sorry about all that.

Woman: No, I understand.

Man: So, what was the problem you encountered?

Woman: There were two things that disappointed us, actually.

Man: Right.

Woman: In the first place, we were told that when we arrived at the station, a <u>taxi</u> would meet us and take us straight to the house, but in fact there wasn't one there. We had to wait for ages, and then pay for one ourselves. So that was inconvenient and expensive.

Man: Oh, I'll look into that, see what went wrong.

Woman: And the other problem was that we'd been promised there would be a <u>bicycle</u> for each of us stored at the house, ready to use, but there were only three, which is no good for a family of four.

Man: No, it wouldn't be. OK, well I'll check into that as well. Now, if you can give me a few hours, I'll get back to you this afternoon, and then we can discuss ...

Presenter: I'd like to welcome you to the presentation. It's nice to see so many of you here, and I hope that everybody ends up with suitable employment as a result of attending. Now, as you know, we at Select Hotel Recruitment are able to offer a range of work at the better hotels in the area. This month is no exception, and I'll take you through some of what we have on offer. The first job is Reception Assistant, and there are three vacancies for this position at the Park Hotel. This is quite a varied job, and in fact I should point out that at certain times of the day it would involve <u>heavy lifting</u> when guests' luggage arrives or perhaps deliveries come in, so bear that in mind when deciding whether to apply for this post. The Park Hotel has quite an international flavour, so you'll need to speak at least two foreign languages. Many guests, of course, travel by car, and you may have to take their vehicles around to the car park, so you will need to have a valid <u>driving licence</u>, and you will not be allowed to do the job if you haven't. They also say that basic computer skills such as word processing would be an advantage, although this isn't a requirement. OK, now the next job is General Assistant, and there are four vacancies for this at the Avenue Hotel. To be honest, the pay is rather low, but there are compensatory factors that you should bear in mind when considering whether to apply. The hotel will <u>provide</u> you with all your <u>meals</u> while you're working, and they will also <u>train</u> you in all the aspects of the job and then issue you with a <u>certificate</u>, which, of course, could be very valuable to you in the future. Right, the third job on offer is Catering Assistant, and Hotel 56 are looking for four people to fill these vacancies at their smart new premises. As you know, this hotel is popular with exclusive travellers and so you'll need to wear the distinctive staff uniform – which you're provided with. Don't consider this job unless you're fairly flexible about when you work, as the hotel will require you to <u>work nights</u> for this job, and you will need to travel to and from the hotel, as it's situated just outside the city. Well, that's some basic information about the opportunities we currently have on offer.

Now, if you would like to apply for one of these jobs, you will need to follow our recruitment process. It might seem complicated, but we guarantee the hotels we work with to provide carefully vetted staff. So the first thing you'll need to do is fill in one of these – a <u>personal information</u> form. It's pretty straightforward and should only take you a few minutes. Once you've done that and handed it in, we'll give you a questionnaire about your <u>skills</u> to do. Again, I don't expect this to take you very long. We then look through the information about you, and pass on our recommendations to the relevant hotel. Hopefully, you'll be accepted by your chosen hotel. Assuming you are, you will then proceed to the next step of the process and attend a <u>general</u> course of training. This is designed to be helpful and realistic, so an important part of the course is <u>role-play</u> activities. You should have some fun while you learn! OK, and after that, the final step is that you will be contacted by the hotel you're going to work for, and they'll post you a <u>video</u> about themselves and the work involved. Watching this will constitute further, specific training for your job. Well, I hope that's reasonably clear at this stage. Are there any questions on what I've said so far?

Dr Wilson: Hello David, Jane.
Jane: Hello.
David: Hi.
Dr Wilson: So, how's the local history project going? Are you making good progress?
Jane: Yes and no.
Dr Wilson: Oh?

David: Well, we anticipated problems of various kinds. None of the group has much experience of collaborating on projects. But we spent some time discussing how to go about it, and thrashed out what seemed a useful approach, but it seems that Jane and I are the only ones actually <u>following the plan</u>. That's meant that the whole project has been lacking co-ordination and so we've fallen behind our schedule.
Dr Wilson: I see … that's tricky.
Jane: Yes, it is. We felt that the targets had been defined, so we'd all know what to deal with, but, looking back, we probably should have really specified <u>individual responsibilities</u>. As it is, we only have a loose sense of what should be done by who.
Dr Wilson: Well, this is quite a common problem, actually. I take it that you've had enough group meetings, so you're looking for an effective solution. If you go to the Resource Centre, I think you'd find the <u>advice service</u> they provide there helpful at this point.
Jane: Thanks – we'll go there later.
David: On a specific note, I think we've got carried away with recruiting people to interview at the expense of building up the <u>reference section</u>, which I don't think is going to be solid enough. Do you think that'll be a major problem?
Dr Wilson: Hmm, I'd have to see how much is there to be sure, but, well, you'll have to be pragmatic at this point, I think. What you'd better do is ensure your <u>methodology</u> is really strong, so at least you can't be faulted on that front. Then, if people challenge your results, at least you've carefully reported how you reached them. Do you see what I mean?
David/Jane: Yes.
Dr Wilson: So …
Jane: Yes, I think one resource in relation to that that we haven't exploited as fully as we might is the internet. I've taken a lot of journals off the library shelves to go through, but, actually, there are <u>websites</u> where you can call up lists of approaches or data sets really quickly.
Dr Wilson: I think that's a good idea, yes.

Dr Wilson: Now, let's think about the field trip, and at least make sure that goes as well as possible. You're going to Cambridge on the twenty-second?
Jane: The Monday, yes.
David: It's quite soon, now.
Dr Wilson: And in the morning, you'll be travelling and then getting settled into the hotel.
Jane: Uh-huh.
Dr Wilson: But you need to get down to work after lunch, of course. Now, I've arranged for you to have a look at some useful visual material, especially photographs and old magazines and newspapers, which is included in <u>an exhibition at the library in the university</u>.
David: That sounds like a good starting point.
Dr Wilson: There's quite a lot on show, so that'll occupy most of the afternoon. Then the following morning, I want you to go and <u>talk to</u> someone in the City Library. His name's Jarvis Gregson. He works in the Education Section there, and he's <u>an expert on the area's history</u>. Don't, of course, forget to take a tape recorder with you so that you can record what he tells you.
Jane: And to have our questions ready.
Dr Wilson: Indeed. OK, and the afternoon's free for you to wander around, get the feel of the place.
David: Do some sightseeing …
Dr Wilson: As you wish – it's a beautiful city … But it's back to

work on Wednesday morning. Concentrate on <u>the central area, and walk around</u> methodically. You'll have the <u>plans</u> I'm getting ready for you <u>from different periods</u>, and your task is to <u>compare those with the make-up of the city today</u>. Make notes on how different kinds of shops and businesses have grown up, what's gone, and so on.

Jane: I hope the weather's good!

Dr Wilson: Yes. And in the afternoon I want you to think about producing your own records, along the lines of the ones in the City Library's archives. The history of the <u>castle</u> is very important to the city's development, so <u>use a camera to get some pictures</u> that reflect that if you can, showing it <u>in relation to the buildings and spaces around it</u>.

David: We'll try! And when do we travel back?

Dr Wilson: That's up to you. You can either …

Section 4

Lecturer: Today I want to focus on some of the major sights that attract tourists to cities, and I'm going to begin with the London Eye. This giant wheel has in a very few years become one of the major attractions of London, and thus in the world. It's both simple in concept and awesome in delivery. Its creators are husband and wife architects David Marks and Julia Barfield. It was on their kitchen table in South London in 1993 that the first drawings for the London Eye were made, as the couple, who usually worked directly for clients, were entering a <u>competition</u>, the brief of which was to design millennium landmarks for the capital. In fact, nobody won, and the whole idea was scrapped, but the couple remained convinced that their dream should be pursued. They started to piece the project together, and were soon attracting the attention of the press, and it wasn't long before <u>British Airways</u> had started to show an interest and then became a partner. As the project unrolled, everyone involved began to realise the sheer scale of what they were undertaking. It would be the largest observation wheel ever built, and over 1,700 people from a total of 5 countries would play a part in its construction. Nearly every one of its many parts and techniques needed to be <u>invented</u>, simply because they had never existed before. Transportation of the components would be on a scale reminiscent of pyramid building. Bringing them in meant that large parts had to fit under the various bridges of the River Thames, so this had to be timed to coincide with <u>tides</u> along its length. And even when completed, the Eye continues to be huge in its requirements. A small army of people are employed to look after it, with 350 hours' maintenance being required every week, and apparently strange demands such as washing all its glass with nothing but <u>distilled water</u> having to be met. But the views the Eye affords across London make it all worthwhile, and it's easy to understand why the Eye has become one of London's chief tourist assets.

So, how is that great wheel held up? How did it get there? The starting point was, of course, the ground, and while parts of the wheel itself were still being constructed in various countries, <u>tension</u> piles were being driven into the ground beside the River Thames. This was the first step, and once these were securely in place, a <u>base cap</u> was installed over them as a kind of lock, with two giant plinths pointing up, onto which an <u>A-frame</u> was attached, like a giant letter. All this took many months and incredible effort, but meant that the spindle could be installed, around which the great wheel would turn. Now the project really was in business, and the vast rim with spokes like an outsized bicycle wheel could be brought in. The passenger capsules were assembled and hung onto the rim, each one linked by mounting

<u>rings</u> that would support eager viewers as they rose above London. And the last thing to be built is the first thing the visitor encounters, the <u>boarding platform</u> laid down underneath. The whole process employed thousands of people in total, and was avidly watched by millions. How long the Eye will stay is uncertain, but any talk of dismantling it always meets with immediate protest.

TEST 3

Section 1

Man: Cuxford Cycle Club.

Woman: Oh, yes, hello. I'm calling to enquire about joining the club.

Man: Fine. What would you like to know?

Woman: Well, I wanted to get a picture of what the club is like. For example, how big it is.

Man: Now that changes each year, of course. Cycling is growing in popularity …

Woman: I'm sure …

Man: So, last year we had nearly 70 members, which was a record in itself, but this year there are <u>76</u> people on the list and I'd say at least 60 of them come to events regularly. I should think something like 85 is a likely figure by next year.

Woman: That's bigger than I expected.

Man: Yes, there are plenty of opportunities to meet people.

Woman: And how much does it cost to join?

Man: It depends. £40 is for standard members, and there are reductions for certain categories. For example, Veteran and Youth members pay £10 less, <u>£30</u>, and family membership works out at £25 per head. All those charges are <u>per year</u>.

Woman: And Youth means?

Man: Under 18.

Woman: Oh, that covers me – at least at the moment!

Man: Then, for safety reasons, your application will need to be endorsed, so your <u>teacher or parent</u> needs to sign your form.

Woman: No problem. So, what happens after I've sent the form in to you?

Man: We deal with it and get a confirmation of acceptance with a membership card out to you in <u>3 weeks</u> and then you're ready to ride. It lasts a year, and we send you a renewal one month before it's due to expire.

Woman: OK. And can you tell me something about the activities you do?

Man: Yes, there's a range of things, to reflect the varied membership. There are the family rides, which are pretty popular, held <u>every month</u> … and that might get increased to every two weeks.

Woman: I don't know if that's really for me.

Man: Mm, you might prefer the Saturday rides, which are more popular with the Youth members. We don't go huge distances, 100km or anything like that; <u>60km</u> is about average … But the pace is fairly brisk.

Woman: Let's hope I'd be able to keep up!

Man: Oh, actually, there's something I should have mentioned before. We've got to be sure everyone's bike is roadworthy, so you'll need to have your bike checked and obtain a <u>safety certificate</u> for it. Most bike shops'll do that for you.

Woman: Fine. Do you do any longer tours, like holidays?

Man: Yes, there's a camping tour at least twice a year. There's one on <u>July 14</u>th, though it'll get booked up very soon. If you miss that, then there's another on August 17th.

Woman:	Oh, good.
Man:	But obviously there's plenty going on before then. You might want to come along on May 5th. Your membership should be through by then, and that's when we have a picnic. Everyone brings some food to share, and we go out to the hills and eat there.
Woman:	That sounds fun. I'm going to fill in my form as soon as I get off the phone.
Man:	And a further benefit of membership is the discount with Wheels.
Woman:	The shop on Mill Road?
Man:	Yes, the manager's a member of the club, and he'll give you a 15% reduction ... it means membership can pay for itself.
Woman:	Great. Well, you'll be getting my form soon.
Man:	Good, I look forward to meeting you ...

Section 2

Woman:	And next on City Life this week, we have with us in the studio Harvey Bowles, Head of the Park Arts Centre. He's here to tell us about forthcoming events at the Centre. Harvey, welcome.
Man:	Hello. Thank you.
Woman:	So, what can we look forward to first at the Park Centre?
Man:	We've got a very exciting programme lined up for you. The next event will start on the 18th of February and run till the 24th. Times for the event? Twice each day, at 2.30 and 7.30 p.m. There'll be a folk music concert, and we're sure this is going to be very popular. A range of excellent musicians are coming, some playing for the first time in this country. And for those who want a souvenir or for people who don't manage to get to the performances, the foyer shop will be selling a CD, showcasing the great talents of the performers.
Woman:	Sounds good!
Man:	Yes, and then after that, our next event is starting on the 1st of March and runs for 8 days. There's a lot going on, so you'll need to look in the separate programme, which shows all the various times and so on. It also includes details of performers and ticket prices – you can pick one up from the foyer at the Centre. Yes, this year we're hosting the dance festival again, and it's going to be even bigger than last year. It's become a major feature of the arts year, and many of the performances will be recorded on video and DVD – but nothing can beat the thrill of attending the events live. We have a great range of styles, performed by over 100 groups representing as many as 4 continents. All I can say is book early, because many of the shows are going to sell out quickly.
Woman:	I'm sure they will. And what do you have for us after that?
Man:	Well, then things get a little quieter, but no less interesting. From the 14th to 20th March, every evening at 8, we go into cinema mode and we're showing a fine new film. I expect you've seen reviews of it – Love and Hope.
Woman:	Oh yes, wonderful!
Man:	Yes, and it's not just an ordinary screening. We're delighted that each screening will be introduced by a short lecture by the producer, who will also leave a little time for questions from the audience. Again, I recommend early booking for this – it's bound to be popular.
Woman:	I'll be there. Anything else lined up at this point?
Man:	Yes, we've got a special one-day event on April 2nd. The times aren't fixed yet, but I can tell you that we're having a singing competition.

Woman:	Oh yes?
Man:	There'll be a large number of entrants, and the talent should be impressive. And Channel 6 are coming, so the event is going to be shown on TV. So come and be part of the audience!
Woman:	I'm sure people will want to. Well, Harvey, thank you very much for coming in and telling us all this. Details of all the events are on your website, aren't they?
Man:	Yes, the address is www ...

Section 3

Ben:	So, Tom, did you manage to get all your reading done?
Tom:	Yes, Ben, I did. What about you, Jane?
Jane:	Me too, though it took much longer than I thought it would.
Ben:	Yeah, some of those dissertations are really long, aren't they?
Tom:	Mm, I'm not looking forward to having to write mine ...
Jane:	Well, that's not till next year.
Ben:	So, shall we compare thoughts about our reading? Let's start with *Twentieth Century Architecture* ... I thought it was pretty impressive.
Tom:	There was quite a bit of detail ...
Jane:	Yeah, all very relevant. I enjoyed the pictures, the diagrams and photos.
Tom:	Mm, they were quite strange, not what you'd expect to find in a dissertation – but very helpful.
Ben:	Whereas sometimes I couldn't really follow the arguments.
Tom:	Yes – a bit of a mixed bag, really. While *Modern Construction* was very serious and thorough, wasn't it?
Jane:	Indeed. Actually, it was rather dense – I didn't find it particularly easy to read, either.
Ben:	The index was excellent, though, so I used that to guide me around.
Tom:	I still think it was a bit high-level. I certainly wouldn't have wanted to try and cope with it in the first year.
Jane:	No, that's not who it's aimed at, of course. What about *Steel, Glass and Concrete*? Not the world's most interesting title, of course.
Ben:	Again, the index was helpful, though I think we could have done with more photos – there weren't really enough to support what he was saying in places.
Jane:	Yeah. But what he was saying was easy to follow, wasn't it? He takes you through step-by-step.
Tom:	It was hard to believe it had been translated – seemed very natural.
Ben:	Actually, it was better written than the next one, *The Space We Make*.
Jane:	But we're supposed to be thinking about architectural ideas, not being literary critics! I liked that one.
Ben:	Really? I just didn't think it covered the whole situation.
Tom:	Mm, it didn't put the question of housing into the context of the time.
Ben:	You mean how in the fifties economic austerity limited the finances available, while a growing population needed housing quickly?
Tom:	Exactly.
Jane:	Again, I think you're asking too much of these dissertations.
Ben:	Perhaps you're right. Well, I did like *Change and Tradition* anyway. Very focused.
Tom:	Yes, although I did think it was oddly arranged in some ways. When you went to the index to track something down, you couldn't necessarily find what you wanted.
Ben:	I know what you mean. But, I have to say, I'd be very proud if I'd written any of these.

Jane: True.

Tom: And you will next year!

Ben: Never mind next year, it's this year that's the problem. I'm never going to get this assignment done.

Jane: Yes, you are.

Tom: Come on. Let's make a plan for you.

Ben: Please. I'm just not sure where to go from here. I could look at city plans, study the layout of housing developments.

Jane: I think you need a closer focus. The approach to small houses won't necessarily tell you what you want to know. You'd be better to concentrate on <u>large private houses</u>, study the drawings of those.

Ben: OK. Though I don't know how much useful detail I'll be able to get from the kinds of plans that are easily available from that period.

Tom: It's true, they can be limited. But what you could do as a next stage is go on to the web – there's loads of useful stuff there.

Ben: More detailed plans you mean?

Tom: Well, I was thinking more of illustrations, that kind of thing. Do a search for <u>window designs</u> … I'm sure you'll find some good ones.

Jane: I agree. And not just online. See what you do find there, and then, for your next step, check both campus libraries – I think you'll be able to get hold of books which will give you further information, and you need to know more about <u>typical furniture</u> of the time.

Ben: This is all very helpful – thanks guys. I'm beginning to think I should be able to get something done for Dr Forbes after all. At least I can see I'll be in a position to tell him the section headings.

Tom: Well, a bit more than that would be better. Put your <u>outline plan</u> together, and give him that to look at.

Ben: Mm, yes. But I'll still need to keep reading, won't I?

Jane: Yeah. Once Dr Forbes has okayed what you've done at that point, you could then go and see Dr Gray – he's very approachable, and I'm sure he'd be happy to provide you with further <u>references</u>, and then you could take it from there.

Ben: That'd be really useful. Well, thanks again – let me get you both another coffee.

Section 4

Lecturer: Now, we all take the wonders of the cinema very much for granted these days, but cinema really is a very recent phenomenon. It has moved from its origins in the simple still camera to the dazzling computer-generated graphics of today in little over a hundred years. Perhaps the real beginning of cinema was the Cinématographe, a moving camera invented by the Lumière brothers. As the excitement at the early screenings of short, simple moving pictures spread, competition developed rapidly and soon cameras such as the American Biograph were on the market. Advertisements asserted that the Biograph did not <u>shake</u> as much as the Cinématographe. Meanwhile, permits were required for outside filming, and import licences were difficult to obtain for equipment. And there were other difficulties for cameramen. When the Lumière brothers went to film the crowning of Czar Nicholas II in Russia in 1896, the camera's ticking noise led people to believe it was a <u>bomb</u>. Although this confusion was resolved, disaster struck at the ceremony when a stand of spectators collapsed and the huge crowd panicked. The cameramen kept filming. It was the first time such events had been filmed and this marked the beginning of a new concept of <u>journalism</u>. Well, the technology continued to develop rapidly – and often secretly. The thrill of invention and the prospect of riches to be made drove experimenters along. But historians of cinema face difficulties in establishing if an apparatus <u>functioned</u> in the way that its makers asserted. Everyone was keen to say that their machine was the best, of course. In some cases, however, we do have reliable records or evidence in the equipment itself, and then we can see the details of the evolution of the technology. By about 1890, for example, the Frenchman Marey had arrived at results of startling clarity in sequential images. He also had the idea of recording images on a long strip of paper that unrolled in front of the lens instead of on separate plates – but he found it impossible initially to ensure that this strip would have <u>regular movement</u>. As we step into the twentieth century, however, we see much progress has been made and there are many examples of what we would today recognise as films. Questions of the art form were now as important as questions of what was technologically possible, and film-makers searched around for ideas to draw on.

Comic strips were very popular at the time in newspapers, and their <u>structure</u> was applied to the planning of films, which were now being mapped in a series of picture panels. Different innovations were achieved by different types of film-maker, with a certain amount of rivalry between makers of documentaries and makers of fiction films. One area where documentaries led the way was in the use of <u>travelling</u> shots, although, of course, fiction films adopted this technique in due course. Various sources for stories were developing, and each would have an impact on the way the story was filmed. For example, film-makers started to use greater numbers of shots when <u>chase</u> films became popular, because they wanted to show the various stages of the policeman running after the bandit, and so on. And it wasn't just different kinds of story that were driving film-makers to think up new techniques. Other technology also played its part. The telephone was growing in use, and film-makers came up with the idea of splitting the screen image into two parts to show <u>telephone conversations</u>. All this growing sophistication in the shooting of films began to make the whole process of creating them more challenging. The very first films consisted of single shots, and were straightforward to take from shooting to showing them to audiences. However, as the filming developed into multiple shots, then <u>editing</u> emerged as an essential ingredient of the process. Cinema was growing up. Well, next I'd like to turn your attention to some of the issues that I believe were …

TEST 4

Section 1

Woman: Able Employment. How may I help you?

Man: I saw your advertisement in the Daily Gazette.

Woman: Oh, yes.

Man: And I'd like to register with you. I'm a student, but I've got the long holiday coming up.

Woman: Certainly. I'll just get the form ready … OK. Let me take your details.

Man: Sure.

Woman: Can I have your full name?

Man: It's Bowen, <u>James</u> Bowen, <u>B-O-W-E-N</u>.

Woman: Right. And your address, please.

Man: Well, just now I'm staying at the Youth Hostel …

Woman: I see.

Man: But I'm moving into a flat on Friday.

Woman: Well, give me that one, then.

Man: It's <u>4 Lion</u>, like the animal, Road, Melford MF4 5JB.

Woman: OK. And then I need to have a phone number for you.

Man: Er, I don't know the number at the flat yet, but I could give you my mobile, that's <u>09954 721822</u> – would that do?

Woman: For the time being. But if you can let me know your new number when you can …

Man: Of course.

Woman: Now … qualifications. What qualifications have you got – I mean post-16 qualifications?

Man: Well, I stayed on at school till eighteen and got my A levels.

Woman: Fine. Anything else? You said you were a student?

Man: Yes … and then I've done two years at college, so I've got my History Diploma – though I don't know how useful that'll be for getting a job!

Woman: Well, it depends – everything counts in some way.

Man: And I also did an IT course this year, and that got me my Computer Skills Certificate, which I certainly hope is relevant. It's different anyway. That's all, really.

Woman: That's quite a good range. And what about on the practical side … What work experience have you got?

Man: Well, not too much, because I've mainly been studying.

Woman: Yes.

Man: But two summers ago I worked, just as general assistant, in a hospital for about three months. It was quite hard, but very interesting.

Woman: OK. Anything else?

Man: If you include part-time work …

Woman: Oh yes.

Man: I've often worked in the college holidays as a tour guide, showing visitors round. That's quite enjoyable, meeting people.

Woman: I'm sure. Hmm, now onto interests. There's space here for two – what would you say?

Man: Two … er, well, I like various sports … but I suppose we should put that I'm in the swimming club, I'm pretty committed to that.

Woman: Yes, that sounds good. And for the other one? Something different?

Man: I'm very keen on music too, and I love playing piano – I've been doing that for over ten years now.

Woman: Yes, I'll put that down. Well, that's more or less it for the time being.

Man: Uh-huh.

Woman: Just one more thing. What I do need is your availability.

Man: Oh yes – um, the college term finishes on June 20th, and then I'm going to visit my parents, but I can be back and ready to start on June 28th, if that seems OK?

Woman: I'm sure it is. Now, what happens next is that I process this information and then …

Section 2

Guide: Thank you everybody for your attention. I hope you're all looking forward to arriving at the town. I thought you might like to know a few things while we're still on the coach – and it'll help to pass the time on our journey! OK, as you know, we're staying at the Park Hotel. It's comfortable and friendly. We're booked in for three nights. Now, I'm aware that not everyone wants breakfast there, so if you do want it, you should tell the Hotel that you do the night before. We're making our own arrangements for dinner each evening, and there's a café open at the Hotel most of the time if you want a drink or a snack. There's also a very pleasant lounge on the ground floor, with a collection of fascinating paintings. And then I hope you're going to enjoy the various activities that are lined up. However, I do have to tell you that there have been some changes since the original programme. For one, because it's been restored and is therefore closed to the public, we won't be going to the castle after all, I'm afraid. However, there's plenty else to see, and the gardens are still open. Something we've been able to add to the programme is for

Saturday, when a local historian will give us a lecture on famous people from the town. I don't know who that includes yet! So, to free up the time for that, we've made another little amendment, and changed the trip to the antiques show that was due for then on to Sunday – actually, I think that'll make for a more relaxed programme, anyway. We're leaving the rest of Sunday free for you to wander around as you wish. One place you might like to try is the art gallery, because it's got a huge display of old postcards – you can't really send them home to your family and friends, but it's interesting, and sometimes funny, to see what people used to send. Well, that's the lot on changes.

I thought it could be useful to try and get your bearings now, before we actually arrive, so I'll give you a few pointers on your maps. OK, first things first – the Park Hotel, because I assume you'll want to deposit your luggage before anything else. We'll be driving into the town from the west, and stopping at the bus station. To get to the hotel, just go straight down the High Street towards the railway bridge, and after the bridge, if you go left, you'll soon see it on the right. As I say, it's a nice place. You can check in, see your rooms, relax a little. There are a couple of interesting little shops nearby. There aren't any internet facilities at the hotel, I'm afraid, so if you want to send any emails, you'll need to get yourselves to the internet café. In fact, if you want to do that first, it's easy, because it's near the bus station, on the corner towards the right, of Curtis Lane and Cramer Street. So, once you've done that – if you do that – then I suppose you'll be ready to do a bit of exploring. You've got your basic maps, but you may want to get more information, and the Tourist Information Office is the place to do that. It's up around the train station area. From the bus station, you could go up any of the streets to the left – Cadogan Road, Earl Street or Duke Street. The Office is directly facing the train station, on the corner with Earl Street. They've got all sorts of brochures and leaflets about local attractions, and tickets for sale. They even sell some locally-produced jams and chocolates. And a last pointer at this stage is our venue for dinner tonight, the Royal House Restaurant. This is conveniently located in the very centre of town. In fact, you'll no doubt pass it as you're walking around beforehand. In relation to the bus station, it's not far. Going down the High Street, if you pass the corner with Cromwell Road, then the next junction is a crossroads with Duke Street and Runton Road, and it's there – you'll be able to see its rather grand entrance over on the left corner. The food and the service there are both excellent, so it promises to be an enjoyable evening. Well, we're just coming into the town now, so …

Section 3

Dr Smith: Right, well, David, I think it's a good idea to talk a little about your plans for going on to do an MA. Now, I understand you're thinking in terms of either Forth College or Haines College?

David: That's right – well, so far, anyway.

Dr Smith: No, I think that's a good choice to have narrowed it down to.

David: I'm interested to know how the services to support students work in both places.

Dr Smith: Yes, I know you've needed to make use of those here in the last year. I have to say I'm not absolutely sure about the situation at Haines. I expect they're alright, but certainly Forth has a good reputation in that regard. They have a large number of students from abroad, and they have to make sure they're OK.

David: That's reassuring. And then I'll be moving city again, obviously, whichever college I go to, and I hope that the room or flat I could expect would be nice.

Dr Smith: Very important, yes. These days, actually, all colleges tend to have decent quality rooms or flats for their students, and Forth and Haines are no exception.

David: Right. Well, what about comparisons on the academic side of things?

Dr Smith: Mm, well, I know you're an avid user of the limited online provision we have here. I think you'll find Haines is about as developed – or not – as we are here, and that Forth has developed some pretty impressive stuff, which I'm sure you'd make the most of.

David: Well, I'd certainly try!

Dr Smith: But that doesn't mean that the more traditional information sources, such as the good old-fashioned library, should be forgotten …

David: No, of course not …

Dr Smith: While Forth has recently had a very splendid law library opened, that isn't particularly relevant for you, and I think you'd find Haines' general university and faculty collections better suited to your needs. But that's something you could check for yourself if you visit both places.

David: Which I'm planning to do next month.

Dr Smith: Good. Now, there's the question of the lecturing staff, which is clearly going to be key to your progress. I think you'd find them adequate at Forth – there are some solid people working there – while Haines have recently taken on some inspirational people, very cutting edge. It's a little hard to judge, though, because as a research student, it's not as if you have teaching all day every day.

David: No, I guess not. But I'll need to consult …

Dr Smith: Yes. And on the subject of research, in terms of the colleges' reputation for results, again, neither place is bad in any way, but I think you'll find – and you can check this on the Research Council's website – that Haines has consistently scored very well. There's perhaps a little bit of an issue with non-completing doctorate students at Forth.

David: Well, I'll certainly look at the website as you suggest.

Dr Smith: Fine.

David: I'm still a bit anxious about making this next step. I know the level of competition is very high, especially in my area. It makes me feel rather daunted, and I wonder if in a new place I may be out on my own, if you know what I mean, compared to the sense of community here. I suppose it'll be down to my determination to succeed to get me through.

Dr Smith: Hmm, well, do remember how you felt when you arrived here – I'm sure you'll get on anywhere in the end.

David: I hope so.

Dr Smith: And, of course, you still don't know exactly where you want to end up. By the time you've completed your masters, you'll have a clearer idea of whether you want to progress to doctorate level. It's possible, I suppose, that you'll begin to see how much you might be interested in picking up some bits of lecturing earlier than that, since your area's fairly specialised and may put you in demand sooner than you think. To establish yourself in your area of expertise, it would be sensible to think in terms of getting your stuff into one or two of the journals, converting parts of your dissertation into suitable formats for them – that'll stand you in good stead, whatever else you decide to do.

David: That sounds like good advice, thanks.

Dr Smith: Actually, I think masters' level studying has improved in some ways over the last few years. The internet you love so much was always going to make all kinds of studying easier, or that's the idea anyway … I'm not sure it really has the impact you might think. What I've found impressive is the way courses have developed to be more adaptable, more able to fit in with all the other demands in people's lives. So, while the exams and assignments you all have to do may not have shifted much, at least a wider range of students are now able to benefit from education at the higher levels.

David: Mm. I just wish I could be sure I was always making the best use of my opportunities. At the end of each week, I usually feel I could have got more done, arranged things differently, been more efficient somehow. I've got a lot better at taking down notes during seminars and lectures, which means, I think, that my written work has benefited to some degree, so there's progress on some fronts, at any rate.

Dr Smith: Yes, it's interesting seeing …

Section 4

Lecturer: So, I'm now going to say a few words about the various different kinds of writing you may want to consider. Each has its own challenges and rewards, and it's really a question of seeing what suits you best. There are no rights and wrongs here. Let's start by considering the short story. Remember that a short story isn't just a very concise novel. There are three basic styles, the story itself, the slice of life section and the surprise type, and all of them are equally valid as treatments of the genre. When producing a short story, you don't have time for a slow build up of interest, so you need to get in there straightaway and begin with a crisis. Then there's non-fiction, which can sell very well, with biographies in particular frequently hitting the best-seller lists. It's important, however, to be sure your chosen topic is genuinely interesting to people and you know enough about it to do it justice, so when you're submitting your idea to a publisher, it's worthwhile to give them details of specialist knowledge you have. What about articles? Now, this is a very wide area, of course, going from the very learned and obscure to the populist gossip type. Articles based on giving advice are a proven area, and to give them a sufficient focus, you should produce your article for a definite market – that will help to define your purpose. Turning to something different, there's the question of poetry. It's often hard to define what poetry is exactly – maybe it's easier to say what it isn't! But it should be subtle, so the message of a poem oughtn't to be overly obvious. True poems let the ideas sit there, for the reader to ponder. What they must do is sound good, like singing, so I recommend reading what you write aloud to yourself, to check the melody. Well, then there's plays, which are basically novels but told only through conversation. A playwright includes minimal instructions for actions – but not for every small action the actors will perform – things such as 'moves towards sofa' and so on are for the director to come up with. If you're thinking of trying your hand at a play, a good starting point would be to educate yourself a little in the art of acting, so that you know what the people who deliver your work can and can't do with it. What next? There's radio, of course. Radio uses an enormous range of material, and the BBC Writing for Radio Handbook contains information about all of this. To begin with, I suggest regional stations for sending your stuff to – the competition for national radio is extremely high. OK, another interesting area is children's literature. Now, very few, if any, children's books are published without pictures, but this doesn't mean that you, as writer, have to draw them – that's for the illustrator. What you do need to do is be clear who you want to write for, so fix on one age group and then aim your stories at that.

Right, I've saved what I consider to be the best – and the hardest – till last. The novel. Very long and very difficult to do well. But certainly not impossible, as any bookshop's shelves will confirm. One of the first things to decide is from what point of view you will tell your story. A popular choice is the first person, and this technique certainly gives a sense of immediacy for the reader, while many new writers find it easier to project themselves into their main character if they can write in his or her name. But that assumes, of course, that the main character is somehow like the writer, which may or may not be the case. Meanwhile, if your book is all narrated by 'I', you <u>can only put into your story things which are experienced by that character, which may prove to be rather restricting</u>. Now, there are all sorts of pitfalls for the novelist, and many of them relate to the issue of providing a balanced narrative. Every time you introduce a character into the story, you have decisions to make. Of course you want to populate your landscape with a variety of people to maintain interest, but don't feel you have to decorate every one of them in elaborate detail. The same goes for irony. All too often, an inexperienced writer will <u>create a strong ironic situation, and then spoil it by spelling out what they mean by it,</u> as if readers were too stupid to understand. A few contrasting details should serve to make the point clear. A big challenge for new novelists is dialogue. What is the relationship between conversation as people really speak and as it is in novels? Well, it depends. If you recorded actual conversations and copied them straight into your narrative, readers would get confused and bored – all those unfinished sentences going nowhere. On the other hand, you don't want to write out <u>page-long utterances by characters</u>, as these will seem unrealistic to an extreme – but you can <u>insert minor descriptions and actions</u> to vary the pace and add interest. Well, I hope what I'm saying is encouraging and not too off-putting about the various difficulties. Are there any questions at this point?

TEST 5

Section 1

Man: Hello, this is Tidborough Tourist Office, Derek speaking. How can I help you?

Woman: Good afternoon. My name's Clara Swift. I'm the secretary of a social club, and we're planning a visit to Tidborough.

Man: Oh, yes.

Woman: So I'd like to ask you some questions, if I may, to help with our plans.

Man: Of course. We're here to help.

Woman: Now, we're thinking of staying in the youth hostel, as we'll be a group and it's quite cheap.

Man: Yes, and comfortable, too.

Woman: But could you tell me how far outside the centre it is?

Man: Oh, it's not too bad. It's only 1 km from the station, which is very convenient, and <u>2 km</u> from the very centre of town. There's a frequent bus service.

Woman: That doesn't sound too bad. Actually, I've tried phoning them, but had no reply.

Man: Ah. You can check out everything you need to know if you go to www.cheapstay.com – that's their own site. It's quite new. And you could email them with your requirements directly from it.

Woman: That sounds good – thank you. We'll be staying in the third week of March. Will there be any special events going on then?

Man: Er … yes, that includes the 22nd, doesn't it? Good, that's when the <u>street festival</u> is held. It's great fun, lots going on. It's held every year.

Woman: OK.

Man: And when that's finished, if you've any energy left, you and your group might enjoy a concert we're putting on.

Woman: Is it classical music? Or rock?

Man: Well, quite a mixture, actually. The point is that it's all performed by <u>local musicians</u>, and between them, they'll be playing most things.

Woman: It sounds a little strange, but I guess it could be interesting. It seems we've chosen a good week to come! Is there anything else on?

Man: Yes, indeed. The City Museum, which was recently completely restored, often has interesting exhibitions. There are some weird and wonderful modern paintings at the moment. That's a good exhibition. Then, opening on March 24th, when you'll be here, it changes to <u>natural history</u>. I'd recommend it.

Woman: I've made a note of that. Now, some of our group are quite young, and they may prefer to do things that they feel are more active than walking round museums and so on. What will they be able to do?

Man: Ah, throughout March, in fact, the <u>sports centre</u> is going to be closed, but the swimming pool will remain open, and there's the park for general relaxation.

Woman: That sounds alright.

Man: And were you planning to go on any excursions while you were here?

Woman: Yes, I was going to ask you – I gather there's a very picturesque train journey out along the coast?

Man: The Beach Express, yes, it's lovely. It's an old-fashioned train … not an express at all, in fact, but it chugs along giving you marvellous views.

Woman: Does it go often?

Man: No, it's just a tourist special, really. But <u>it sets off in the morning at 9.30</u> and it's very popular, so I'd get there no later than 9.15 if I were you. The station opens at 9.00, so you can get a coffee or something while you wait.

Woman: It sounds lovely. And for tickets?

Man: Well, as I say, it may be crowded at the station, so <u>it's probably more convenient to get them beforehand from us at the tourist office</u>. The youth hostel may sell them too – you'd have to check that.

Woman: OK, I will, thanks. How much are tickets?

Man: £5, although students get 20% off, and <u>if there are more than ten of you travelling together, you get 15% off</u>, so it's very reasonable.

Woman: Yes, that's not too bad. And is it a long ride?

Man: Er, not really. I think it's about three hours actually in the train. You'll be back for lunch about <u>four hours</u> later – it stops twice for half an hour so you can stretch your legs, have a little stroll on one of the beaches.

Woman: I see. Well, you've been very helpful, thank you.

Man: Not at all. I hope you enjoy your visit. Contact us any time.

Section 2

Director: Hello everybody, and welcome to Hawkins. I very much hope you will enjoy working here, and indeed that some of you may take the opportunity to join our permanent staff. Now, my purpose this morning is to give you a short overview of Hawkins and a few pointers about working here. Then I'll hand over to Celia, Head of Human Resources, to begin the training proper. Right, now we've seen quite a mixed history in sales recently at Hawkins. Five years ago, we saw the beginning of a success period, <u>as sales climbed at an exciting rate, but then they went flat again for a few years, although we're delighted that they've recovered in the last year to rise again, so the future looks bright</u>. As a company, we have to watch and be pro-active about where these sales are coming from. All of you here will be allocated to different departments, but you may be interested to know where your area stands in relationship to others. Hawkins was traditionally basically a clothing retailer, and clothes remain an important part of our business, but over recent years we've seen that reduce as food and electrical have both grown, leaving us equally balanced on all fronts at the present time. This is a situation we'd be pleased to maintain, although the general increase in food spending is predicted to affect all major players in our sector. Well, that's us. What about you, as temporary staff? Where do you fit in? Any business that operates in a changing climate must rely heavily on contributions from a flexible proportion of its staff, and Hawkins is no exception. Last year, we recruited temporary staff into every department, and this year we've done that again, actually increasing the numbers, and we expect to take on an even higher proportion next year. So, you'll be playing an important part in our success.

We regard the Hawkins approach to the retail business as something special. Our mission statement – the guiding idea behind everything we do – is based on quality and is phrased 'creating value for customers', and this belief applies to every customer and every purchase, however large or small. Happy customers means good business for us, and your main aim must always be to keep customers happy. If any kind of problem or complaint arises, don't try to resolve it yourselves or simply leave it to a colleague, but get the assistance of your line manager. It's his or her responsibility to sort it out. A properly resolved problem will mean we get a loyal customer for life, and that's why we need to make sure that everyone who shops here feels they have had a positive experience, not just a routine transaction. We like to remind customers that everything we sell in Hawkins is high quality – it's the basis of our advertisements. But keep customers informed – let them know about special offer products. To keep yourself up to date about these and all the other aspects of the company, please look carefully through the newsletter that we publish each month. And something else you'll need to do regularly is to talk with your section supervisor, and you do this in your progress meetings, which will be every Thursday. OK?

Right, just a few last things, and then I'll hand over. I think you were all asked for details of your certificates when you filled in your initial application form. Can you make sure that you provide the Human Resources office with copies of them by the end of the week? There's a pile of information videos on the table at the back there, and I'd like you to take one each, and please make sure you watch it carefully when you get home this evening. It contains lots of important facts and advice. Will you also pick up your security pass by the end of the day from the office on the fourth floor, as you'll need it to get in tomorrow? Don't forget you'll need it to obtain your staff discount when you make any purchases. OK, that really is it from me, so now, Celia, if you'd like to …

Section 3

Woman: So, Brian, how have you been doing with your reading on penguins?
Man: Not too bad, Emily. And you?
Woman: Yeah, OK. I hadn't realised there were so many differences between the various types of penguin.
Man: No, nor had I. Anyway, I started with the Gentoo.
Woman: And me with the Rockhopper.
Man: And it turns out they're rather cautious.
Woman: Not scared of swimming, I trust?
Man: Oh no, but they don't like going about at night – scared of the dark, I suppose – and if they're climbing over some rocky landscape, they'll only jump if they have to. And even then they'll look carefully down and spend time deciding whether to or not. Is that common?

Woman: I don't think so. The Rockhopper will have a quick look if it's somewhere they haven't dropped down before, but they don't seem timid. In fact, they're pretty determined and if they're trying to get up somewhere, they grip onto the stones with their slightly hooked bills as well as their nails when the surface gets very steep. Nothing stops them.
Man: Interesting, because the other type I looked into, the Magellanic, tend to stick to the beach rather than going inland, so you see them walking along with their flippers at their sides or a bit forward. If they come across something they haven't seen before, they cock their head first to one side then the other, peering out of each eye in turn, as if they don't quite believe anything until they've double-checked it. And then, when they call to each other about anything, they arch their backs strangely first before making a very loud noise indeed.
Woman: Oh, because the King Penguin stands very upright when it calls. And they have the longest flippers, which they hold towards the ground, as if they're worried about falling over. But it's quite dignified, too. I think they're my favourite type.
Man: Uh-huh.
Woman: Anyway, there are some things that they all do the same, aren't there?
Man: Oh, yes. Eating fish, for example!
Woman: Well, of course! But sleeping, say.
Man: Yes, occasionally, you might see one stretched out flat in the sun for a snooze …
Woman: But normally, you see them standing at night, even though they're sound asleep.
Man: It seems odd, doesn't it? And then they're all liable to get aggressive if they feel invaded, aren't they?
Woman: Yeah, not quite so sweet then … And with the Rockhopper …
Man: The one with the distinctive black and yellow feathers on its head?
Woman: That's the one. If it gets annoyed about something, then the black feathers on the head point upwards and the yellow feathers stick out. It all makes it look bigger, or tougher.
Man: I wonder how often they get annoyed.
Woman: Well, I don't know about annoyed, but they've plenty to get frightened of. They've got predators in the water and on land – well, in the sky, anyway.
Man: Oh yes, the Great Skua bird. It's after the eggs.
Woman: So, the penguins have to keep a careful watch for the Skua all the time, especially when they're nesting.
Man: They can spot the white patches in its wings, can't they, as one flies over.
Woman: Yes, and then they sit very closely on the eggs to protect them.
Man: Not an easy life, really.
Woman: No.

Woman: So, what else have we found out?
Man: Well, I was interested to see that although they nest individually, they always go into the sea together, in large numbers.
Woman: Even though it might make them more obvious to predators?
Man: That's the price to pay for the best way to find food. It means a bigger catch from each trip.
Woman: I see. I watched a video, too, just showing them on the beach, and I was struck by how calm they seemed to be. I thought they might have looked frightened.
Man: Perhaps it's because there are so many of them, maybe that gives them a sense of security. In fact, all the types have a social nature.

Woman: Mm, I guess that's why we humans find them so fascinating to observe.

Man: I guess so. So, shall we start to put all our notes together, and then …

Section 4

Lecturer: Now, a key issue in the ability of cities to grow is the question of housing. However, quality is as important as quantity here. But that isn't to say that this is easy to guarantee, and the development, or at least the spread, of many modern cities is marked by the sprawl of slum or shanty town housing. Governments are, of course, keen to address this, but the tendency to <u>demolish</u> them has often proved disastrous, as it doesn't solve the problem, unless satisfactory replacements are ready for the inhabitants. What I'm saying is that suitable housing projects have to be lined up to accommodate these otherwise displaced people. And suitable is the key word here. All too frequently, there isn't <u>real consultation</u>, only token gestures. If the residents aren't fully involved, they are unlikely to find the resulting development appropriate to their needs. People need to feel reasonably independent, and strategies for providing accommodation schemes work much better if an approach rooted in <u>self-help</u> is applied. People value things more when they have been part of bringing them into being. At the same time, residents can't do everything for themselves, or not well enough anyway, and so governments need to accept that a number of <u>services</u> will always have to be laid on. These would include electricity and water and so on. From the other side, residents need to feel able to commit. Migrants are essential to the growth of cities, bringing rapid increases in population, skills and income. But they need to have a sense of security, of long-term commitment to the city if they are to <u>invest money</u> in building or buying houses. Developing this sense of commitment isn't straightforward, and it takes time. It's complex and involves several factors. People need to feel they belong and, unfortunately, too many governments fail to appreciate that <u>community values</u> are a crucial component of that. Sadly, there are too many housing schemes which don't work – people drift away, or the whole place becomes crime-ridden. It's easy to be wise after the event, but it is worrying that a lot of housing is put up without analysis having been carried out to examine how much <u>employment</u> is going to be available for people.

But I don't want to labour the negatives too hard. Such difficulties as there are are challenges, and challenges that can be, and often are, overcome. And cities are, I believe, a good thing. Urbanisation – the process of developing cities and the societies that comprise them – may not be everyone's dream, but it has a huge impact on the economy and also benefits each and every person's <u>freedom</u>. Furthermore, the sheer volume of people means that work can be differently distributed. In villages, people need to be multi-skilled in order to be autonomous, but in cities you can see the evolution of a variety of <u>specialist activities</u> and this means people live in a more sophisticated way. It's not only tangible phenomena – there are all sorts of other, equally important benefits, too. Residing in cities brings us face to face with many different ways of thinking or going about things, and this increases our degree of <u>understanding</u> – something which is hard to measure in scientific terms, but which surely makes better people of us all. Right, well, now I'd like to turn our attention to …

Section 1

Man: Hello, you're through to Go-Travel. This is Darren speaking. How may I help you today?

Woman: Hello. I'm calling to book a holiday.

Man: Great. May I take your name please?

Woman: Yes, it's <u>Grieves, Anna</u> Grieves.

Man: Is that G-R-E … ?

Woman: No, G-R-I-E-V-E-S. And Anna is with double N.

Man: Right, thank you, Anna. Now, we're delighted you've called us. Can I ask where you heard about us?

Woman: It was your advertisement, in, er, one of the magazines …

Man: Was it <u>Holiday World</u>?

Woman: Yes, that's the one.

Man: Good, thank you – it's useful to know.

Woman: Of course.

Man: And did you have a particular holiday in mind? Or was it a general enquiry?

Woman: I think I've chosen. I like the look of the one with the code <u>FT4551</u> – the right destination and the prices seem reasonable.

Man: Right. Now was it for yourself only, or …

Woman: Oh no, I want to go with a couple of friends, so there'd be <u>three</u> of us going.

Man: OK. Now there's a choice of dates, as you know.

Woman: Yes, I think, well, we've got to back by the end of August, so if we say going on <u>August 16th</u>? That would work fine.

Man: No problem. And you can also choose the length of your holiday. There's, let's see, 7, <u>11</u> or 14 nights.

Woman: We thought the middle one would be great. Longer would be nice of course, but …

Man: Maybe next year!

Woman: Yes.

Man: And you do need to have insurance.

Woman: Uh-huh.

Man: We've three levels, Standard, Super and Superplus.

Woman: Standard seems a bit basic – let's say <u>Super</u>, that should be sufficient.

Man: Fine.

Man: Well, that's all good so far, and the availability's OK. Have you looked through the list of options they're in the advertisement?

Woman: I have, and I've got the list here. Some of them do seem a good idea.

Man: Which ones would you like to take?

Woman: In terms of the hotel, the offer of picnic lunches, we'd leave that. We'd rather go to cafés. I think <u>a balcony for the room is a must</u> – it's so nice to sit out, enjoying the view.

Man: Oh, yes.

Woman: And then the trips. Er, I think we'll pass on the night bus one – I never really enjoy the commentaries. And museums aren't really my sort of thing, to be honest, any more than dance is.

Man: Uh-huh.

Woman: But I like practical things, so I think <u>the demonstration of local arts could be fun</u>.

Man: Yes, I would think so.

Woman: And then, in terms of getting out of town … <u>going up the river on a boat sounds delightful, and I wouldn't want to miss that</u> … but the mountains, well, sitting in a coach on those winding roads …

Man: I understand. OK, well, that's all I need for the booking at this point. Just a few details for you, and then we'll check the payment …

Section 2

Presenter: I'm very pleased to have this opportunity to tell you something about the Run-Well charity and the work we do. I'll give a brief overview of what we do, and I hope you may be able to help, and then there'll be time for questions at the end. Run-Well's founder, Mike Hughes, took up long-distance running in 1987, raising money by doing sponsored half-marathons, and in 1992 established the charity as we know it today. By 1997, the runs were being filmed by local TV and today they appear on national TV every year. All the funds collected by Run-Well go to the hospital, with the idea that those fit enough to run use their energy to assist the provision of people who are unwell for whatever reason. Now, if you want to race – and I assume that's why many of you are here – let me explain a couple of the basics. Races are run by teams, so you need to form and register a team. What you wear to run in is up to you, and I know some teams come up with some pretty wacky ideas. We have a standard design for your numbers, which we ask you to reproduce … So, you make them up according to that standard. We don't want to spend valuable funds on doing that ourselves. Now, the race is run as a kind of relay, so, while you won't actually compete side by side, we do recommend that you train as a group – this helps to optimise performance and build team spirit. It will also give you a fair idea of how much you need to eat and drink over the race distance. This is clearly essential for an effective performance, so please make sure you come along to the race with sufficient food and drink – again, we don't spend money on providing that, but you do need to keep yourself going for the 20 km course. The course goes through the town, then out through Highfield Park, concluding in the main square, where the applauding spectators will be ready to greet you! There are many different prizes, including oldest runner, youngest runner, team with the most sponsorship, team with the best costume – that one's donated by Zoom Fashions. The Mayor will introduce the Minister for Health, who will hand over each prize to the winners, and then the hospital President will make a short speech.

OK, that's the big race. But I know there are many people who don't feel they are up to running a 20 km race, but who would nevertheless like to raise money for Run-Well. Over the years, we've had experience of many ways of trying to collect money, some very successful, others less so. Now, of course, 20 km is too far for children to run, but there was a sponsored swimming event at the local school last year, and that did very well. People have also tried to organise food-based events, such as selling homemade cakes and bread and so on at the market, and there was a large picnic arranged in Forbright Gardens, although these events failed to justify the efforts put into them – though I'm sure they were very tasty! These days, so many people are out at work all day that going from house to house to collect money isn't very effective – but it is possible to raise useful funds by selling small promotional items, such as badges with the Run-Well motif on them. We're currently checking to see if postcards, perhaps showing the race's winners each year, might also be a good idea or not. We do appreciate the efforts that have gone into selling second-hand goods, but, to be honest, the returns have not been very high on this. One very dedicated group organised a team quiz recently, which went very well, and it would be good to see more such activities. There's also been talk of a concert, but we'll have to see how plans for that progress. Now, are there any questions at this stage …

Section 3

Joe: Hi, Martin. Hi, Angela.

Martin: Hi, Joe.

Angela: Yeah, hi, Joe. So, you're really worried about your presentation? The one about names?

Joe: I am.

Martin: Well, you know your stuff on names pretty well, so it's just a question of selecting what you want to use …

Angela: That's right.

Joe: But there's so much!

Martin: Well, you don't have to include everything. Let's start somewhere.

Joe: Well, for example, there's a lot to discuss about people's names in terms of culture.

Angela: It would be a good way to start, bringing in issues of religion, society …

Joe: I thought so.

Martin: As long as you can keep it concise, since it's potentially a large area.

Joe: I'll pick out some key points.

Angela: Good. Now, that will tend to be about differences – what about something on ways in which naming practices are often similar across different languages?

Martin: Mm, that sounds good.

Joe: I'm not sure how much I could say that's really about just names, and not really general language.

Angela: Maybe you need to give that some more thought.

Joe: Yes, I'm not ruling it out.

Martin: Well, what about what first names mean? That's got to be specific to languages, or language groups …

Joe: Yes, there are all sorts of different principles at work. It's a rich area for discussion.

Angela: And you can present lots of examples.

Joe: Hmm, it would mean a good slide or two – I'll enjoy making those up.

Martin: Don't forget to put our names in!

Joe: No, OK! Right, where have we got up to? Yes, now there's the question of place names.

Angela: Ones where the name of the place is the word for the situation, like something to do with sea or mountain et cetera?

Joe: Yes, people often don't realise the origin.

Martin: It sounds like it's just a translation issue to me. Don't you think you might give that a miss?

Joe: Given the time limit, perhaps you're right.

Angela: You need something on place names – could you get history in?

Joe: Actually, the way migrants often used to name places after somewhere in their country of origin is interesting.

Martin: Sounds a bit narrow to me.

Joe: Well, I'd hope to build it up a bit.

Angela: Perhaps you should make a final decision on that later.

Joe: OK, I'll see how the rest of it goes first.

Martin: Is that the lot?

Joe: No, there's still country names, the origins of those. I think that's an interesting area.

Angela: Yeah, because it's something we often don't think about.

Martin: It'd be a way to bring in various aspects; history, certainly …

Joe: I could project a map of the world, and have people match the original meanings to the countries.

Angela: Well, that seems to be a foregone conclusion.

Martin: Fine.

Joe: Yes, I'm feeling clearer already.

Joe: You know, there's another aspect that I think I'll cover.

Martin:	Yes?
Joe:	Brand names.
Angela:	Isn't that more to do with business studies?
Joe:	Well, international companies are finding it increasingly important to have brand names that can be used in many different countries.
Martin:	Oh, so they can advertise the same product everywhere?
Joe:	Yes, and it seems that brand names are very special in our brains.
Angela:	How so?
Joe:	Well, there was a research study recently, carried out on a group of about 50 students. They showed them 108 words and the students had to say whether they recognised them as real words or not. The list included, all mixed up, ordinary nouns, brand names and meaningless words, and they were shown all the words quickly. And the brand names seemed to be recognised strongly and in the emotional right-hand side of the brain. It was interesting that the brand names were recognised more readily if they were displayed in capital letters rather than lower case – something which doesn't apply to normal words.
Martin:	How strange! What else did the researchers find out?
Joe:	Of course, it's a relatively small study. But they suspect that other visual features are at play, and so that, for example, colour has a major effect in helping us to store brand names in a special way in our brains.
Angela:	I suppose that's logical. But what do you, well, they mean by a special way?
Joe:	I'm not saying I understood everything about this study!
Angela:	Of course not.
Joe:	But they seemed to be saying that the power of brand names is that they conjure up a range of associations inside our brains, more so than ordinary words or names do.
Martin:	I guess this is great news for international companies.
Joe:	Potentially, certainly. Though exactly what they do …

Section 4

Lecturer: Now, balloons and airships are worth consideration because, while on the one hand they represent humans' first successes at air flight – after centuries of less than successful theory and experimentation – they also on the other hand continue to be used today. We may have appeared to have moved on to jet planes and space rockets, but you can still see these more 'primitive' fliers in the skies. OK, er, gas balloons first. France saw the first balloon flight in 1783 and this began a process of development. By 1862, in the Civil War in the United States we find Thaddeus Lowe replacing spies with balloons to go behind enemy lines. The success of this led to the continued use of balloons in peacetime, and they were employed in the creation of maps. And such applications continue to this day, with balloons assisting in increasing our knowledge and understanding of the world we live in. Unmanned balloons are still widely used to collect data to inform scientific research of various kinds. You'd be surprised at how much they contribute. All sorts of instruments can be mounted in a balloon, and ongoing investigations into climate benefit from the information that can be gathered from a flight. Well, that's gas balloons. Now, the increase in the popularity of ballooning as a sport or leisure activity has been mainly due to the development of the modern hot air balloon, being cheaper and safer than the gas balloon. Heating air rather than using potentially explosive gas is what makes these rise, although the process doesn't generate as much lift as with gas balloons. But this is a small price to pay for its other benefits, and this type of balloon is no doubt here to stay.

Airships are also fairly old in their origins. The idea for a balloon that could be powered and steered was first published in France in 1784, although 1852 was the date of the first successful airship flight. The first airships, like the first aircraft, didn't provide any weather protection for their crew – so it must have been rather uncomfortable up there! But designs continued to develop in sophistication. It was realised that the ships would drift about if they weren't strengthened, and that to work effectively, they would have to have a framework. Once designs started incorporating this, flights became longer and more reliable. Airships were deployed for various uses in the First World War, and once peace returned, designers began to turn their attention to ambitious plans for regular intercontinental flights. However, in the 1930s this programme more or less came to an end. For one thing, the speed and popularity of airliners meant that the airship appeared superseded. They just couldn't compete. And as if that weren't enough in itself, another factor in the decline of the airship was an alarming number of crashes, and this of course put people off. Nevertheless, several countries have continued to build smaller airships for various uses, such as naval observation or publicity purposes. In fact, their popularity seems set for a slight revival and in the past few years there has been renewed attention paid to the possibility of using them to transport cargo. Who knows? Maybe the twenty-first century will be the age of the airship. Now if you look at your handouts, you'll see that I've included some …